INTER-DIMENSIONAL PRAYER

DR. LARRY EDWARD BIRCHETT, JR

Contact and booking information:

harvesthouserestorationcenter@gmail.com

www.harvesthouserestorationcenter.com

 Scriptures are taken from the **Holy Bible, The King James Version** unless otherwise marked.

ISBN – 978-0-9896249-7-8

Library of Congress Number – 2018913282

Printed in United States of America

November 2018

Table of Contents

DEDICATION

This book is dedicated to Arlene and Larry Sr., my Mother and Father, who taught me how to pray. The best way to teach someone how to pray is to model it in front of them, and I praise God that they did that for me. I dedicate this book to you both because if you didn't teach me how to pray, I wouldn't be here today. You prayed for me and with me before I went to school. You prayed for me and with me before we ate our food in the evening. You prayed for me and with me before I went to sleep. And many times, I heard you praying for me when you thought that I had went to sleep and at other times I heard you praying and crying out my name to God when I would sneak in the house from off the street. Thank you. Thank you for loving me and imparting in me the special gift and weapon that we call prayer. I love you both.

FOREWORD

I was elated to read this great book on prayer, written by my Son, Dr. Larry E. Birchett, Jr. All the principles contained in this book are simply inspiring. Especially, considering the changing times that we live in. Unfortunately, there are families that have lost focus and need these principles on prayer. There are new ministries that have been born that have lost focus. More than ever believers need to return to God in prayer. The Bible explains that we should pray with power for a deeper purpose helping the least of these. This book is simply saying that if you believe God and take the time to pray, you can trust that God's power will be released in your life.

Larry's faith is an uncompromising faith and he prays about everything. Larry's strong faith knows the power of prayer. God is able to do exceeding and abundantly above all that we ask or think according to the Holy Spirit's power that works in every believer. It all started in the home. Someone great has said, children learn what they live. If a child lives with approval they learn to like themselves. If a child lives with praise, they learn to appreciate. If a child lives with security, they learn to have faith. Being a resilient teenage mom my love for my only son compared to no one. Larry was born not with a silver spoon in his mouth but a veil over his face. A visible sign of God's anointing and favor. This author is authentic wearing humility with honor; yet his commanding spirit is captivating hearts to pray with power and this is a greater working of the Spirit.

Also, I learned from my beloved mother Barbara who taught me to pray, which greatly influenced my parenting. So, I taught my son his first bedtime prayer such as, "Now I lay me down to sleep, I pray the Lord my soul to keep and if I should die before I wake, I pray the Lord my soul to take."

It is nothing like a mother's love for her child to know her Lord and to lead him in the greatest prayer is a joy. Larry at an early age of 6 or 7 prayed to Jesus for his own salvation while in my kitchen at our first home on Frazier Street in Philadelphia. Ever since that great day Jesus captivates his heart and many lives have been transformed by Jesus. It is hard for most people to live in the moment and think of themselves as royalty. He is being loyal to the royal inside of him, which makes him understand that being true to self is not about ego. Never underestimate the power of a healing prayer.

One more thing, I remember Larry praying for me after being diagnosed with Sarcoidosis, an incurable disease. I knew what it felt like, dying, even before the doctors confirmed it. But Larry, along with his dad and sister by the laying of hands on me, pulled on God's power and God's presence was with us in that living room on Wilton Street in Philadelphia. My faith is not small. That secret closet moment prepared me to hear from God saying, "No, you will live and not die." You don't have to stand in a special prayer line for God to hear your prayer. You don't have to even be in a sanctuary for God to respect your prayers. Where ever the Spirit of the Lord is you should seek the Lord and I've learned that the sanctuary that you pray at the most should be your home.

Age has taught me to never underestimate God. God is greater. It was never about me. My child needed his mother to live and not die. As result practicing his mustard seed faith he grew to be a great man of God, able to move mountains. All praises to God. Being a mom there is no greater role worthy of double honor. One of the rare advantages of growing gracefully old now in my 62th year is to have the opportunity to celebrate my son's dreams and living his passions as result of prayer. I am not surprised that great people around the world will buy and train leaders using this powerful book.

Nothing is impossible when you believe in a higher purpose. What a Great and Mighty God we serve.

Reverend Dr. Arlene Paulette Birchett
DMin. MDiv. M.Ed.
www.womenofgreatprice.org
drapaulette.birchett@gmail.com

Luke 1:35 (NIV)

[35]The angel answered, "The Holy Spirit will come on you, and the power of the Most High will overshadow you. So the holy one to be born will be called the Son of God.

Thank you, Son, for becoming the holy thing that was born. You have answered the prayers of your grandmother Elizabeth Birchett, whose desire was to see you in the conflict and say, "Faith cometh." You are my faith that cometh. Stay true to the Holy thing and continue to be at one.

Larry E. Birchett, Sr.
Father of the Author

ACKNOWLEDGMENT

I'd like to thank the Holy Spirit for pulling out the grace that God has attributed and imbedded in me while I was in my mother's womb for the purpose of this book I have been inspired to aspire for my highest self in God as He continues to reveal to me and in me His purpose for my life.

I'd like to thank my gorgeous and gifted wife, Joanna, for her love and support of me via this book and everything else that God has placed in my heart. You're always there my love and it means the world to me. It's you and me to the end of time *babygirl.*

I'd like to thank my children who inspire me with their very existence and unconditional love towards me. I love you all so much and I pray that as your father that I've been the champion that every father is supposed to be for their sons and daughters.

I'd like to thank my parents Dr. Rev. Arlene Paulette Birchett and Reverend Larry Birchett, Sr. for pure love and dealing with me in love even when I didn't deserve it. I love you two so much and I'm blessed that Mom you weren't just a Mom to me you were a Mother. And Dad you weren't just a Dad to me, you were a Father. I honor you both for rearing me and my beautiful sister, Nija Birchett, in the way that we should go.

I dedicate this book to you both for being my first examples of what real prayer looks like. From prayers in the morning, when you woke me up, to praying before breakfast, lunch, and dinner, to the prayers holding hands at our family meetings, to praying before I went to sleep; you guys always had me and Nija in prayer. Love you both. I'd like to thank my spiritual father and mother Apostle Earl Palmer and Pastor Maria Palmer for always being there for me and my wife, Prophetess Joanna, and for always being a source of encouragement and strength. I praise God for you both and your labor of love concerning me.

I'd like to thank my church, Harvest House Restoration Center, the greatest church in Pennsylvania, for encouraging, inspiring, and obliging me to explore what God has for me. It is an honor to be the under-shepherd of such an awesome congregation. You all are such a blessing to me.

Lastly, I'd like to thank the Holy Spirit for equipping me and defending me during the arduous process of putting this book to paper. During the writing of this book I came under serious spiritual attacks from witches and warlocks all over the world. One night, I was even visited in my dream, which wasn't a dream, it was real, by a warlock from London, who stabbed me from the back, through my heart, right while I laid next to my wife. The Holy Spirit took me through everything that I've been teaching my own congregation to bind, renounce, rebuke, and recover from that attack. Thank you, Holy Spirit, for comforting and defending me for the glory of God.

INTER-DIMENSIONAL PRAYER

Earnest Prayer

God answers the prayer of a sincere heart.

Apostle Dr. Larry Birchett, Jr.

Prayer in its purest form is the verbal and sometimes non-verbal expression of your heart. However, do you know what happens to your prayer once it leaves your lips? Does it just go into the atmosphere where God hears it, blinks His eyes if He approves, nods His head if He really approves, or anything else to the contrary if He doesn't approve? Have you ever meditated on the actuality of what is really occurring in the spirit realm concerning your prayers? What happens when you say "grace" over your dinner? What happens when you say prayers with your children before they go to sleep? Does God really hear you when you ask Him to protect you before you're put to sleep before that surgery? Have you ever seriously thought about it? Well fortunately, the Bible gives us a little inclination as to what transpires once we pray to God in faith. We can find it in one of the most overlooked passages of scriptures in the Bible.

Revelation 8 New International Version (NIV)

1) When he opened the seventh seal, there was silence in heaven for about half an hour.

2) And I saw the seven angels who stand before God, and seven trumpets were given to them.

3) Another angel, who had a golden censer, came and stood at the altar. He was given much incense to offer, with the prayers of all God's people, on the golden altar in front of the throne.

4) The smoke of the incense, together with the prayers of God's people, went up before God from the angel's hand.

5) Then the angel took the censer, filled it with fire from the altar, and hurled it on the earth; and there came peals of thunder, rumblings, flashes of lightning and an earthquake.

This text gives us a snapshot as to what will take place at the very inception of the opening of the Seventh Seal. The beauty of this text is that it also gives us a glimpse of what our prayers literally look like once our words hit the air, as it ascends, if it ascends and makes its way to Heaven. We get to learn a little bit regarding who handles them and at least a glimpse of what is done with them, literally, at this point of history, the last chapter of the age of mankind.

One summer, my wife and I took our family to the Hershey Amusement Park in Hershey, PA along with a very good family friend. And I sat back and observed how my children along with our friend's children were playing in the water park portion of the park. There was a lot going on in that portion of the park to include water rides, fake kiddie streams and kiddie ponds, large swing sets that would totally soak the kids before they were done, large nets that would soak the children as they climbed up them, and then my eyes got fixed to one particular spot amongst all of the joyous chaos. There were large buckets of water suspended high in the air that were being filled little by little with trickles of water from various places of the elaborate water park. Our children along with many other children stood for about fifteen minutes or longer in one general spot, looking up at these huge buckets of water as they bulged with refreshing, liquid anticipation.

At certain times the buckets seemed to strain and almost tip to one side or the other and then it would upright itself. Then it would do the same thing to the other side and then it would again upright itself. Every time it almost tipped, you would hear collective "Ahhhhhhhhh" or "Oooohhhhh" or even "Uh Ohhhhhhhh"! I've never seen anything like it and at the allotted time the few children that were under the buckets were very many and it wasn't just the small kids now it was the teens, the young adults and even some adults almost pushing the little kids out of the way. And then, the water stopped, and you hear a very brief silence for about two seconds. All of the kids and teens and adults hear the silence and start remarking, "Here it comes!" and put their hands up or bend down or some of them even closed their eyes by putting their hands over their eyes. That is when you can hear the strain of these huge buckets one by one tilting, screeching even and clicking into place. The enormous amounts of cold and refreshing water comes pouting out of the enormous containers into the atmosphere, cascades downward through the air and soaks every boy, girl, man and women that is in the proper place to be soaked. Never have I seen so much joy because of an essentially oversized bucket being tilted for the purpose of being poured.

In the Book of Revelation, the Bible describes golden bowls full of incense, which are the prayers of the saints (Revelation 5:8). In other words, the prayers of God's people collectively fill heavenly bowls with sweet aroma, much like the burnt offerings did in days of old. In Revelation 8, we discover what these bowls are used for:

Revelation 8:3-5

3 Another angel, who had a golden censer, came and stood at the altar. He was given much incense to offer, with the prayers of all God's people, on the golden altar in front of the throne.

4 The smoke of the incense, together with the prayers of God's people, went up before God from the angel's hand.

5 Then the angel took the censer, filled it with fire from the altar, and hurled it on the earth; and there came peals of thunder, rumblings, flashes of lightning and an earthquake.

In short, the image that we're given of where our prayers end up in Heaven is much like the water park buckets. The prayers of God's people that actually make it into Heaven, which is an important topic that we will discuss later, because most prayers don't even make it this far, are compiled by powerful angels and taken into the very throne room of the Almighty God. They are then placed in huge golden bowls which seems to be right in front of the Mercy Seat in the midst of the throne room, where the Almighty God of Heaven and Earth sits. As these bowls are filled the scriptures say that "another angel" besides the seven angels that are in the throne room with their seven trumpets, comes forth with a golden censer with "much incense to offer". Which lets us know that **even our best prayers stink before God.** It's a little tip to us to inform us that even our most earnest prayers are not worthy to be presented before God without a little bit of help from God's holy angels.

These priceless and select prayers are mingled with incense which undoubtedly creates a pleasing aroma to God that goes forth directly from the angel's hand. Then as the bowls fills up with the effectual and fervent prayers of the righteous saints, it gets full to capacity and then starts to brim over. The select angel then takes the censor dipped in incense and prayers with fire from the altar of God and showers the fire of God on the earth. The NIV version actually reads that the angel "hurled" this powerful concoction of earthly and heavenly elements that creates thundering and lightning and earthquakes. Beloved, have you ever been in a storm that seemed supernatural? Have you ever thought of the fact that maybe God was answering your prayers? What if that lightning and thunder that is causing traffic jams, electrical disturbances, and certain trees being struck, really is God answering the prayers of the Saints? Next time you're in the midst of one of these occurrences think about this text and let it be a reminder to you to not fear the wind and rain but instead have reverence for the storm.

God said, *"If my people who are called by My name will humble themselves, and pray and seek My face, and turn from their wicked ways, then I will hear from heaven, and will forgive their sin and heal their land"* **(2 Chronicles 7:14).**

The "fire from the altar" is the power of God released from heaven to change the earth. In order for the “fire” to reach its intended recipient it has to go through principalities, powers, rulers of darkness in high places, and every other demon in the lesser heavens and kingdoms that exist in and outside of our human realm. We’ll get to all of these throughout our discussion in this book. But for now, let’s just say that as our prayers are lifted up to God, the golden bowls are filled until they reach a point when the bowls tip and pour out God's power and provision on the earth.

When God's people pray earnestly, the ***"effective, fervent prayer of the righteous"*** avails much (James 5:16). I'm not talking about begging God. Because begging God is not the same as believing God, taking God at His Word, and praying in faith. But one should know that one variant meaning of supplication, which is what God tells us to do in Philippians 4 along with our prayer, means to beg. However, let’s not digress in this initial chapter. Effective and fervent prayer are always filled with faith. But to be effective, our prayers can’t be like bullets, popping off toward God like He's a target. No, our prayers must be spirit-led and intentional.

James 5:16 (Amplified Bible)

16 *Therefore, confess your sins to one another [your false steps, your offenses], and pray for one another, that you may be healed and restored.* ***The heartfelt and persistent prayer of a righteous man (believer) can accomplish much [when put into action and made effective by God—it is dynamic and can have tremendous power].***

Beloved, please understand the simple truth regarding what literally takes place when you pray. When you pray, you are filling the prayer bowls of heaven. When you pray, in the spirit realm, your prayers look like ascending incense. In the Old Testament we constantly see visual images of incense ascending in the Temple as a representation of the effectual and fervent prayers of the Saints. The burning of the incense was symbolic of the prayer of the people rising up to God. We see David, literally praying this way in Psalms 141:

Psalm 141 King James Version (KJV)

[1] *Lord, I cry unto thee: make haste unto me; give ear unto my voice, when I cry unto thee.*

[2] *Let my prayer be set forth before thee as incense; and the lifting up of my hands as the evening sacrifice.*

So, David was literally saying let my prayers be sweet in your nostrils oh Lord and may my praise be counted as a sacrifice on your holy altar. This sounds so cliché for those of you who have been in church your whole entire lives. However, consider what the Bible teaches us about the layout of the throne room of God, in the Third Heaven. You just read it a few chapters ago, but I'm sure you missed it:

Revelations 8:3 (KJV)

[3] *And another angel came and stood at the altar, having a golden censer; and there was given unto him much incense, that he should offer it with the prayers of all saints upon the golden altar, which was before the throne.*

What do we see? We see that the altar is right in front of the throne. Depending on what the Apostle John really saw, the throne and the altar, probably are even combined. This is amazing because we see that our prayers are being conditioned right before the throne of God. I'm not sure about air conditioning in God's throne room but one thing I do know is that there is prayer conditioning in the throne room of Heaven. Couldn't resist that attempt at humor beloved. But isn't amazing that God the Father, sits there and watches every prayer that makes it to this point be prepared for Him. As He watches the angel prepare this gourmet, I believe that He starts to smell which ones He wants to consume and address first.

In Exodus 40:9, we see that Moses consecrated the altar with the anointing oil when the Tabernacle was being dedicated to the Lord. And in this snapshot, we see that incense was burned daily on that altar during the morning sacrifices and the evening sacrifices. This might be a hard scene to picture if you have never seen a very well-endowed church with a real altar and pulpit. But, the Old Testament altars were very substantial. The first altar ever constructed was made by Noah after God spared him and his family after the flood (Genesis 8:20). We see after that, Abraham, Isaac, Jacob, and Moses all erected altars unto the Lord. However, when it came to the temple, the altars were very prominently made and very prominently placed within the temple. The temples were made with two altars; the Altar of Burnt Offering and the Altar of Incense.

In the Mosque of Omar, immediately underneath the Great Dome, which occupies the site of the old temple built by King Solomon, King David's son. This is a place that is currently controlled by the Muslim population in the Middle East, but some of the prominent features of the prior temples are still there. One of the most revered features is the altar. There is a rough projection of natural rock, of about 60 feet in its extreme length, and 50 in its greatest breadth, and in its highest part about 4 feet above the general pavement. This rock seems to have been left intact from when Solomon's temple was built. According to leading archeologist and theologian it was probably the site of the Altar of Burnt Offering. It is said that underneath this rock is a cave, which leads many to believe that it was probably the granary of Araunah's threshing-floor. Refer to 1 Chronicles 21:22 to learn about Araunah.

We see another perspective of the Receiving Department for our prayers in Heaven in Revelations 5:

Revelations 5:8 King James Version (KJV)

8 And when He had taken the book, the four living beings and the four and twenty elders fell down before the Lamb, having every one of them harps and golden vials full of incense, which are the prayers of saints.

In God's perfect timing, your prayers are mixed with the fire of God, which symbolizes His power, and cast back down to earth to change your situation. Even if you don't feel like anything is happening in the natural world, when you pray, you are filling the prayer bowls in the spirit realm. When they finally become full they will tilt and that is when you will experience the "**pouring**" of God on your life. Somebody needs to shout right now; God **pour** out your blessings on me right now in the name of Jesus! Lord **pour** your will! Lord **pour** your response! Lord **pour** your direction into the atmosphere right now in the name of Jesus!

Revelations chapter 8 shows us the critical elements that are vital to having your prayer make it from your lips into the atmosphere, which is the first dimension, into the second dimension and all the way through the subsequent 12 dimensions. Some of you might be saying to yourself right now, twelve? Yes, twelve. In the 1990s, mathematicians working on the string theories of physics discovered the likelihood of there being at least ten dimensions in existence, not just the four dimensions that we had acknowledged before. Since then, we now have discovered that there are at least twelve.

There are some things that we have to consider as foundational. Firstly, all matter is energy. The entire universe is energy. And behind that energy is the consciousness that created it. To really understand this principle, we must also realize that the universe exists within the consciousness of the Original Creator. Our thoughts and intellect beloved, should be thought of as mental activity in a linear direction. The next paragraph is from an article named the *12 Dimensions of Creation*, written by Owen Waters.

"Physics has already proven that physical matter is energy, i.e. electro-magnetic energy held in a state of tension. Therefore, if the wooden cube is made up of electro-magnetic energy, then electric energy and magnetic energy are two more measurable dimensions. An object has so much electric energy and so much magnetic energy. Dimensions are measurable variables affecting the existence of objects, therefore electric energy and magnetic energy are two of the dimensions of existence. They usually express themselves in an entwined, electro-magnetic form, but underneath they are two distinct forms of energy."

Beloved, our thoughts are actual things. They are matter, comprised of energy because again, all matter is energy. So much so, that in experiments with subatomic particles, the consciousness of the observer often affects the outcome of the experiment. Did you know that? If you already knew this, then you are one of the few that understand how powerful our thoughts are. They are the only things that God has given us the ability to create. If I put a picture of your mother, father, son or daughter that passed away suddenly or something to that effect, it would mean more to you than a person who never met the child and/or doesn't have any emotional attachment to the child. So, while, something (love, remorse, regret, pain, anger, emptiness, confusion, happiness or peace) is actually leaving you in the direction of that picture, nothing has to be happening for the individual that didn't love the child or parent. Get it? Your energy towards that photo can be so intense that it could cause the photo to fall of the table or move and more.

Now, you should really be starting to come to the understanding that your thoughts are so critical, because your thoughts after being filtered through your heart comes forth as words which become the very things that will shape our lives. Which is why I don't believe in wasting my thoughts and/or words on frivolous and foolish things because if you think on a thing hard enough you literally will it into being and initiate its occurrence in your life. This is why I intentionally reject negative, silly, and foolish emotions as they are directed to me and/or launched in my atmosphere. I don't have time for it and it offends me as it should you. **2 Corinthians 10:5** says it this way, ***Casting down imaginations, and every high thing that exalteth itself against the knowledge of God and bringing into captivity every thought to***

the obedience of Christ. How is this connected to prayer? Well, if you haven't figured it out by now, your thoughts to Heaven can be a prayer. The process of the words or "groaning" and "moaning" that proceed out of your spirit are a function of your thoughts and is in essence matter in the form of energy that is launched and transmitted into the atmosphere.

What I am explaining to you is the thing that holds us as humans back, because we don't understand our full capability even in our human form. Human consciousness consists of the fundamental building blocks of thought and feeling, so these are also dimensions of reality. Consciousness goes far beyond just the realm of human thought. In fact, the entire universe is constructed of the original consciousness of the Creator. So why do we limit ourselves to the limits of our own individual consciousness which is limited to our respective intellect and experiences, when in fact, we are already logged into the consciousness of the creator, which is infinite? The sooner that we free our minds and dare I say our soul and spirit from the bondage of the flesh that contains them, the sooner that our thoughts, words, and prayers turn into something that makes the very Kingdom of Hell tremble. I believe that we can develop our prayer life to such a level that we can simply think of something and God will bring it to pass. I had a dream once where it seemed like I was in a part of hell and huge demons were trying to catch me. As they got close to me, for some reason I couldn't speak the name of Jesus, but I was able to think it and immediately as I thought it, I woke up and I was in, or should I say back in, my bed. Somebody needs to shout, JESUS! Now shout Glory Hallelujah!

The Bible, via James the half-brother of Jesus, lets us understand that there are three elements necessary to produce effective prayer. They are confession, relationship, and intense earnestness. The last element necessary to produce prayers "that availeth much" as it is stated in the King James translation is effectual fervent prayer. However, I like the New Living Translation version of this scripture:

James 5:16 ~ *Confess your sins to each other and pray for each other so that you may be healed. The earnest prayer of a righteous person has great power and produces wonderful results.*

So, let's just reword the third element of prayer that works to read thusly, the earnest prayer of a righteous person. Maybe the reason that your prayer is not being answered is because of your spiritual state in the eyes of God. I say in the eyes of God, because a lot of people are basing their righteousness and spiritual status on how they are perceived in the eyes of men. Many people think that just because they have fooled all of their family, friends, and associates into believing that they are in right standing with God, that they really are. Never forget that God knows the real state of your heart.

The earnest prayer of a righteous man or woman are the only prayers that even penetrate Heaven beloved. Earnest is the adjective in this scripture, which means it is describing the subject. And what that means as it applies to this scripture is that it is put here to describe how we are supposed to pray. We are to pray earnestly. I didn't say loudly, I said earnestly. The definition of the word earnest is the following: resulting from or showing sincere and intense conviction. Synonyms of the word earnest are serious, solemn, grave, sober, humorless, staid, or intense. To pray earnestly means to pray with sincere and intense conviction. Again, I'm not saying that all prayers are audible and have to be loud but I believe that little and continual weak prayers are muttered by little and weak people. And let me qualify the aforementioned statement with saying that there is such a thing as Heart Prayers or Heart Praying, which we will talk about later in this book which has its place and is just as powerful.

However, show me a person that is never serious when they pray and I'll show you a defeated person. Show me a person that shouts and cheers for their favorite game or TV Show but has to hide and become embarrassed when it comes time to pray and I'll show you a person that has a repressive relationship with the Lord. If you scream when your favorite secular song or video comes on and know all the words to that song but almost whisper every prayer that you dare pray to God, you do not have a healthy relationship with God. You are ashamed of God and you are wasting one of the mightiest weapons that he's given His children while we're on the planet Earth, which is prayer. Beloved, if your corporate prayer partners are people that practice small and mundane prayers that the person sitting right next to them can barely hear, you are under a mantle of shame. I'd like to encourage you to switch prayer partners, because birds of a feather do flock together.

We must assimilate with people that have effective prayer lives and that have regular times of communicating to God. To be very basic, we have to associate with those that can get a prayer through. Get in the company of people that have a real relationship with the Lord. Never stay under a mantle of leadership that does not put prayer on the highest level of priority in the ministry. Never regularly blend your time of prayer with those who don't hold it to the same regard that you do. If you continually do this, the fire that you once have will be diminished because birds of a feather do flock together. Eagles fly alone, but pigeons fly in flocks. Those with strong prayer lives are like eagles, they don't just fly, they soar. Pigeons have to work very hard to reach the levels that an eagle can reach and honestly most pigeons can never ascend to the height of the strongest eagles.

Unless you are strong enough to influence or at least impact the group that you're connected to in such a way that their prayer life comes up a little bit it will go the other way and you will soon find yourself praying just like them. Be unapologetic about your commitment to effectual and fervent prayer because pigeons fly in flocks, while eagles fly alone.

Jesus never had a problem disassociating Himself from others. He had an awesome prayer life with His father, the Almighty God, and He was not ashamed to break away from all His disciples and get with the twelve. He would then break away from the twelve and be with His most spiritually mature three, Peter, James, and John. He did this to differentiate between their roles amongst the other disciples after He would physically be taken out of the equation and because their faith levels were the highest.

Then there is the word "fervent" in there. Literally the etymology of that word is "boiling, hot, glowing." Figuratively it means "violent, impetuous, and furious." Another use of the word in the early church would've been impassioned. Which eludes to being passionate about our time of communicating with God.

The reason why many people start to lose their fervency for prayer is because their definition of prayer isn't correct. Many people will simply say that prayer is only limited to communicating with God. But if we understand the totality of the process it will change our mindset and our approach to the ordinance of prayer. When we pray, we have to understand that just as thoughts are things, refer to *Proverbs 23:7*, our prayers are literal things. Our words go into the atmosphere as an element. We have to understand that when we pray we put the angels to work to carry our prayers to Heaven safely and return with the reply.

Prayer is interdimensional warfare between a created being and the creator of all things. It is the convergence of the natural and spirit world. You might be saying but isn't that a little much? And the only reason why you would ask that is because you're stuck on the definition of communication with God. However, I would ask you to consider that God is omniscient. Meaning that He knows all things even before they're done. So, He knows every thought before they are thoughts. He knows every word that we will speak before we speak them. And this means that He knows and hears every spoken and unspoken prayer, meaning the silent prayers in our hearts. This means that it's not a matter of communicating because trust me beloved, God knows every thought and prayer you have ever muttered. It's a matter of our tangible prayer making it into the Holy of Holies literally, so that God can legally grant us those things that are prayed in accordance to His will. This is why in *John 11*, Jesus said that He was praying for the sake of those around Him, when it came to the resurrection of Lazarus, because He knew that God had already heard Him.

When our prayer leaves our lips, it takes on the form of vapor, smoke, or fire in the spirit realm. We can't see it in the visible realm but every angelic being and every spiritual being can. The difference between the forms of prayer depends on the purity of heart of the person praying, along with a few more critical factors and things that we will be discussing in this book.

Taking the whole phrase "effectual, fervent prayer" we can draw some thoughts to apply to our prayer life. No matter how long, loud, or hard that we pray, our prayers may not always be effectual. The next thing we see is that to be effectual, prayer should be passionate. If you do not have a passion regarding the thing or things that you're praying about, you are wasting your time and you're just going through an academic activity that won't profit you anything.

The Bible lets us know that Jesus prayed until He sweated blood in the Garden of Gethsemane. Which shows that He was engaged in an intense battle as He prayed for further encouragement and direction from Father God. Jesus was praying with passion. It physically affected Him. So, don't ever apologize for the passion that you have towards the things of God. Passion mixed with righteousness and faith produces the elements necessary to make a regular prayer catch fire! Jesus was praying so intensely that He got Heaven to respond right away. Can you imagine that? God sent Moses and Elijah to Jesus as a result of the His prayer. God authorized them to walk into our earthly and human dimension just to encourage Jesus. To give Him the perspective of 'Hey this is only temporal Jesus, look at us now!'. I believe that they were also preparing Him for what was going to literally happen to His body at the point of death. I believed they evened discussed the process of what exactly would happen regarding His Spirit and Soul, because even though He was and is the Son of God, I believe these certain things had to be shielded from Jesus so that He could face and conquer the challenge of death in the same way that any of us would.

Jesus prayed and prayed and prayed and His choice disciples couldn't even stay awake with Him. The truth is, we're guilty of not lingering in prayer long enough. The people at the water park who became weary of waiting for the buckets to fill missed an outpouring. The same is true and applies in prayer. However, it's not about works, whereas you're trying to make something happen, it's about diligence. It's about earnestly presenting yourself before Almighty God. This kind of prayer is genuine. This kind of prayer is real. It's not about how many words are prayed or the way we pray, as long as our prayers are heartfelt, faith-filled, and authentic.

The earth needs saints to be fervent in prayer. If there was at least one righteous person praying for the city and the people of the city, God would not have destroyed Sodom and Gomorrah. How many of us know that a prayer of deliverance and grace is not normally a small prayer? Normally, it's a loud conversation because of the grace that you know can only come from God. When Peter was walking on the water and his faith waned and he started to sink and almost drown he cried out Jesus save me! His prayer was short, focused and fervent. He needed an answer right away. The same is still true today. If God's people start praying in earnestness an overflow will occur. I believe there is a revival of the intercessor in this generation, a remnant that is praying. And because of this remnant, God is getting ready to tilt the prayer bowl and pour out divine blessings and occurrences on this generation. So be encouraged in your prayer life, because I'm here to tell someone that the golden bowls are being filled and the fire of heaven is about to fall!

Prayers of the Righteous

Prayer is the bridge that connects Heaven and Earth.

Apostle Dr. Larry Birchett, Jr.

I Timothy 2:1-2 (KJV)

I urge, then, first of all, that petitions, prayers, intercession and thanksgiving be made for all people—for kings and all those in authority, that we may live peaceful and quiet lives in all godliness and holiness.

We've established the fact that everything is dimensional and even the fabric of the air is dimensional. God doesn't only exist in our dimension, He exists outside of our dimension and in every other dimension at the same time because He is the creator of dimensions. So, we have to learn to approach Him in a manner conducive to the interdimensional King of all Kings that He is and remember that He is Omnipotent, Omniscient, and has already figured and planned everything out. When we look at God in the right way our prayer life changes. **Prayer is an act of faith, but prayer is also an attitude**. Let's discuss this. First, we must understand that He is spiritual:

John 4: 23-24 (KJV)

[23] But a time is coming and has now come when the true worshipers will worship the Father in spirit and in truth, for the Father is seeking such as these to worship Him.
[24] God is Spirit, and His worshipers must worship Him in spirit and in truth."

Beloved, you are not doing anything if your prayer life is wrapped up in your own efforts, understanding and flesh. I want to bring balance to what effective and dimension breaching prayer really is so that the effectual and fervent prayer as discussed in the first chapter is not misconstrued as a fleshly and emotional act. You have to breach the physical and enter into the spirit realm.

The number one question is how do we do this? Glad, you asked. First, we much go to God in faith. Everything as it relates to God, in His spiritual realm, is accessed by faith. Without the element of faith, prayer doesn't work. Now, I know that this is not a sensational statement, but one must understand that everything that gives us power in God is invisible. Love is invisible, sincerity can't be seen, and faith can't be proven until you're tested.

We believe on God via faith. There is an awesome quote from a man of God named, Leo Tolstoy, the acclaimed Russian Christian writer, which says "Where there is faith, there is love; where there is love, there is peace, where there is peace, there is God, and where there is God; there is no need." It's all initiated via our faith men and women of God. Hebrews 11 is known as the hall of faith chapter. Let's look at just a few scriptures:

Hebrews 11:1-7 (KJV)

1) *Now faith is the substance of things hoped for, the evidence of things not seen.*

2) *For by it the elders obtained a good report.*

3) Through faith we understand that the worlds were framed by the word of God, so that things which are seen were not made of things which do appear.

4) By faith Abel offered unto God a more excellent sacrifice than Cain, by which he obtained witness that he was righteous, God testifying of his gifts: and by it he being dead yet speaketh.

5) By faith Enoch was translated that he should not see death; and was not found, because God had translated him: for before his translation he had this testimony, that he pleased God.

6) But without faith it is impossible to please him: for he that cometh to God must believe that he is, and that he is a rewarder of them that diligently seek him.

7) By faith Noah, being warned of God of things not seen as yet, moved with fear, prepared an ark to the saving of his house; by the which he condemned the world, and became heir of the righteousness which is by faith.

It was by faith; the ability of being sure in your beliefs and convictions even when you can't see them manifesting, that all of these great men obtained a good report from the Lord and the chapter goes on and on, however we won't cover the whole chapter. But just as verse 3 states, we must understand that we believe in the very existence of God through our faith in His Word and creation. Not because He has physically manifested Himself to all of us in this realm or dimension. However, when we think about how everything on earth and in the sky and beyond the sky are in total order and synchrony, we realize that there is a God. When we think about how the waters stay in their place and the earth never moves off its axis, we realize that there must be a God. When we think of the fact that this air that we breathe was specially blended just for us and can't be found anywhere else in this universe, that God created this world and everything in it on purpose and for a purpose. Therefore, when we go to God, we must focus on who He is and realize that we are speaking to the most powerful spiritual being that there is, was, ever have been, or ever will be.

Your focus thrusts you into faith which streamlines you into the spiritual realm. What am I saying? I'm saying that words are merely words until belief, passion, and faith are put behind them. I'm saying that your words don't have power unless they are focused. Faith that has not been tested is not faith. ***Likewise, a*** **faith that is not focused can't be faith, because faith is a streamlined belief in that whatever you're hoping for will come to pass.** Faith and doubt can't exist in the same place. Faith and fear don't mix. All of the men mentioned in just the first seven verses of *Hebrew 11* were not extraordinary, because if they were then God would have to level the playing field. They were ordinary men just like me, just like you if you are a male reading this book, and just like any other female that has walked this earth, they were normal human beings. The thing in them that transcended them into the "Hall of Faith" was that they were empowered *by their faith* to do exploits according to the wisdom and will of God. Ordinary men and women become extraordinary to God when their focus is all about Him and their faith matures to the level of action.

Whenever you focus on something, energy transfers. Therefore, make sure your faith is focused. It sounds easy, but in actuality, this takes a great deal of effort and sometimes effort defeats skill. I know that sometimes you feel like your efforts are being wasted. As if it's doing no good. However, I'm here to tell you that success doesn't have business hours. Our efforts are never wasted. Therefore, be encouraged and know that your continued labor in prayer is changing some things in the spirit realm beloved. Keep on pushing. Keep on praying until something happens.

What do we also learn from this chapter in Hebrews? Enoch was translated simply because his ways pleased God. The term translated means that he never experienced death in the way that our great grandfathers and great grandmothers did. God took him straight to Heaven probably in the same way He took Elijah, but the Bible doesn't mention how Enoch was translated. But it does let us know the reason why. This is interesting because we don't see a reason in the Old Testament but the fact that the writer of Hebrews knew the reason lets us know that Enoch's story had been communicated down through the ages and even at the time of the writings of the canonized New Testament, people knew.

If God would translate the men of God that pleased Him so that they could be with Him faster, it is only common sense that He answers the prayers of those who please Him first as well. Not only would you surmise that God probably answered almost all of Enoch and Elijah prayers, but God took them early so that they could be with Him. We know that God hears everything including all prayers but because of His nature He distances Himself from some of them because some prayers are evil or offered from a wicked heart. This is why we have to live a life that is pleasing in the eyes of God. **When a man's ways please God, their prayers are prioritized in the Heavenly realm and God answers them first.** This is not my opinion beloved, this is Bible. Consider the wisdom of Solomon in the book of Proverbs:

Proverbs 15:29 (KJV)

The LORD is far from the wicked, but he hears the prayer of the righteous.

Do you feel like God is not paying your prayers any attention? Well, if you're shacking up, fornicating, cussing, smoking, drinking, killing, raping, envying, backbiting, gossiping, hating, lying, cheating, bullying, sowing discord, lusting, lazy, fake, lukewarm, bitter, angry, adulterating, disbelieving, and plain not living according to God's commandments and precepts, He probably isn't! Sorry, but I just have to keep it real.

Don't look for a magical method of getting your prayers answered, start living a life that is pleasing in the eyes of God. And guess what? We have to watch our words. Watch your words men and women of God because God is judging you by each and every one of them. You can't bless God and curse God with the same lips and expect results. Your words, which are originated from your heart, shapes your life.

Psalms 34:13-14 (NKJV)

13 Keep thy tongue from evil, and thy lips from speaking guile.
14 Depart from evil, and do good; seek peace, and pursue it.

An essential point is that your heart, when you go to God, matters. An unclean heart will not produce any goodwill in the economy of God and your frustration level will only increase as you keep operating in this way. One of the ways to identify insanity is when someone does the same thing all the time but expect different results. That's insane, so stop acting in this manner.

Faith without works is dead and until you are operating in total faith unto a faithful God you and your words don't possess any power and consequently don't possess any life. We all know the story about the sons of Sceva in ***Acts 19***, where it gives us a glimpse of a group of people who tried to operate in the things of the spirit without any power. The sons of Sceva saw people getting healed by the handkerchiefs and aprons of Paul that he used on himself. They saw sickness, diseases, and demons leaving people because of these effects. The Bible says that itinerant Jewish exorcists, the seven sons of Sceva, and a Jewish chief priest, then took it upon themselves to call the name of the Lord Jesus over those who had evil spirits, saying, *"We exorcise you by the Jesus whom Paul preaches."* In verse 15 of the same chapter the evil spirits talked back and said, *"Jesus I know, and Paul I know; but who are you?"* Which leads us to the fact that head knowledge does not mean that your heart acknowledges the power behind the information that has entered your mind.

Information that has not been "IN FORMED" does not take root and therefore does not produce any power. You can say get out in the name of Jesus all you want, but if you don't really believe that Jesus is Lord and that there is power in His name nothing will happen. If you're trying to cast out demons but you don't really believe in them, meaning that demons exist, it won't work. And if you believe but can only focus on the fear produced by the situation, instead of the faith that supposed to lie inside of you, it won't work. How can you cast out big bad demons and at the same time be scared of little roaches? That is not consistent at best and it won't work. It's almost like having information on making a good cup of coffee in a coffee making machine. You can read the instructions, turn it on, and even clean it up all nice. But if you don't put the adequate amount of coffee beans in the machine along with a proper filter for the beans with the proper amount of clean water, you will not get the rich and robust coffee that one could produce if they know how to make a good cup or pot of coffee. The blessing behind the cup of coffee is not the machine or beautiful mug or cup to hold the coffee. It is the essence of the coffee bean that needs a few factors to be in place to get the power, genius, and essence out of it.

The coffee bean in this illustration represents our faith. Without the proper motivation those beans wouldn't know its own genius. Without the proper mechanisms and pressure, the essence of the bean would never be produced and brought forth. And so, as we implement the process necessary, utilize the ingredients necessary, apply heat and ingenuity, and be prepared to catch what will come forth from the whole transaction, the miraculous fruit and power of the coffee bean will never be brought forth and enjoyed. Likewise, our faith, without the proper motivation, will never be brought forth. Without the power of motivation our faith will never be evident and/or mature. God is not trying to crush you beloved, He's trying to motivate the divine essence of your spirit, to manifest.

Unless your faith has been processed under the right conditions and brought forth with the proper applications it will never mature and produce the power that it is supposed to. The truth is that everyone has faith. The question is in what? The people in *Acts 19* was easily defeated because their faith was not rooted and grounded in the right thing. **Head knowledge does not produce Kingdom power.** And unless the essence of your faith is rooted and grounded in Jesus Christ and His Word it will not produce any power. The fact that they even thought to say that I cast you out in the name of Paul's God lets us know that there was no personal conviction and commitment. For them it was a simple transaction or means to produce an end, almost like magic words from a magician that makes a bunny rabbit appear in a hat. They didn't understand that the power is not in the words per say, it's in the Word manifest in the flesh, as per John 1:14, His name is Jesus.

In Ephesians 6:10-18 it basically tells us to get in our faith so that we can withstand the fiery darts of the wicked one. So, our job is to make sure that faith has been properly formed **in** us and not just a concept or piece of information. Your focus has to be so laser like that you will not doubt the outcome of your efforts. When you sit in a chair you don't think twice about if the chair will hold you. You just see a chair and know what it is supposed to do and sit down. And just like the faith that you have in the chair you must ensure that you're applying this same focus to your prayers. It's not always easy and in fact it is a lot of work. But the fact that it takes work is one of the greatest revelations that God gives us to achieving the power and seeing the results of prayer because a lot of people believe that our approach to praying and prayer really shouldn't require any real effort. Focus requires discipline which always involves work. Faith, just like discipline, is something that you have to train yourself to have and operate in and the process of getting to this point is a lot of work. Watch what James said:

James 2:14-17 (KJV)

[14] *What does it profit, my brethren, if someone says he has faith but does not have works? Can faith save him?* [15] *If a brother or sister is naked and destitute of daily food,* [16] *and one of you says to them, "Depart in peace, be warmed and filled," but you do not give them the things which are needed for the body, what does it profit?* [17] *Thus also faith by itself, if it does not have works, is dead.*

So, what do we see from the scriptures? We see that faith alone doesn't produce anything. However, faith mixed with work is powerful. So, effective, and focused faith is faith that has been put into action. What does this have to do with prayer? Prayers without faith aren't really prayers, they are vain words, no matter how poetic and biblical they sound. Our prayers are to be always submitted in faith. Faith that someone is actually listening to us, right? Faith that they, meaning our prayers, make a difference. Faith that they are creating a positive change.

Faith causes enthusiasm. The 44th President of the United States of America was presenting the National Teacher of the Year award to a host of the nation's finest teachers. Jahana Hayes, a teacher at John F. Kennedy High School in Waterbury, Connecticut, who could barely contain her excitement, had the honor of introducing him as the keynote speaker. She said to him girlishly, "Please don't kick me out" as she continued to giggle and laugh while introducing him. He hugged her because he appreciated her genuine reaction to him being there and doing what he was doing, and so he said, "You can't be great if you're not enthusiastic." She started clapping and smiling from ear to ear and he said to her kiddingly, "Now you need to settle down." Everyone erupted into laughter as did she because she knew he was joking and he came over and gave her another hug and continued on with his speech. Her enthusiasm changed a boring and dull and mundane moment to something special that is all over local and international news as well as social media due to her enthusiasm to her particular duty and who she is doing it for. This type of enthusiasm and respect is what changes our words from being placating to powerful. Effectual and fervent prayers coupled with the work of faith and righteous living are our number one spiritual weapon against the forces of the enemy and we have to know how to use them.

Our prayers can be dangerous if we know how to use them and more importantly if we know how to pray. When I was a Commissioned Officer School in the United States Army, we did a staff ride to Gettysburg, Pennsylvania, the bloodiest and most deadly place of the American Civil War of the 1800's. There were many original canons and model canons out there on the now beautiful and peaceful battlefields. God gave me a revelation about them. A person that knows of prayer but never prays is nothing but a canon that has never been fired. The unused canon always looks nice but can't hurt anybody unless someone would happen to trip over it. It takes a little effort to prime the canon, fill the canon, point the canon, and light the canon. But if you do all of these things, you have a weapon that can cause havoc on the enemy.

Prayer is a weapon and the utilization of a weapon requires some form of training and preparation to know how to use it effectively. So, before you go into the most holy act of prayer, spend some time **preparing** your spirit, your soul, which can be looked at as your mind, intellect, your body with all its sensualities, feelings, and negative emotions, before going to God. It takes effort, which we aptly use the term work. For our prayers to affect anything other than the air that is front of our mouths and break through to the dimension where prayers are answered it sometimes takes a lot of effort and work. A lot of times our efforts are being used and wasted in things that won't produce results. James talked a lot about praying and submitting prayers that are effective.

James 4:1-3

[1] What causes fights and quarrels among you? Don't they come from your desires that battle within you? [2] You desire but do not have, so you kill. You covet but you cannot get what you want, so you quarrel and fight. You do not have because you do not ask God. [3] When you ask, you do not receive, because you ask with wrong motives, that you may spend what you get on your pleasures.

If you are praying with hate and anger in your heart, this is not faith, even though a lot of people think that it is because anger does focus you. But the truth of the matter is that anger, hate, jealousy, and envy are the opposites of the Godly faith attribute that moves the heart of God. You can't pray a prayer that is asking God to exalt you to show everybody that they were wrong and make everybody feel bad, because, that is a battle that is raging within you that has nothing to do with God. You can't pray oh

God bless me with the hottest car, nicest house, and biggest church, so that people will have to show me deference, because that is a prayer of covetousness, pride, discontent, and it even shows low self-esteem. So just like the scriptures say, you do not have initially because you do not ask God, but then when you do ask, you're asking with wrong motives, to feed your flesh and fleshly desires and pleasures.

Let's break down a little bit more about interdimensional prayer. A pre-approach is just as important as the approach. Your pre-approach or preparation period should focus on consecration. Holiness is still required and in fact, still right. Remember I started this chapter talking about Enoch and Elijah and how they were pleasing to God. We must be pleasing to God to expect a difference in God's response to our prayers as per someone else. As we are in the flesh we will not reach the level of being pleasing in the sight of God unless we're in the practice of living a consecrated life. Consecration is an act of removing any impurity from our hearts, minds, body, soul, and spirit. This is critical to the necessary function of being pleasing in the sight of God. God is spirit and we must connect with Him via a life of integrity and truth. Therefore, we must clear our heart and all the while wrap all of these elements of preparation under the umbrella of faith.

The Old Testament priest in **Leviticus 11** had to be consecrated before they functioned as actual priests. God told Moses to kill a ram take out its entrails, boil some of it, along with the holy oil, Aaron and the priest were to eat some of the boiled pieces along with the shew bread, and many more things, including that Aaron and the rest of the priests couldn't leave the tabernacle for a full 7 days after everything that was prescribed was completed. Every word that God spoke to Moses had to be carried out or the whole ordination process of the Levitical priesthood would've been invalid.

Words matter. God told Moses specifically to sacrifice a ram, not just any old lamb or sheep. A ram is an uncastrated male lamb. If he would've just said bring me a lamb he would've done all that work for nothing. If they would've brought him a castrated male lamb, he would've been in disobedience and all that work would've been for naught. God used specific words to describe what He wanted for this consecration process.

God has never uttered a word that He didn't mean. It is said that several misconceptions can come when trying to translate a concept from one language to another. This is because words matter in the spiritual and in the natural. The Pepsi Cola Company found this out when mounting an ad campaign in Taiwan. The slogan was supposed to read "Come Alive with the Pepsi Generation." Unfortunately, translated into Chinese it read, "Pepsi Will Bring Your Ancestors Back from the Dead."

Needless to say, the advertisements were canceled due to the fact that even Pepsi couldn't quite live up to that claim. The resurrection from the dead is possible but only through the Lord Jesus Christ!

I Thess. 4:13-14 (NKJV)

[13] *"Brothers, we do not want you to be ignorant about those who fall asleep, or to grieve like the rest of men, who have no hope.* [14] *We believe that Jesus died and rose again and so we believe that God will bring with Jesus those who have fallen asleep in him."*

So, to be clear, before we even go to God in prayer we should prepare ourselves. We should be just as consecrated and cleansed before God as Aaron and the priests were in the Old Testament. I'm not saying that we have to fast for 40 days and nights or stay in the church for 7 days before we start praying, but there should be a time of acknowledging who God is and then repentance. In the same way that Jesus did when He prayed in Matthew chapter 6; ***Our Father, who art in Heaven, Hallowed be thy name. Thy Kingdom come, Thy will be done on earth, as it is in Heaven. And forgive us our trespass, even as we forgive those that trespass against us***.

Considering Jesus' example, after we square our account with God, so to speak, then we can come to Him as clean vessels covered under the grace of His blood and promise that He is faithful and just to forgive us our sins. Consider the promise that John tells us in his first epistle:

1 John 1:7-10 (NKJV)

7 But if we walk in the light as He is in the light, we have
fellowship with one another, and the blood of Jesus His Son
cleanses us from all sin. 8 If we say we have no sin, we deceive
ourselves, and the truth is not in us. 9 If we confess our sins, He is
faithful and just to forgive us our sins and to cleanse us from all
unrighteousness. 10 If we say we have not sinned, we make Him out
to be a liar, and His word is not in us.

So, because we are all sinners saved by grace and in need of this grace daily, we come to Him in acknowledgement of this fact, which is what He requires. This shows humility and obeisance unto our holy and benevolent God. If we are unwilling to come to God in this way, we are not expecting our prayers to permeate the next dimension to actually produce results. This is why God says that:

2 Chronicles 7:14 (NKJV)

14 If my people, who are called by my name, will humble themselves and pray and seek my face and turn from their wicked ways, then I will hear from heaven, and I will forgive their sin and will heal their land.

We are required to do five things before His promise of the three things that He would do for us if He's pleased. We must first be called by His name, meaning we must be saved. For a lot of you reading this book if you have been praying continually to God for something that it seems like your prayers are bouncing off of the ceiling. You might want to check your salvation. God hears all prayers, even the sinners, but besides the prayer of confession to faith, of which we sometimes call the "Sinner's Prayer", He is not obligated to respond. Why? Because we don't command God. And I'm going to get back to this topic in another chapter. But also, because a shepherd looks after his own sheep. If you are under the authority of another shepherd you should be praying to him, not God. Why do we think that God is a magical genie waiting to be commanded to act on our behalf? However, if you are under the banner of Christ, Jehovah Nissi, He is obligated to honor His Word concerning you. This is true of all the sacraments and ordinances of Christ, such as communion and baptism, they are for believers and those who has received Him.

The next step for us after we are saved, is for us to humble ourselves. Which is why our position, in the spiritual and natural is important to God. We can pray anywhere and anytime but there are times when God wants reverence which stems out of the word humility, like we just read about in 2 Chronicles chapter 7.

Humility is not weakness, humility is controlled strength. It's knowing that you have to power to do something, but you don't, for the better good, the bigger picture. This is the humility that is required to please God. If we cannot live a life that is pleasing unto the Lord, then we can never expect our prayers to avail much. If our humility does not reach the level of not only **not doing** what we shouldn't, but over powering our flesh to the point that we don't **want to**, our prayers will never leave the first dimension, let alone the twelfth.

One of my life scriptures is **Proverbs 18:12 (NIV)** - *Before a downfall the heart is haughty, but humility comes before honor.*

Humility comes before honor beloved. Prayer is a conversation with God, but it's not a conversation between two equals, it is a conversation between a superior and an inferior. We are subject to God and when we pray we are showing even more so, our dependency on an Almighty God. We bow down and lower our heads in an act of humility. It is an act of obeisance. We are inferior to the supremacy of El Elyon, which is one of the names of God which is translated to mean, the Most High God. When one would approach a King and even a Queen in ancient times you would first have to kneel or bow and lower your eyes so as not to make eye contact with the subject. Our approach to God in prayer is similar to this kind of courtesy. If we can spend time in submission to God, He will exalt us in due season. Remember, we're not witches or warlocks, and our words are not magical incantations. The formula of having an effective prayer life is rooted in the working power of the Holy Spirit.

1 Corinthians 4:20 (NIV)

For the kingdom of God is not a matter of talk but of power.

Lastly, regarding the approach to prayer, we must understand that our position determines our condition. Daniel prayed to God in Daniel 10 and the result of the story in scriptures is that his prayers were heard and answered immediately by God but was held up by the Prince of Persia, which is and was the devil. God dispatched the archangel Michael to defeat the Prince of Persia and then the angel Gabriel delivered the message. The moral of the story is that 21 days later, Daniel was still on his knees praying and expecting God to deliver. If he had turned back on his beliefs or started living a less than holy life, his delayed response to his prayers would've turned into a denial and deemed null and void or cancelled. What am I saying? I'm saying that sometimes the enemy will delay the blessings that are trying to make their way to you because he is counting on you to change your position. He is counting on you to backslide. He is counting on you to fail and let God down. He is counting on you to get weary. Don't ever give him that satisfaction beloved. Stay the course, and let your position remain constant. If you go to God on your knees so to speak, then stay on your knees until God sends the answer.

The story of Daniel and others allow us to know that when we're really serious about communicating to El Elyon, the Most High God, that we should take on a position of submission and even obeisance. Because it is only He that has the power to answer our prayers. Bended knee for example is always a good start. However, if your heart is not right you can bend lower than everybody else and your prayer still won't even dent the most outer layer of Heaven. If bending down is too much for you. If this progression is too fast for you, how about starting with the down casting of your eyes and the lowering of your head. These simple techniques or methods are a good start. Whatever you do beloved, let your approach be in submission to a God that without His help and grace over your life, you wouldn't be here. And lastly, let the truth of the last sentence create a humbleness of spirit that gets God's attention. Remember how David prayed in **Psalms 51:15-17(NIV)**.

15 Open my lips, Lord,
and my mouth will declare your praise.
16 You do not delight in sacrifice, or I would bring it;
you do not take pleasure in burnt offerings.
17 My sacrifice, O God, is a broken spirit;
a broken and contrite heart
you, God, will not despise.

Warfare and Deliverance

A man who wars in prayer will never bleed in battle.

Apostle Dr. Larry Birchett, Jr.

There are some powers that are only accessed by knowledge. But more important than that, I want to talk to you about a certain kind of knowledge, that is called tacit knowledge.

The term "tacit knowing" or "tacit knowledge" is attributed to Michael Polanyi in 1958 in Personal Knowledge. In his later work The Tacit Dimension he made the assertion that "we can know more than we can tell." He states not only that there is knowledge that cannot be adequately articulated by verbal means, but also that all knowledge is rooted in tacit knowledge.

In order to defeat your foe, you have to have knowledge of who your foe is, what they are comprised of, their strengths and weakness, and how they fight.

What is understood, doesn't need to be explained. For example, we all are alive because of the breaths that we take to pump the oxygen into our body. There is no class that we have ever taken or will ever take to make us understand this better because it is tacit knowledge to all of us. It was written in our

DNA and we do it by instinct. We breath before we even know how to spell the word or define it. Therefore, tacit knowledge is knowledge that is hard to communicate or express with words.

Another example of tacit knowledge is dance. You ever notice that when a groovy beat is on around a little baby that can at least stand, they just start dancing and grooving. The start bucking and bobbing and it's always so cute. No one had to teach them the art of dance and explain what rhythm is, it's just something that they do.

Prayer is similar, and I believe falls in the category of tacit knowledge because believe it or not we all know how to do it, in one form or the other. From when we were little, and we wanted a certain Christmas gift and we would say God please allow Mommy and Daddy to get what I asked for. Or if you were one of them children that was strung along with the belief of Santa Claus, you would say Lord, please let Santa bring me this toy or that toy.

The part of this that is tacit is the fact that we know that there is a God listening and hence, demons that are listening as well. How many of you had to cry for mommy or daddy to leave the light on when they put you into bed because you didn't want the "boogeyman" or something else to come out and get you? Hopefully, you're smiling beloved, but you know that what I'm saying is true. More children than not are afraid of the dark. The tacit knowledge that I'm alluding to here is that of a demonic force. None of us needed a class on demonology to understand that something made you feel uneasy when all the lights were turned off.

Tacit knowledge is good but explicit knowledge is necessary to access dimensions in the spirit realm. Let's talk about some explicit knowledge, such as the organization of the forces of the enemy:

- 1 demon can be anything from a singular soldier demon to a strongman ***Luke 11:18-22***

There are three levels of strongmen: rulers over principalities or wide geographic areas on earth; rulers over people, churches, families, communities and other specific groups or individuals; and rulers who dwell within people. Principalities are ruled by princes, also called strongmen. These are the gods and goddesses of the underworld.

- 300-600 demons are a cohort (some translations use the word band instead of cohort) ***John 18:3***
- 3000 to 6000 demons are a legion (which was the typical size of a Roman Legion during those days) ***Matthew 26:52-54***

The following are possible descending levels of satanic authority. No one knows definitively no matter what they say, but the rest of this book will delineate and explain more concerning these seven levels listed. These demonic authorities can be set over cultures, nations and regions of the earth. They can also be behind natural and supernatural government.

1. satan (commander-in-chief)
2. Thrones
3. Dominions (lordships)
4. Principalities (rulerships, princes)
5. Powers (authorities)
6. Rulers of Darkness of This World
7. Spiritual Wickedness (wicked spirits) In High Places (heavenly places)

Without explicit knowledge you can't conduct warfare. Which is why Intelligence is the primary commodity needed to win wars in the physical and spiritual. Without the CIA, FBI and other unnamed agencies, America would never be able to remain the world's superpower. Strategically speaking, you have to know your enemy and how they roll if you ever really want to put up a defense against them or go on the offensive against them. I gave you the name of each demonic formation that any deliverance minister will run into because you have to know how deep, so to speak, we have to go to defeat them from this realm. What am I saying? I'm saying that there was an instance in the Bible, specifically the book of Matthew 17, where Jesus' disciples could not cast out demons that were in a man. Jesus came on the scene and cast the demons right out of the man. Later, in private, the disciples, who would later become Apostles, asked Jesus, why they couldn't do it. Jesus said in **Matthew 17:21**, *Howbeit this kind goeth not out but by prayer and fasting.*

The words imply degrees in the intensity of the forms of evil ascribed to demons amounting to a difference of approach. We need to be strategic because the demonic realm is always operating against us in a strategic manner and we need to know when to pray strategic prayers. The point is that the Kingdom of darkness work as a team, therefore we need to work as a team.

You will never see demons fighting each other in the scriptures. You won't see this because they are highly organized and each one knows their place. However, unfortunately, you won't see this Kum Ba Yah type of spirit in the Kingdom of Light. Because too many people want to be in charge and due to power struggles, we have fractured into denominations, sects, clubs, and clicks that mocks the original intent of the warrior remnant that God truly wanted to inhabit the Earth.

How can you effectively go to war when you don't know the level of opposition that you're dealing with? I want to add a little more information on the number provided for legion because it's warranted.

In Mark 5, we see Jesus in the region of the Gadarenes, where He was encountered by the demoniac that was possessed by demons that described themselves as legion. A legion was the largest unit in the Roman army. At that time, a legion averaged about 5,000 fighting men. However, it is proposed that a legion could be a lot less, anywhere from 2000 to 6000 men.

The scriptures let us know that Jesus cast the demons into "about" 2000 pigs, and they all went to their death by drowning themselves in the sea. Why did the scriptures tell us that part? I mean Mark could've just said that he sent the spirits into some pigs and we all know the rest. However, the scriptures explicitly said, "about 2000". God wanted us to know the amount of demonic presence that could comprise of what is called legion. He casted about 2000 demons, a small legion, out of the demoniac and every one of them lived up to their true identity and destroyed the hosts that they were sent into.

Those that are possessed with these amounts of demons, that the Bible refer to as legion, are normally those people that are obsessed with death, graveyards, darkness, and depression. That's why we see this demoniac coming out of the tombs with enormous strength. He was right next to his base of power. For example, watch out for people that have tattoos of skulls and things like that. However, Jesus, the Light, the Life, the Truth, and the Way, had walked on the scene and we all know the rest of the story. The reason why Jesus even asked the question of "What is your name?" is because He wanted it to be a teaching moment for His disciples and Apostles in the future. Normally, Jesus told any demon that tried to hold a conversation with Him to shut up, which is what I would recommend to anyone trying to engage in any kind of deliverance; but this time, He didn't.

No amount of demonic presence can withstand the delivering power of Jesus Christ, the in the beginning Word, the Light that takes away the sins of the world. A thousand demons can't keep you bound beloved. Not even two thousand demons can withstand the power of God. Therefore, some of you reading this book, need to give up your excuses for being all messed up because it's not biblical.

One of the reasons that Jesus didn't mind casting out the already cursed demons into the pigs because the pigs were still accursed at that time as well. Jews, at that time were not to eat of the swine or handle them, however, we see that someone in that region had a whole bunch of them. Which is another key. Whenever there is presumptuous, willful, and blatant disobedience against a direct command of God, a portal for demonic oppression is opened.

Now that we've gotten through all of that, let's get to defeating these demons. First of all, whenever Jesus came against any of the fallen angels that had actually possessed a human being, notice that He never killed any of them. So, stop trying to kill every demon that manifests in your meetings and start commanding them to leave its host. Their time of destruction is set, and you and I won't be doing the destroying.

Let's refer to **Mark 5** once again. When Jesus was casting out demons in the region of the Gadarenes, they cried out, **"Son of God, what do you want with us? Have you come here to punish us before the time for us to be judged?"** Most of the encounters between Jesus and demons described in the gospels are typically brief and cryptic, but we can at least tell from this one that God has set a time for demons to be judged and punished. The other thing that we can derive from this particular encounter is that these demons knew, that time had not yet come during the ministry of Jesus. This in itself is interesting because it means that even the demons know that some things have to take place first before their time of reckoning is to take place. One of them things that they're counting on is the rise of lucifer himself. So, as was discussed earlier, they successfully appealed to be sent into a herd of pigs instead.

The knowledge of not trying to kill the demons should allow some of you to stop wasting precious energy with useless words and pointless actions. The reason why God can't and won't destroy any demon before their time is because He honors His Word more than His name and there is a time set for all of the fallen angels to receive the consequence of their defection.

Another secret that we learn from this instance of Jesus delivering this demoniac can be found in Matthew 8, which depicts the same exact scene by Matthew. The legion of demons within the demoniac asked a question:

Matthew 8:29 (KJV)

And, behold, they cried out, saying, What have we to do with thee, Jesus, thou Son of God? art thou come hither to torment us before the time?

You might be asking what is the significance of that question? The significance is that one must understand that demons can be sent for early torment. If they couldn't they would have never mentioned it. So, this means that we can pray for tormenting angels to be sent for early torment according to Matthew 8:29. It would go something like this,

Father God, according to the principle that I understand according to Matthew 8:29, I send every tormenting demon that is oppressing me right now for early torment in Jesus name. I apply that scripture and I pray that each and every one of them be rounded up by mighty warring angels, chained, and taken to the place scheduled for their torment right now. God, you said that greater works shall we do than even our Lord and Savior Jesus Christ and by His very blood we consume every work of the enemy and burn every chain by fire and break its grip by force.

The other reason that I believe that God will allow many of the demons to run free on the earth is because the freedom of every human being must be challenged and tested. Only those who can withstand the pressure of sin that comes from demonic oppression and influence are worthy to be called overcomers. Of course, God could've removed all of the demons, sin, temptation, and suffering from the world, but He didn't and won't and you have to understand that He wants you to learn how to maneuver through this realm **with** all of these stressors and external pressures.

So, remember these imps, strongmen, and legions have a right to roam this earth until their time is up. What they don't have a right to do is occupy the same place as the Holy Spirit. Therefore, if the Spirit of God is within us, there is no authorized way that any demon can inhabit any space within us. Our job is to do what James told us to do in **James 4:7 (KJV)** - *Submit* *yourselves therefore to God. Resist the devil, and he will flee from you.*

See, just because they don't have authorization doesn't mean that they won't try. Adam and subsequently Eve had all power and dominion on the earth but because Eve didn't really know her worth she allowed satan, the serpent, to beguile her; which means *wholly seduce.* The serpent seduced Eve into thinking that she was missing something and there was more that she could experience that God was withholding from her and Adam and she partook. If she would've resisted satan, he would've had to leave her alone. But because she didn't resist, his seduction was completed. She then went and seduced her husband Adam, who was not deceived, as the Bible says, but he was seduced, which caused him to give into the spirit that was now controlling his wife. Immediately after their actions their eyes were opened.

Because of the fact that Adam and Eve acquiesced their authority to satan, it gave him authority over the air and atmosphere of this earth. **Ephesians 6:12 (NIV)** - *For our struggle is not against flesh and blood, but against the rulers, against the authorities, against the powers of this dark world and against the spiritual forces of evil in the heavenly realms.*

Now, we covered some reasons why Jesus probably decided to grant the demons their request of being sent into the swine. **However, the question that you should be asking yourself, is why did the demons ask Jesus to send them into the herd of swine?** The reason is because they were afraid that Jesus was going to send them into the Abyss.

Now, you're asking what is the Abyss? The Abyss is a place, under the middle eastern desert, as I will show you from scripture, where certain chief demons that were running rampant upon the Earth before the flood of Noah's day, has been bound, awaiting the day of judgment. We'll get to more about this in this chapter. Let me take my time, because I'm about to stretch your mind.

What's the lesson? Demons like to go into places that they don't belong. Take the planet Earth, for example. I'd like to throw out just a little bit of extra knowledge for the average believer that I know has no clue or point of reference as to what I'm going to briefly discuss. We all know that one third of the angels left Heaven, their native habitat. Or better stated, they were defeated by Michael and his angels and kicked out of Heaven and fell to the Earth. Now the next few chapters, I want to give you a disclaimer, you don't have to read if you don't want to be stretched, however, some of you will find it interesting and this knowledge will help you as you develop your acumen and propensity for spiritual warfare and prayers that really penetrate Heaven.

The canonized Bible consists of 66 books, however, it's important to know that there were other books that were included in the holy writings throughout all of the Old Testament and even while Jesus walked the Earth. Yes, while Jesus walked the Earth, He was teaching His disciples from the full plethora of spiritual knowledge that was present during His time, whereas the Council of Nicea and all of the rest of the councils hadn't happened yet to take away some of the spiritual literature out of the mainstream that Jesus and the Apostles were reading and learning from during their time. satan managed to take away 33 books that was once a normal part of our holy Christian literature. Wow is right beloved. So, for all of you King James Version or nothing, check yourselves at the door because King James ain't God. One of these books is the Book of Enoch. In the book of Enoch, a story is recounted of an angel name Azazel.

In the Dead Sea Scrolls the name Azazel occurs in the line 6 of 4Q203, The Book of Giants, which is a part of the Enochic literature found at Qumran. I'm going to give you a little bit of this story along with the references whereas you can go a little further and then I will get back to the more main stream traditional Christian references. But let me caveat this knowledge with a statement, all you need is the canonized Bible to live a free and powerful life in God. Some of the restricted books do not need to be read at all and hold no value and may even not be authentic.

But if you know anything about the Dead Sea Scrolls, many biblical literatures was found, including almost the whole book of Isaiah and the whole book of Enoch. Now, that I got that disclaimer out of the way, let's get to it.

According to the Book of Enoch, one of the fallen angels named Azazel is introduced to us as one of the leaders of the rebellious "Watchers" in the time preceding the flood when the "demons of old" would congregate on Mt. Hermon. (Enoch xiii.; compare Brandt, "Die mandäische Religion," 1889, p. 38) It is penned that Azazel taught men the art of warfare, of making swords, knives, shields, and coats of mail. He also taught women the art of deception by ornamenting the body, dyeing the hair, and painting their face and eyebrows. Which is why some of our "Holiness Churches" forbid makeup and the sort completely. But probably the most egregious of his transgressions was that he also revealed to the human race the secrets of witchcraft hence, corrupting the nature of man, leading them into wickedness and impurity until God Himself commanded that he be bound hand and foot by the Archangel Raphael. He commanded Raphael to chain him to the rough and jagged rocks of [Ha] Dudael (= Beth Ḥadudo), where he is to abide in utter darkness until the great Day of Judgment, when he will be cast into the fire to be consumed forever. (Enoch viii. 1, ix. 6, x. 4–6, liv. 5, lxxxviii. 1; see Geiger, "Jüd. Zeit." 1864, pp. 196–204).

Enoch 8:1 *And Azazel taught men to make swords, and knives, and shields, and breastplates, and made known to them the metals of the earth and the art of working them, and bracelets, and ornaments, and the use of antimony, and the beautifying of the eyelids, and all kinds of costly stones, and all 2 colouring tinctures. And there arose much godlessness, and they committed fornication, and they 3 were led astray, and became corrupt in all their ways. . . .* ***(The Apocrypha and Pseudepigrapha of the Old Testament)***

Enoch 10:1 *Then said the Most High, the Holy and Great One spake, and sent Uriel to the son of Lamech, 2 and said to him: 'Go to* **Noah** *and tell him in my name "Hide thyself!" and reveal to* *him the end that is approaching: that the whole earth will be destroyed, and a deluge is about to come 3 upon the whole earth, and will destroy all that is on it. And now instruct him that he may escape 4 and his seed may be preserved for all the generations of the world.'* ***And again the Lord said to Raphael: 'Bind Azazel hand and foot, and cast him into the darkness: and make an opening 5 in the desert, which is in Dudael, and cast him therein.*** *And place upon him rough and jagged rocks, and cover him with darkness, and let him abide there forever, and cover his face that he may 6,7 not see light. And on the day of the great judgement he shall be cast into the fire. . . . 8 . . . the whole earth has been corrupted 9 through the works that were taught by Azazel: to him ascribe all sin.* ***(The Apocrypha and Pseudepigrapha of the Old Testament)***

Why do I give you this extra knowledge? Because the truth has been hidden systematically by satan himself from generation to generation to keep the human race limited. My assignment, given to me by God Himself, is to expose the ignorance and inform His people once again. How does the scripture, we wrestle not against flesh and blood, but against principalities and powers and rulers of darkness in high places, etc. make any sense if all you know about in the angelic world is Michael, Gabriel, and satan. If that's your only reference you have no clue and your power concerning mental assent is weak, because of lack of knowledge.

John 8:36

So if the Son sets you free, you will be free indeed.

The early disciples, turned Apostles, was taught by Jesus Himself, and all of the secrets that were written and undoubtedly unwritten, were taught to them. Which is why when they prayed a prayer of deliverance, for example, results had to occur. Which is why even when they were threatened with losing their lives, they never faltered, because they had all of the knowledge and proof that they needed, or in plain terms, the truth. And this truth produced what I like to call perfect faith. When you have perfect faith, you can literally say unto a mountain, be thou removed unto the sea, and it has to happen. When you have perfect faith, you can speak to the Sun and command it to stay still and God will honor your words. When your mind and more importantly your spirit is expanded via the truth that can only come from the Holy Spirit, nothing can make it shrink back to its former limits.

Let me show you this particular angel in the Bible and explain the place of the Abyss.

Leviticus 16:6-10 (ESV)

6 And Aaron shall offer the bull as a sin offering for himself, and shall make atonement for himself and for his house.
7 Then he shall take the two goats, and set them before the LORD at the door of the tent of meeting;
8 and Aaron shall cast lots upon the two goats, one lot for the LORD and the other lot for Azazel.
9 And Aaron shall present the goat on which the lot fell for the LORD, and offer it as a sin offering;
10 but the goat on which the lot fell for Azazel shall be presented alive before the LORD to make atonement over it, that it may be sent away into the wilderness to Azazel.

As this passage of Scripture shows, the high priest was to enter into the Most Holy Place of the Tabernacle, and later the Temple, **only** one time per year. The day that they were to do this on was on the Day of Atonement, which is 10 Tishri on the Hebrew calendars. This entry into the Most Holy Place was allowed so atonement could be made for the people, to cleanse them of their sins so that they would be clean before the LORD [***YHVH***] (Lev. 16:30).

The ceremony with the two goats is the main focus of the rite conducted on the Day of Atonement. In addition to the information recorded in Leviticus 16, we are given additional details about this observance in the ***Mishnah***, which is the body of Jewish oral law recorded in the 2nd century CE. The tract ***Yoma*** describes this ceremony in detail.

In ***Yoma*** we are told that a box was brought to the high priest which contained two lots, one marked "for ***YHVH***" and the other marked "for Azazel." The high priest put his hands in the box and brought out a lot in each hand; he held up the hand which contained the lot for ***YHVH***. The high priest then tied a crimson thread on the head of the goat which was to be sent forth (the goat for Azazel), and another crimson thread around the throat of the goat which would be slain as a sin offering (the goat for ***YHVH***).

After the high priest atoned for his own sins and those of his family by the blood of the bull (Lev. 16:6, 11-14), the goat which had been designated "for ***YHVH***" was brought to him. The high priest then slaughtered this goat, and its blood was used to purify the Most Holy Place from the uncleanness of the Israelites. Who or what did this goat represent? The author of Hebrews clearly shows us the answer:

Hebrews 9:11 - *But Christ came as High Priest of the good things to come, with the greater and more perfect tabernacle not made with hands, that is, not of this creation. 12 Not with the blood of goats and calves, but* ***with his own blood he entered the Most Holy Place*** *once for all, having obtained eternal redemption.* ***(NKJV)***

Unquestionably the goat chosen "for ***YHVH***" was symbolic of Yeshua, which is the Hebrew name for Jesus, who of course is the Messiah. As the High Priest of the New Covenant, he entered the Most Holy Place in the heavenly Tabernacle and cleansed us of our sins with his own blood, not that of a goat:

HEBREWS 9:24 - *For Christ has not entered the holy places made with hands, which are copies of the true, but into heaven itself, now to appear in the presence of God for us; 25 not that he should offer himself often, as the high priest enters the Most Holy Place every year with blood of another. 26 He then would have had to suffer often since the foundation of the world; but now, once at the end of the ages, he has appeared to put away sin by the sacrifice of himself.* ***(NKJV)***

Through our acceptance of the sacrifice of Jesus (Yeshua), we have access to the Most Holy Place in heaven and can go into the very presence of God our Father:

Hebrews 10:19 - *Therefore, brethren, having boldness to enter the Holiest by the blood of Jesus, 20 by a new and living way which he consecrated for us, through the veil, that is, his flesh, 21 and having a High Priest over the house of God, 22 let us draw near with a true heart in full assurance of faith, having our hearts sprinkled from an evil conscience and our bodies washed with pure water. **(NKJV)***

Now after the goat for the LORD had been slain and its blood sprinkled on the mercy seat, the goat for Azazel was brought to the high priest. He laid both hands on its head and made the following confession:

"O Lord, your people, the house of Israel, has committed iniquity, transgressed, and sinned before you. Forgive O Lord, I pray, the iniquities, transgressions, and sins, which your people, the house of Israel, have committed, transgressed, and sinned before you, as it is written in the Torah of Moses, your servant, *For on this day shall atonement be made for you to clean you. From all your sins shall you be clean before the Lord*" (*Yoma*6:2, ***The Mishnah, A New Translation***)

According to Bryan T. Huie, who is the Elder and bible study leader of the Derek LeChayim Bible Study Group in Central Arkansas, at that time, the high priest gave the goat for Azazel over to the man who was to lead it out into the wilderness. Anyone could be chosen for this task, but later high priests made it a practice of selecting someone other than an Israelite to lead the goat. The goat was taken to a ravine, **thought by some scholars to be a precipice about 12 miles east of Jerusalem.** At that time, the man leading the goat divided the crimson thread on the head of the goat. Half of it he tied to a rock, and the other half he tied between the horns of the goat. He then pushed the goat backwards until it fell into the ravine. Because of the steep and jagged nature of the chasm, the goat for Azazel was usually dead before it had fallen halfway down the mountain.

This precipice about 12 miles east of Jerusalem or wherever the place really is where the demons of Mark 5 didn't want to be sent. They were saying to Jesus, send us anywhere except the place where Azazel and the rest of these very, very bad demons are being held. Let's read this again from Luke's perspective:

Luke 8:26 – [26] *Then they sailed to the country of the Gadarenes, which is opposite Galilee.* [27] *And when he stepped out on the land, there met him* ***a certain man from the city who had demons for a long time****. And he wore no clothes, nor did he live in a house but in the tombs.* [28] *When he saw Jesus, he cried out, fell down before him, and with a loud voice said, "What have I to do with you, Jesus, Son of the Most High God? I beg you, do not torment me!"*
[29] *For he had commanded the* ***unclean spirit*** *to come out of the man. For it had often seized him, and he was kept under guard, bound with chains and shackles; and he broke the bonds and was driven by the* ***demon*** *into the wilderness.* [30] *Jesus asked him, saying, "What is your name?" And he said, "Legion," because* ***many demons*** *had entered him.* [31] *And* ***they begged him that he would not command them to go out into the Abyss****.* [32] *Now a herd of many swine was feeding there on the mountain. So they begged him that he would permit them to enter them. And he permitted them.* [33] *Then the* ***demons*** *went out of the man and entered the swine, and the herd ran violently down the steep place into the lake and drowned.* ***(NKJV)***

As the passage of Scripture above shows, the demons who inhabited this man were terrified of being banished by Jesus (Yeshua) into the Abyss.

So, what have we learned here? Some demons and fallen angels are free to spawn evil in the physical world. However, there are Scriptures which confirm that a portion of these evil spirits and angels are currently restrained in darkness and chains. Let's look at what a few of the New Testament Apostles had to say about the subject:

Jude 6 - *And* ***the angels*** *who did not keep their own position, but left their proper dwelling, he has* ***kept in eternal chains in deepest darkness*** *for the judgment of the great Day. 7 Likewise, Sodom and Gomorrah and the surrounding cities, which,* ***in the same manner as they*** *[the angels], indulged in sexual immorality and pursued unnatural lust, serve as an example by undergoing a punishment of eternal fire.* ***(NRSV)***

II Peter 2:4 - *God did not spare* ***the angels who sinned****, but cast them down to hell and delivered them into* ***chains of darkness****, to be reserved for judgment;* ***(NKJV)***

I Peter 3:19 - *He [Messiah] went and preached to* ***the spirits in prison****, 20 who formerly were disobedient, when once the Divine longsuffering waited in the days of Noah, while the ark was being prepared, in which a few, that is, eight souls, were saved through water.* ***(NKJV)***

The Scriptures above basically are reiterating what I've already shown you from the ***Book of Enoch***. Notice that the Apostle Jude specifically states that it was those angels who committed sexual sins with human women that were being kept in chains until the end of this age in utter darkness. And then furthermore, these same angels are referenced by the Apostle Peter in his second epistle as well. And then the kicker is that Peter, the Apostle who Jesus built His church on, let us know that the preincarnate Messiah, who is our Jesus (Yeshua), went and preached to these imprisoned angels during the days of Noah, while he was preparing the ark. Are you getting goosebumps yet?

In short, the ceremony on the Day of Atonement depicted the sacrifice of the goat as a representative of Jesus (Yeshua) and His sacrifice for our sins on the cross. And the other goat was representative of the soon coming victory that Jesus will claim over Azazel and the forces of evil at the end of this age.

I'm going to take you a little further, because I showed you in Enoch 10 the fate of all of these chief demons, however, I'd like to show you something else in the book of Revelation regarding the unsealing of the Abyss.

Revelation 9:1- *And the fifth angel sounded, and I saw a star from heaven fallen unto the earth: and there was given to him the key of* ***the pit of the Abyss****. 2 And he opened* ***the pit of the Abyss****; and there went up a smoke out of the pit, as the smoke of a great furnace; and the sun and the air were darkened by reason of the smoke of the pit. 3 And out of the smoke came forth locusts upon the earth; and power was given them, as the scorpions of the earth have power. 4 And it was said unto them that they should not hurt the grass of the earth, neither any green thing, neither any tree, but only such men as have not the seal of God on their foreheads. 5 And it was given them that they should not kill them, but that they should be tormented five months: and their torment was as the torment of a scorpion, when it striketh a man. 6 And in those days men shall seek death, and shall in no wise find it; and they shall desire to die, and death fleeth from them. 7 And the shapes of the locusts were like unto horses prepared for war; and upon their heads as it were crowns like unto gold, and their faces were as men's faces. 8 And they had hair as the hair of women, and their teeth were as teeth of lions. 9 And they had breastplates, as it were breastplates of iron; and the sound of their wings was as the sound of chariots, of many horses rushing to war. 10 And they have tails like unto scorpions, and stings; and in their tails is their power to hurt men five months.* ***(ASV)***

Revelation 9:11 - ***They had for their king the angel of the Abyss****, whose name, in Hebrew, is* ***Abaddon****, and in Greek,* ***Apollyon****, or the Destroyer.* ***(NEB)***

The "star" which falls from heaven to earth is an angel who has the key to the pit of the Abyss. This angel has the authority to open the Abyss and release the demons and evil angels imprisoned there. He does it and they go on to torment all of humanity. God uses them for five months as an instrument of His wrath; they are allowed to *inflict pain on those on the earth who don't have God's seal on their foreheads* **(Rev. 7:2-8)**.

Abaddon or Apollyon both mean destroyer. As you should remember from a few chapters prior, Azazel's most egregious crime was teaching mankind warfare. One would surmise that these Angels that will be released are one and the same and will one day be released upon the Earth to just go ballistic on all of humanity. It won't be an easy time for anyone who has not been raptured up to this point.

I needed to go through all of that with you beloved, because you need to understand that there are forces on the Earth, under the Earth, and in the Heavens, that are first of all real, and secondly, very powerful. The Bible says in **Hosea 4:6** - *My people are destroyed for lack of knowledge: because thou hast rejected knowledge, I will also reject thee, that thou shalt be no priest to me: seeing thou hast forgotten the law of thy God, I will also forget thy children.* You don't overcome these forces by accident, you overcome them on purpose through the power of the name of Jesus and His redeeming blood. If you don't have respect for that fact you might as well close this book and go back to reading about prosperity and getting rich, because that's the only god (mammon) that some of you care about.

So, you have a little bit of extra knowledge about the state of affairs regarding the historic makeup of principalities and powers and spiritual wickedness in high and low places, even though I'm going to go a lot deeper in this book. If you have the correct knowledge this will change your prayer life. Now, I'm not going to go any further, in this book, with that kind of knowledge (extra biblical), because if you're immature, the knowledge can stain and skew you from the truth, which is not my point. Let's look at something else regarding special knowledge that Jesus revealed to us regarding the activity of demons when they are kicked out of or off of a human host.

One of Jesus' parables shows how God wanted people to respond instead to the fact that demons remained at large even after they had been cast out of their victims. Jesus said, in **Luke 11:24** ~ *When the unclean spirit is gone out of a man, he walketh through dry places, seeking rest; and finding none, he saith, I will* *return unto my house whence I came out.* One must know that during the time of Jesus it was common knowledge that disembodied demons inhabited desolate places, such as the deserts of Syria, Arabia, and Egypt. If you remember, Jesus Himself was approached by lucifer himself after he fasted for 40 days and 40 nights in the desert. I could give you reference to other demons being caught in the desert and bound by Godly Angels at God's request, but I won't because it involves other non-canonical books. However, tacit knowledge, lets us know that there is an atmosphere in dark and desolate places that are conducive to fear, lunacy, and despair. Again, this is why a child normally doesn't like to go to sleep with all of the lights off.

One of my prayers when I am in a serious encounter with a demonically possessed or oppressed person is this:

Father God, I now cover myself with the blood of Jesus Christ, and pray that the Holy Spirit would bring all of the work of the crucifixion, resurrection, and glorification over my life right now. I affirm that I have all the dunamis power that was received by men at Pentecost (Acts 1:8) and in the name of Jesus, I command any ungodly spirit to leave this man or woman right now. I command you to a dry and desolate place. Go and never return, in the name of Jesus!

The reason why I say this is to one free the host, but two, make sure the demon knows that I have the knowledge of God, Who has the power, and faith to deal with him. I even sometimes literally say, ***in the name of Jesus Christ, I command you to leave him or her and go to the Abyss.*** You are guaranteed to either encounter a full manifestation after this or the demon will immediately leave.

Why do I include the power of Pentecost? One must understand the scripture in **Acts 1:8** (MEV) which says, *"But you shall receive power when the Holy Spirit comes upon you, and you shall be My witnesses in Jerusalem, in all Judea and Samaria, and to the ends of the earth."*

As you know Jesus said that He had to leave so that the Holy Spirit can come, and greater works shall we do. This is the same power that Acts 1:8 is referring too. The Koine Greek word being used for power here is dunamis, which the Analytical Lexicon of the Greek New Testament defines as thus: "able to produce a strong effect power, might, strength and "supernatural manifestations of power miracle, wonder, powerful deed." Dunamis is used 10 times in the Acts of the Apostles and is always used in reference to God's power, miracles, signs and wonders.

One must understand that whenever the Bible uses the word dunamis, it is always referring to the power of God not ours. It never refers to our strength or ability but rather to His power through us. It is His power alone that keeps us, and it His power that forms our character as we walk in His power and glorify Him. So, if you include this in your prayer, you are using all of the ammunition given to us by God at one time; the Blood of Jesus, the Name of Jesus, and the Dunamis power of the Holy Spirit combined in Faith that nothing and/or no one can stand against the power of God.

Now, let's keep progressing. Because there are levels to this thing. The next level that I've arrived at after mastering what I've already taught you was revealed to me by the Holy Spirit Himself after much meditating and prayer. What the Holy Spirit has taught me since engaging in these types of activities is that I don't necessarily have to say go to a dry and arid place in the deliverance process. And I've learned this through the conduct of Jesus in these situations. The reason I've used the story of this particular demoniac in Mark 5 is because it's the only time Jesus sent a demon to a specific location. Every other time He just said leave, go, get thee hence, etc. Jesus never told the demons where to go, He just told them to leave its host. Sometimes he even told them to shut up first and then leave. I pondered this and prayed about this and what the Holy Spirit revealed to me is that we don't have to tell the demons to go to a dry place because as soon as they are extracted from us, they are already in dry places, whereas we must remember that we are made up of at least 70% water.

Remember that God separated the heavens from the earth and the sea from the land.

The other thing to learn from the actions of Jesus is that we should never negotiate with the enemy. The United States has a policy of not negotiating with terrorists and guess what beloved? So, do we. The Kingdom doesn't negotiate with terrorist. Demons exist to create terror. Don't negotiate with demons. This isn't the movie, The Exorcist. Just tell them to leave in the mighty name of Jesus.

The most important thing after a demon is cast out of a person is to fill the once occupied place that is now empty. We have to fill those empty, once occupied places, with truth, healing and new revelation. We must do this right away, because Jesus taught us in Luke 11:24-26, that the demon that has been evicted will always try and return, and if the demon is successful in his attempt to return he will bring with him seven more demons, even more wicked than before.

"When an unclean spirit goes out of a man, he goes through dry places, seeking rest; and finding none, he says, 'I will return to my house from which I came.' And when he comes, he finds it swept and put in order. Then he goes and takes with him seven other spirits more wicked than himself, and they enter and dwell there; and the last state of that man is worse than the first" **(Luke 11:24-26, NKJV).**

The truth of the matter is that simply just asking the Holy Spirit to fill these empty places will not be sufficient to keep the newly freed man or woman from being re-inhabited. The only way to ensure that the evil spirits will be defeated when they return is to make sure that the door is shut. We shut the door by getting with the freed man or woman and discuss where the point of entry may have been for them to come in, in the first place. Was it through witchcraft? Was it through abuse? Was it through bitterness and unforgiveness? Has someone given you an item that you haven't asked for lately? Was it through the eye gate (pornography, murder/horror movies)? Was it through the ear gate (Rock, Heavy

Metal, Hard Hip-Hop, Metallica)? And on and on and on. I think you get the point. We need to have the total revelation and understanding of the lies that opened the door, so that we can come into agreement with God's truth. That is the only way to fill the empty space. ***And you shall know the truth and the truth shall set you free (John 8:32, NKJV).*** The truth will close the door and keep the light on in the room so that no darkness can ever come in again. That's why the scripture says that Jesus is the light of the world.

And the light shines in the darkness, and the darkness did not comprehend it **(John 1:5, NKJV).**

For you were once darkness, but now you are light in the Lord. Walk as children of light **(Ephesians 5:8, NKJV).**

Keep the light on beloved, because thieves like to break in during black outs and at times when they think that people are not home. By the way, if you are an adult and have issues with being attacked by demons in your dreams or feel like you're being choked or can't breathe. Pray this prayer on bended knee before you even get in your bed

:

Father God, as I lay me down to sleep cover me deep in the Blood of Jesus. Blood of Jesus fight for my physical body, spirit, and soul, right now in the name of Jesus. To any and EVERY dark power pressing me down in my dreams, I command that you die by the power in the blood of Jesus.

Father God, I put on your armor that you said is mine in Ephesians 6 and I ask you to fight for me.

I lay a fire to EVERY agenda of the enemy for my life through EVERY satanic oppression. To EVERY satanic power, your time is up, the blood of Jesus is against you, and by the authority of the name of Jesus I command that you die by fire, in the name of Jesus. By the power of the blood of Jesus and the authority of His name, I declare that EVERY

power that is sitting on my peace, good, and expected end, be unseated by fire, in Jesus name.

If you are ever a victim of this kind of event, make no mistake that you have been targeted in the spirit realm for warfare. This is a classic spiritual attack that has been initiated by someone who is jealous and for some reason has hate and/or maybe unforgiveness in their heart against you. If this is happening to you, understand that you have been targeted by witchcraft. Let me clarify, if you don't have emphysema or asthma, which are spirits as well, you are the victim and target of a witch or warlock. These powers cannot be seen with your physical eyes, however, when your spiritual vision becomes developed you will see them in realms and spheres of the spirit. Some of you are even seeing the faces of people that you know choking you or sitting on your chest. Am I correct? You have been targeted and you must take action against the attack. If you ever have this type of dream and you can't see their faces in your dream or their faces was blurred it could mean that the people that are performing witchcraft on you or sending demonic darts your way are people that you know. Please note that sometimes people enact witchcraft and send bad energy and spirits our way unknowingly. This is why you should distance yourself from individuals that does not have a certain discipline of speech that would yield positivity over negativity.

The purpose of the attack is to stop you from progressing in life and being blessed. To the person that doesn't know how to warfare, they can expect this to be a sign of some very negative things to follow. Fight, pray, and resist the devil and his cohorts and they will flee. Even in your dreams, you can fight. Just speak the name of Jesus! Apply the blood of Jesus to every nefarious spirit and they will disintegrate, and rest assured you will wake right up. Pray the prayers prior to going to sleep and you will never have these attacks again.

If you keep the light of Christ burning bright within your heart, there is NO WAY that you can ever become subject to a possession or anything of the sort. The only people that in any way that can be inhabited by these foul and nasty spirits are people that commonly keep dark things in their heart. Such as hate, unforgiveness, depression, low self-esteem, jealousy, envy, lying, lust, murder, and on and on and on. Somebody just got delivered just now! Hallelujah! Glory to God! The truth has made you free beloved and the "strongman" has been evicted. Now, walk as a child of light and let's learn more how to create havoc in the kingdom of darkness.

Your heart matters and seeking the spiritual first is a key ingredient in getting more from God. When you pray your heart opens up and is an open book to Heaven. When God told Solomon that he can ask for whatever he wanted so that He could grant it to him, Solomon asked God for wisdom. It pleased God that He asked for the spiritual instead of the material and God gave him all the material that he could handle. Solomon became the richest man that ever lived.

When Elijah asked Elisha what he wanted, Elisha said that he wanted a double portion. Elijah said you have asked for a hard thing, but if you see me when I'm taken up, it will be so. Elisha stuck with and served the man of God and because he asked for the spiritual God allowed Elisha to do twice the number of miracles than Elijah. Seek the spiritual before you seek the material. *Seek ye first the Kingdom of God and all of these things shall be added unto thee.* **Matt. 6:33**.

Exousia

The anointing is a powerful force that is always present. However, it takes faith to activate it.

Apostle Dr. Larry Birchett, Jr.

Luke 10:19-20 (NKJV)

19 Behold, I give you the authority to trample on serpents and scorpions, and over all the power of the enemy, and nothing shall by any means hurt you. 20 Nevertheless do not rejoice in this, that the spirits are subject to you, but rather rejoice because your names are written in heaven."

In order to be an effective prayer warrior and intercessor you have to know what kind of authority you have before you pray. I want to drop this chapter right here in this book because prayer is more than just a bunch of cleverly chosen words and scriptures that will produce an effect, which is nothing but witchcraft by the way. Prayer is of no effect if you don't know your rights within it. A more direct way to say this is that you have to know your power. The word that Jesus used when He taught and educated His disciples was exousia. Exousia is a Greek word most often translated into the word "authority" or "power." This term is not exclusive to just a natural authority but also a moral authority. Exousia can also be thought of in terms of jurisdiction or dominion over a certain realm, right, privilege, or ability.

When you think of moral authority you think of an entity or a person that possesses an integrity beyond reproach that has a mastery of the moral principles that comprise what one would call spiritual ethics. To narrow down the scope of what we really need to master in regard to talking about wielding biblical authority in the earth realm, we'll call it biblical ethics. Ethical thinking leads to ethical living and without a moral compass that comprises of everything ethical one cannot obtain the moral authority that the spirit world even must respect. The important feature to identify in this conversation of ethics is what set of ethics are you being governed by. That's why biblical ethics is critical, because biblical ethics lead to biblical thinking.

Right up front, one must understand that there are principles that exist in the atmosphere that is universal regardless to belief or whatever you think about God. For example, whatever goes around comes around. This is basically Jesus's principle of *Do unto others as you would have them do unto you.* One false religious tradition, called Buddhism, even calls it Karma. Also, I believe that everyone would agree that slavery is wrong and inhumane. Additionally, most of the modern world believes that supremacist and extremist views are wrong and dangerous. To not like, not hire, or want to kill someone because of their racial origin is wrong. Wouldn't you agree? We all know that it is wrong to kill another human being. It doesn't matter if you are a Muslim, Buddhist, or Christian we all know that it is wrong to bully someone because they are weaker than you or to abuse a child in any way. And I can go on and on and on, but I think you get the point. All of these things are wrong irrespective of your belief regarding theological issues.

Ethics are moral principles that govern a person's behavior or the conducting of an activity. The thoughts or opinions that I just suggested all represent polar extremes of ethical thinking and living. And I used them to zone in on what ethics really is and why it is so important As Christians, our ethics should be based off the Word of God. Anything that the Bible speaks against we shouldn't do it. Anything that it permits we shouldn't feel any condemnation regarding any of the permissible things.

The Name of Jesus

In light of this, understand that we serve a God of principles. One principle that you should adhere too if you want your prayer to travel through dimensions, is that God will not answer your prayers if you are praying in your own strength. We pray in the name of Jesus because it's at His name that all knees will bow and declare that He is Lord. We pray in the name of Jesus because He is the King of Kings and Lord of Lords and all power has been giving to Him in the Heavens and Earth. And to make this point even more simple, we pray in the name of Jesus because the Bible tells us to. Jesus said to His disciples in in the fourteenth chapter of John:

John 14:13 (NKJV)

"Whatever you ask in My name, that I will do, that the Father may be glorified in the Son."

And in the sixteenth chapter of John He said:

John 16:24 (NKJV)

"Until now, you have asked nothing in my name. Ask and you will receive that your joy may be full."

And so, when we pray in the name of Jesus we see that we're doing three things: first, we're glorifying the Father; second, we're increasing the capacity of our joy; and third, we are using the only name that gives us an authority to wield the spiritual power that Jesus Himself say that we have. This is an important teaching because one must understand that God hears every prayer, because if He didn't the sinner wouldn't be able to get saved. However, once we're saved, we have to know that the name of Jesus is in fact, our spiritual ID badge, so to speak, that gets us into privileged places in the Kingdom. The name of Jesus is our security clearance that gives us access to do work (prayer) regarding the deep things (spiritual warfare) of God. Beloved, have you been using your badge, when you go to work?

Another principle is that God will not answer your prayer if there is unconfessed sin that has not been addressed.

1 John 1:9 (NKJV)

> *"If we confess our sin, he is faithful and just to forgive our sin and to cleanse us from all unrighteousness."*

The context of this verse is being addressed to Christians and the promise of God's forgiveness hinges on the word **if**. God offers total pardon for every sin His children commits **if** we confess it to Him. **You have to confess it if you want God's grace and love to address it.** This is such an underrated activity in Christendom, confessing our sins, praying for the forgiveness of sins and asking God for repentance. Consider Jesus's instructions in the first few verses of Luke 13:

Luke 13 New King James Version (NKJV)

1 There were present at that season some who told Him about the
Galileans whose blood Pilate had mingled with their
sacrifices. 2 And Jesus answered and said to them, "Do you
suppose that these Galileans were worse sinners than
all other Galileans, because they suffered such things? 3 I tell you,
no; but unless you repent you will all likewise perish. 4 Or those
eighteen on whom the tower in Siloam fell and killed them, do you
think that they were worse sinners than all other men who dwelt in
Jerusalem? 5 I tell you, no; ***but unless you repent you will all***
likewise perish*."*

Beloved, if you would be free of sin's power and consequence, pray this prayer:

Dear God, in the name of Jesus:

Your Word tells us in Romans 10:9 that if I confess with my lips that Jesus is Lord and believe in my heart that You raised him from the dead, then I am saved. According to Luke 13:3 I repent of my past sins and I admit and confess that I have sinned. I believe that You are faithful and just to cleanse me from all unrighteousness. I call upon You, Lord JESUS to cleanse me from all sin and unrighteousness by Your Blood (1 John 1:7). And as Your word says in Romans 10:13 ***Everyone who calls upon the name of the Lord will be saved.***

I've covered the fact that God is holy, and He demands holiness, so this shouldn't be a surprise. God and sin don't mix and can't mix. So, if you expect God to convene in and over your prayers you have to make sure that you have confessed your sins, cleansed your spirit, and purged your soul before Him. All throughout the Bible we see God operating in this way. He asks us to do something so that we can receive a certain response. Forgiveness and hence prayer are no different.

The other principle that applies to answered prayer regardless of anything else that you're doing right is idolatry. You have to get rid of any idols that you have in your life, known and unknown. An idol is anything that you give preeminence over God in your life. For example, the pride of life could be an idol. Your spouse could be an idol. Your children could be an idol. Your money could be an idol. Your title and perceived stature and appearance could be an idol.

I think I lost some of you. What I'm saying is that if you're so content with things just because of the vast amount of money in your bank account, you have made money your idol. Why do you need to pray to God to do something if you don't need anything from Him? So, you're saying well money is not my issue so I'm good. But what about your children? if you're making statements like, "My children are my world." Or let's try this one, "Nothing comes before my children." You have just set yourself and your children up for warfare, because God does not want to come in second to no one. Are you understanding what I'm saying? If you don't want premature death or sickness to come and take your idol, in this case, your children, out of the way, don't make them your idol. It could be your spouse. It could be your house. It could be your Pastor even. It could even be appearance, always having to appear as if you're living in certain social circles and status. Are you paying a car note that is way beyond your means, just to appear as if you're more successful than you are? I know people, even pastors unfortunately, that live in Thirty Thousand-dollar row homes with Fifty Thousand-dollar cars. Huh? Deal with these things so that God can dress you with the full complement of authority that He said you can have.

Let's look at this word exousia. We see it used in **Matthew 7 (ESV)**, the chapter that starts off with Jesus telling everyone not to judge unless you want to be judged yourself:

1 "Judge not, that you be not judged. 2 For with the judgment you pronounce you will be judged, and with the measure you use it will be measured to you. 3 Why do you see the speck that is in your brother's eye, but do not notice the log that is in your own eye?

It's important for us to know that Jesus started off talking about this, because Jesus was talking about character and making sure that we as individuals are totally cleansed before we start engaging in spiritual warfare with principalities and powers and the rulers of darkness in high places. After He explains to them the things that they shouldn't be doing, and the state of the heart expected, He tells them in verse 24 that anyone who hears these sayings and does them are like a ***wise man who built his house on the rock***; that even the rains, floods, and winds couldn't knock it down because it was built on a good foundation.

We then see Jesus instructing them regarding prayer in verses **Matthew 7:7-12:**

[7] "Ask, and it will be given to you; seek, and you will find; knock, and it will be opened to you. [8] For everyone who asks receives, and he who seeks finds, and to him who knocks it will be opened. [9] Or what man is there among you who, if his son asks for bread, will give him a stone?[10] Or if he asks for a fish, will he give him a serpent? [11] If you then, being evil, know how to give good gifts to your children, how much more will your Father who is in heaven give good things to those who ask Him![12] Therefore, whatever you want men to do to you, do also to them, for this is the Law and the Prophets.

They were astonished at His teaching on prayer because He taught as one who had special insight to the process. And of course, we know now that He did, being as though He was God in the flesh as the Word tells us in **John 1:14**. Of course, Jesus, the one who answers and responds to prayers know exactly what the process is beyond the words leaving our lips.

Jesus clearly let us know that every time we ask there will be a response. Our prayers activate Heaven and creates an enormous amount of activity. He also lets us know that God listens to everyone's prayers whereas *'For everyone who asks receives'*. The question for anyone of average to superior intellect would be or should be, receive what? The answer is in verse 11; good things.

If you ask for something that is in the will of God, God will give it to you. But you have to pray according to the principle that God set forth in **John 16:23,24** regarding praying in the name of Jesus. Everything that we want from God is contained in Jesus. **Every prayer that would make it through every dimension to God's ears has to go through Jesus.**

[23] And in that day ye shall ask Me nothing. Verily, verily I say unto you, whatsoever ye shall ask the Father in My name, He will give it to you.

[24] Hitherto have ye asked nothing in My name. Ask and ye shall receive, that your joy may be full.

So basically, Jesus was teaching that we should ask and keep on asking and in God's timing the prayer will be answered. One note about God's answers is that it's not always yes. He was teaching seek and keep on seeking and you will find. A quick note on that though, is that you may not like what you find. Jesus taught that we should knock and keep on knocking and God will open doors for you. A note of clarification however, God knows what doors are to be opened and which doors are to remain shut. Trust God's judgment in these matters because His ways are not your ways and His thoughts are not your thoughts. **Also, open doors are spiritual indicators of gateways to your ultimate destiny and purpose, so there is no way that God will allow any door to be opened prematurely.**

We can come to God in confidence but don't be discouraged just because it doesn't look like Heaven is addressing your prayer. Just keep on praying and don't change your prayer because every time you change your prayer you negate the last prayer that has activated Heaven. Remember the Bible states in **James 1:8**, that *a double minded man is unstable in all of his ways.* **That's why you must spend time in the Word of God first to know the will of God before you can even pray for God's will to be done in your life.**

After all of this teaching they were astonished at His manner of teaching because He taught as if He wrote the law, not understanding that He was the actual Word in the flesh and the actual fulfillment of the Law. Let's look at verses 28 and 29 of **Matthew 7**:

28 And so it was, when Jesus had ended these sayings, that the people were astonished at His teaching, 29 for He taught them as one having authority, and not as the scribes.

The scripture is saying that He taught with exousia, the Greek translation of the word authority; something that obviously, the other teachers of the law didn't possess. We know this to be true because of the many demoniacs that walked in this region of the earth while Jesus was there. The word is also used in **Matthew**

9:6 when Jesus demonstrates that He has "authority" to forgive sins by healing a paralyzed man. The word is again used in **Matthew 21:23–27** when the chief priests and elders question Jesus's authority.

Now remember that I stated earlier that a person who would wield true authority would have to hold the moral compass of Godly principles that would comprise of them being deemed ethical. Well watch this next point, because interestingly, in **Luke 4:6** it is exousia with which Satan tries to tempt Jesus.

Luke 4:5-7

[5] *Then the devil, taking Him up on a high mountain, showed Him all the kingdoms of the world in a moment of time.* [6] *And the devil said to Him, "All this* ***authority*** *I will give You, and their glory; for this has been delivered to me, and I give it to whomever I wish.* [7] *Therefore, if You will worship before me, all will be Yours."*

How can satan even deem to give Jesus authority while He walked the earth? The answer is simple, he has the moral authority and is the prince ruling spirit of the air due to the fall of Adam in the Garden of Eden. If you notice Jesus didn't quibble about satan's statement, Jesus just kindly took His own authority and reminded satan of who He was, the Living Word:

[8] ***And Jesus answered and said to him, "Get behind Me, Satan! For it is written, 'You shall worship the Lord your God, and Him only you shall serve.'"***

Our authority comes from the scriptures beloved. As a matter of fact, every scripture is a prescription to fight or combat against evilness and wickedness due to the fall. Just like a doctor that would prescribe you antibiotics or some other kind of medicine to fight off an infection or other kind of sickness is the same way that God has given us "scripture" (**pre**-script-ions) to fight off all of the attacks of the enemy is this earth realm.

In fact, God gave us these "prescriptions" before they were ever written. That's why I like to call the holy scriptures, pre-script-ions. See, because Jesus is the Word **(John 1:1.14)**, and He has no beginning or ending, and He was slain even before the foundations of the earth, we understand that they already existed before they were physically written. Therefore, the scriptures that we use is just Jesus (God wrapped in flesh) being thrown back at the devil to defeat his every work. God has prescribed a scripture for every headache that the enemy causes you. God has prescribed a scripture for every illness that you find yourself dealing with. The Bible is full of prescriptions against every condition beloved and the best thing about these prescriptions is that they always work. Rejoice beloved, because whatever you're dealing with right now, Jesus is your prescription. Take a heavy dose of Jesus and I promise you that when you wake up in the morning everything will be alright.

And just to set the record straight for any one just learning about principalities, powers, dominion and authority, in **Ephesians 1:17–23** we see that Jesus is far above all authority, dominion, and power. The following set of scriptures was and is Paul's prayer for the church of Ephesus to receive spiritual wisdom regarding theirs and our authority (exousia).

17 That the God of our Lord Jesus Christ, the Father of glory, may give to you the spirit of wisdom and revelation in the knowledge of Him, 18 the eyes of your understanding being enlightened; that you may know what is the hope of His calling, what are the riches of the glory of His inheritance in the saints, ***19 and what is the exceeding greatness of His power toward us who believe, according to the working of His mighty power*** *20 which He worked in Christ when He raised Him from the dead and seated Him at His right hand in the heavenly places,* ***21 far above all principality and power and might and dominion, and every name that is named, not only in this age but also in that which is to come.***

*[22] And He put **all things** under His feet, and gave Him to be head over all things to the church, [23] which is His body, the fullness of Him who fills all in all.*

I'm giving you all of these scriptures so that you can truly have power beloved. Again, our authority comes through the Word of God, which is Jesus Christ, our Lord and Savior, because true exousia is His. Paul was explaining that through the knowledge and total acceptance of Jesus the Christ, the exceeding great power of God is extended to us who believe that we can possess His delegated power and authority, to apply and use according to His will and unlimited power. Truly awesome and empowering and I also appreciate that the Holy Spirit is being straight forward. Basically, showing us that it's all about Jesus. As verses 22 and 23 states Jesus is the head of all things to the church, which comprises of us men and women of God. We are the ekklessia, or in other words, the church. We are the literal body of Jesus Christ as verse 23 states, the fullness of Him who fills all in all. So, pray with authority against the kingdom of darkness because when you pray the right way, in the right spirit, every demon in Heaven and Earth has to line up according to your words, because you are an emissary or ambassador of the Lord Jesus Christ Himself. **Colossians 1:15–20** and **Colossians 2:10** also affirm the supremacy of Jesus, but instead of going to these scriptures I would just follow up my premise and remind the reader that even the Archangel Michael had to use the name of Jesus when he fought with satan over Moses's body:

Jude 9 New King James Version (NKJV)

[9] Yet Michael the archangel, in contending with the devil, when he disputed about the body of Moses, dared not bring against him a reviling accusation, but said, "The Lord rebuke you!"

So, use the Word of God, in the name of Jesus beloved and watch demons scurry. satan is a Lord with a small l, that has limited authority. But we have to remind him that we're under the protection of the Lord of Lords and the King of Kings, that has all authority, we've been brought with a price, and redeemed by the blood of the Lamb.

Applying the Blood

Which leads me to me my next point on wielding authority while we're in our human bodies. In Galatians 6 it tells us to put on the whole armor of God that we might be able to withstand the enemy. What I'm giving you in this book is the full armor and arsenal, so to speak, for praying and intercession that works and are effective. We have authority through the blood of Jesus.

God gave us this example of sin propitiation in the Old Testament, where believers were able to sacrifice a lamb and utilize the blood in regard to forgiveness and/or repentance of sins. We see it with Cain and Abel. We saw it with the Hebrew people during the event commonly known as Passover. And we see it in many other places in the Old Testament. Everything in the Old Testament pointed to Jesus, the fulfillment of everything written and discussed. John stated in John 6 that Jesus was the lamb that was sent as a ransom for all of us and thus the life that was contained in His blood was the only elixir that God accepted. Jesus's blood is Holy, and its effects are lasting and timeless. It reaches to the highest mountain and it flows to lowest valley. The blood, dear one, can be used against demons and demonic situations, and it will never lose its power.

Unlike what a lot of the "old folk" would say, regarding pleading the blood, the proper term would be applying or appropriating the blood. Who's blood? Jesus's blood of course. The term "Plead the Blood" comes from David's prayer in Psalms 51:7 where he was pleading to God for forgiveness due to his adulterous transgression with Bathsheba. He said to God purge me with hyssop. Which is the substance that God used to mingle with the blood of the Passover lambs that were slain as a substitute for God's judgement on His enemies. David never said, "I plead the Blood." All he said was:

Psalms 51:7

[7] Purge me with hyssop, and I shall be clean; Wash me, and I shall be whiter than snow.

The fact that he said that, let us know that he had knowledge of the hyssop that was used with the sacrificial blood and it served as a cleansing agent along with the substance that God said would be acceptable for protection. Before we get there let's delve in and explain why we don't have to use goat blood, lamb blood, bird blood or any other blood to present before the Lord. The only blood that God honors is the blood of Jesus, Lamb slain before the foundation of the Earth. In **Revelations 12:10,11** it tells us that we overcome satan by the blood Jesus and the word of our testimony:

[10] Then I heard a loud voice saying in heaven, "Now salvation, and strength, and the kingdom of our God, and the power of His Christ have come, for the accuser of our brethren, who accused them before our God day and night, has been cast down. [11] And they overcame him by the blood of the Lamb and by the word of their testimony, and they did not love their lives to the death.

This particular chapter in Revelations is talking about an event that happened prior to us being on this earth, regarding satan being kicked out of Heaven. And one must also understand that this scripture is prophetic pointing to us in our current "Church Age" beloved. John, the Divine, was allowed to witness all of these events, whereas the blood of Jesus was not being applied during His lifetime in the way that it is now. Think about it. The disciples, turned Apostles, didn't use the blood of Jesus. All they used was the name of Jesus and the other deliverance secrets that Jesus Himself taught them to deliver and disciple the world for Jesus. The blood of Jesus couldn't be applied until He actually came to be the "Lamb that taketh away the sins of the world" and His actual blood was shed. So again, John's writing was powerfully predictive to a time when we would use the blood of Jesus as the weapon that it is.

I'm going to take this a little bit further because applying or appropriating the blood of Jesus is not supposed to be a spooky thing. It's not a spell and it definitely is not some sort of magic. It is the actual substance that God looks at when satan tries to accuse us regarding our sinful nature. The enemy says that we are sinners, but God looks at the blood shed on Calvary for our sins that has been applied on behalf of our sins and He says yes, they are sinners, SAVED BY GRACE. Nothing sinful can ever enter into the realm of God, which we commonly call Heaven, so the standard of the sinless blood of Jesus was used to wipe us clean.

We can use this blood against satan and any dark spirit and force beloved. Some of you are shaking your head and saying this is too much for you. But I want you to know that Satanist or those who practice witchcraft and sorcery don't. There is a well-known Evangelist named John Ramirez, who is an ex High Priest of the dark arts, who has testified on numerous occasions that he used to talk to satan himself face to face in his living room to receive the next set of instructions as far as ushering out current principalities and setting in new ones. He testifies that he would commonly be assigned to regions. And his method to cause havoc in these regions were to sacrifice animals and drink some of their blood and then take the rest to the crossroad of the region that he was assigned and apply the satanically blessed animal blood to the four corners of that particular area. After he would curse the ground he would astral project and then curse and set things in place in the air.

Astral projecting is when your spirit leaves your body and travels. For a person that practices witchcraft and divination their spirit is carried by a demon to wherever they want to go or wherever their assignment is supposed to be. Many of you reading this have done this at least once in your life, without spiritual assistance, because we all have the ability to do this, but your mind has told you that it was a dream or a coincidence. Newsflash it was real. We live in a very spiritual world and don't allow your mind to tell you that these things don't exist, because they do.

When I was little, I had an experience of coming out of my body while my body was sleep. I walked through the halls, went down stairs, and how I really realized that I was out of my body, is that I remember floating or walking through the railings of the steps in our house in Southwest Philadelphia. I remember going through the door of my father's room, who's bedroom was downstairs, and I watched him sleeping, I came back out and kind of gazed around the dark house, but I could see everything and then I went back upstairs and laid back in my body. I couldn't wait to tell my dad, who was a pastor as well, what had happened, and he shook his head and said, "Uh huh, you just had an out of body spiritual experience." He proceeded to tell me how these things were in our genes and about my grandmother who was a Preacher as well before she passed and all her experiences. I was amazed.

My experience wasn't initiated by anything that I knew that I was doing, but it happened, and God allowed me to be aware of what was happening and remember. However, let me be clear, when you try to manufacture these experiences you are in sin. You're using demonic, fallen spirits and that is illegal, immoral, and spiritually unethical according to the Kingdom ethos of God. It is an abomination to do anything in the spirit realm without the authorization and power of the Holy Spirit. And believe me the practice of this outside of the realm of the Holy Spirit is an abomination to the Lord. These types of activities are in the realm of the Holy Spirit and only He would have a good reason enough to allow your spirit to leave your body in this way. This gift of an experience like this has been documented in many powerful prayer warriors that know how to intercede. These types of intercessors are people who have a propensity to war in the spirit realm. They have the gift of deliverance which requires an exceeding measure of the gift of faith also.

The Holy Spirit initiates these experiences and it is always for a reason. The purpose is never to be newsy or to become a spy or invade another person's personal space. I believe sometimes God does these things to make a person more aware of their spiritual identity in opposed to their physical one. God always has a purpose behind these kinds of events. God has many exciting ways and methods of equipping and providing information in His kingdom.

I want to be clear that any out of body experience by a Christian is never self-initiated. A voluntary out-of-body experience, or an "astral projection," is different. A person trying to achieve an out-of-body experience in order to connect with spirits or the spirit world is practicing the occult. There are two forms of this. The first is called the "phasing" model, in which the person tries to find new spiritual truth by accessing a part of the mind that is "shut off" during everyday life. This practice is connected to Buddhism or postmodernism and the belief that enlightenment is achieved from looking within oneself. The other form, called the "mystical" model, is when the person tries to exit the body entirely, his/her spirit traveling to another plane that is not connected to the physical world at all, again assisted by demons.

Last thing that I'll say about the spirit leaving the body is that there is a difference between Clairvoyance, Astral Projection and there are other words and functions of this type of activity. For example, law enforcement has a branch of specialized people called remote viewers, which is just another title for a person that practices astral projection. They have witches and warlocks that teach this dark art to people that are "open" under the guise of helping to assist in finding kidnapping victims and murder suspects. See how crafty the enemy is? The enemy likes to play with words. Some people call it postcognition psychometry telepathy, dowsing, and again clairvoyance. All of them have their respective special and unique qualities and abilities.

Paul wrote to the church of Galatia warning against sorcery and the occult and how God is against it. Paul lets us know that anyone who practices these things will not inherit the Kingdom of God.

Galatians 5:19-20

19 Now the works of the flesh are evident: sexual immorality, impurity, sensuality, 20 idolatry, sorcery, enmity, strife, jealousy, fits of anger, rivalries, dissensions, divisions,

God's commands are always for our good, and He commands us to stay far away from occult practices because there is great potential, when trying to access the spiritual world, of opening oneself up to demons who can tell us lies about God and confuse our minds. Let's read an account from Eliphaz, the Temanite, from the book of Job. He was one of the three friends that tried to comfort Job when he went through his calamities.

Job 4:12–21(ESV)

12 *"Now a word was brought to me stealthily; my ear received the whisper of it.*

13 *Amid thoughts from visions of the night, when deep sleep falls on men,*

14 *dread came upon me, and trembling, which made all my bones shake.*

15 *A spirit glided past my face; the hair of my flesh stood up.*

16 *It stood still, but I could not discern its appearance. a form was before my eyes;*
there was silence, then I heard a voice:

17 *'Can mortal man be in the right before God? Can a man be pure before his Maker?*

18 *Even in his servants he puts no trust, and his angels he charges with error;*

19 *how much more those who dwell in houses of clay, whose foundation is in the dust, who are crushed like the moth.*

20 *Between morning and evening they are beaten to pieces; they perish forever without anyone regarding it.*

21 *Is not their tent-cord plucked up within them, do they not die, and that without wisdom?'*

Eliphaz is describing being visited by a lying spirit in a vision that tells him God does not regard humans and that He doesn't care for us, which is false! We have to be careful regarding visions and experiences that we all in some shape or form experience. Not all of them are Godly or have derived from God. The Bible says test the spirit by the spirit. If your vision, experience, dream, or event is not in line with the Word of God it is not from God.

For example, Joseph Smith, the founder of the Mormon religion, claimed that in 1823 he had been visited by a Christian angel named Moroni who spoke to him of an ancient Hebrew text that had been lost for 1,500 years. The text was offered by Mr. Smith as a holy text. It was supposedly engraved on gold plates by a Native American historian in the fourth century, and it related the story of Israelite peoples who had lived in America in ancient times.

Now the Bible lets us know in the Book of Revelations that anyone who adds or take away from the Word of God shall inherit all of the plagues that are in the Bible.

Revelations 22:18

18For I testify unto every man that heareth the words of the prophecy of this book, If any man shall add unto these things, God shall add unto him the plagues that are written in this book:

I could've used any religious book outside of the Bible such as the Koran that was written almost 600 years after Christ because of a supposed vision by Muhammed, but I'll stick with Joseph Smith. First, of all in Smith's "Frist Vision" he tells us that he was visited by God the Father and Jesus Christ at a sacred grove. Stop! Because, my immediate question is where was the Holy Spirit? The Bible is clear whereas it teaches us regarding the tripartite union of the Father, Son, and Holy Spirit. If you were trying to convince the body of believers, which we call today Christians, about a visit from Heaven regarding direction to humanity you would have to come in context with what our God has taught us prior.

1 John 5:5-8

[5]Who is he that overcometh the world, but he that believeth that Jesus is the Son of God? [6]This is he that came by water and blood, even Jesus Christ; not by water only, but by water and blood. And it is the Spirit that beareth witness, because the Spirit is truth. [7]For there are three that bear record in heaven, the Father, the Word, and the Holy Ghost: and these three are one. [8]And there are three that bear witness in earth, the spirit, and the water, and the blood: and these three agree in one.

If Joseph Smith, wanted to say that he had been visited by God, all he had to say was that he was visited by Jesus, because all of the God head is wrapped up in Jesus physically. And He is the only form of God that any human can see while in the flesh. So, right away from there he would lose a real biblical scholar or someone who studies the Word of God and is biblically sound. The other thing is that he would be the ONLY man in history to ever be visited by, God the Father, so to speak, physically. The great men of old didn't see this attribute of God, they saw Jesus in what we would call a Theophany. A Theophany is any visible manifestation of God that can be detected by the human senses before the actual incarnation of Christ in the New Testament. Some are specifically called Christophanies in the Old Testament. Refer to These appearances can be seen in Genesis 16:7-14; Genesis 22:11-18; Judges 5:23; 2 Kings 19:35; and other passages. The great men of the New Testament after the crucifixion and resurrection of Jesus, didn't see God the Father, they saw Jesus. Paul saw Jesus. Doubting Thomas, saw Jesus, John the Revelator saw Jesus, and so on and so on. One of the last things that Jesus told us before He ascended to Heaven was this:

Matthew 28:18-20

18Then Jesus came to them and said, "All authority in heaven and on earth has been given to me. 19Therefore go and make disciples of all nations, baptizing them in the name of the Father and of the Son and of the Holy Spirit, 20and teaching them to obey everything I have commanded you. And surely I am with you always, to the very end of the age."

So why would anyone believe that God the Father and Jesus decided to take a road trip and leave the Holy Spirit to visit some guy who had a problem with the Christian doctrine in the first place and give him a whole new holy book relating just to America? Is this making sense? Anyway, let's get back to what this chapter is being written to explain Exousia, divine authority and how applying the blood is a necessary ingredient in implementing it.

Your knowledge of the Holy scriptures is very critical regarding possessing the spiritual authority to dispel the truth from a lie beloved. Which is why giving you so much scripture in this book. You have to learn to speak the Word over your life. It's the Word that giveth life. It's the Word that demons can't contend with. It's the Word that will shift your destiny. That's why the enemy is always on the prowl for the harvest of your mouth. But before they focus on stealing the harvest of the mouth, they try to kill the seeds in your soul. If there are no seeds, and I should say good seeds being deposited into good soil, there will be no good harvest and therefore, nothing to steal. The harvest of your mouth is based on the seeds that have been deposited into your spirit. When you speak the scriptures in faith, knowledge and context you are speaking power to truth and utilizing your God given authority.

Proverbs 18:20

20 A man's stomach shall be satisfied from the fruit of his mouth;
From the produce of his lips he shall be filled.

Let the produce of your lips be from the harvest of God's engrafted word in your gut. The more Word in you, the more your spiritual guts expands. Hence, the bigger the gut, the bigger the capacity. The more the capacity in the spirit realm equals increased strength.

Proverbs 18:21

21 Death and life are in the power of the tongue, And those who love it will eat its fruit.

There are demons that are dispatched only for your words. If they can catch you in your words speaking death, negative, perverted, angry, lustful, or prideful words; they can use your words as an occasion against you. You give them legal spiritual authority. **The enemy comes for the harvest of your heart; your words! Watch what you say and don't give the devil and his imps more information than they need.**

We have to understand that the enemy of our spirits are not omniscient, therefore they don't know everything. Evil spirits have a huge but very efficient network that takes information on everything that we do and many times they are only using the information that we have either prayed audibly or told someone else. So, speak less and ask God for the Gift of Tongues, so that you can pray in a heavenly language that only you and God understands. In this book there is a chapter regarding "Heart Prayers" that you're going to want to read to get around giving the devil more information than he needs to know. Stop telling the demons every little thing that you're struggling with and just leave it in the hands of God alone. Some of the best prayers are not spoken verbally but more so spoken from the heart.

Back to the blood. We overcome satan by the blood of the Lamb (Jesus Christ) and the word of our testimony according to Revelations 12:11. In this text it states that we're not to "Love not our life unto death", which means it's more important to do God's will than it is to stay alive. From the Ordinance of the Passover that we see in Exodus 12:21-23, we understand that the blood had to be transferred from the basin to the door of the home. This means that your desire to perform God's will over self will prompt you to use the power of the blood of Jesus.

Exodus 12:21-23

[21]Then Moses summoned all the elders of Israel and said to them, "Go at once and select the animals for your families and slaughter the Passover lamb. [22]Take a bunch of hyssop, dip it into the blood in the basin and put some of the blood on the top and on both sides of the doorframe. None of you shall go out of the door of your house until morning. [23]When the Lord goes through the land to strike down the Egyptians, he will see the blood on the top and sides of the doorframe and will pass over that doorway, and he will not permit the destroyer to enter your houses and strike you down.

The blood in itself is powerful, but you have to know how to take the blood from the basin, so to speak, and apply it to the door of your heart: even the door of your spirit. This requires faith. The blood is not just a literary concept to be read about, it is a spiritual substance to be applied literally against the forces of evil. When the fallen angels come to afflict you, cover yourself with the blood. How do you do this? With prayer.

I now cover myself with the blood of the Lord Jesus Christ and pray that You, blessed Holy Spirit, would bring all the work of the crucifixion, all the work of the resurrection, all the work of the glorification, and all the work of Pentecost into my life today. I surrender myself to You.

After you cover yourself in the blood, if you are about to go into rebuking and deliverance mode you want to command your atmosphere. Remember, God has given us delegated authority:

Matthew 10:7,8 (KJV)

[7]As you go, proclaim this message: 'The kingdom of heaven has come near.' [8]Heal the sick, raise the dead, cleanse those who have leprosy, drive out demons. Freely you have received; freely give.

Mark 16:15-20 (NIV)

[15]He said to them, "Go into all the world and preach the gospel to all creation. [16]Whoever believes and is baptized will be saved, but whoever does not believe will be condemned. [17]And these signs will accompany those who believe: In my name they will drive out demons; they will speak in new tongues; [18]they will pick up snakes with their hands; and when they drink deadly poison, it will not hurt them at all; they will place their hands on sick people, and they will get well."

[19]After the Lord Jesus had spoken to them, he was taken up into heaven and he sat at the right hand of God. [20]Then the disciples went out and preached everywhere, and the Lord worked with them and confirmed his word by the signs that accompanied it.

Consider the authority given to us by Jesus Himself in the prior scriptures and then pray thusly to charge, command, and cleanse the atmosphere:

Satan, I command you, in the name of the Lord Jesus Christ, to leave my presence with all your demons, and I bring the blood of the Lord Jesus Christ between us.

After commanding my atmosphere, if I am about to engage in deliverance, I take it a little bit deeper. I normally like to not only apply the power of the blood to myself only, but my family as well, because evil spirits are vindictive and always looking for revenge. Consider:

Father God, I come before you in JESUS' name, and I thank you for giving me all power and all authority over all demons (Matt. 10:8, Mark 16:17). I cover myself in the blood of JESUS and I cover all my family members in the blood of JESUS. I thank you for your giant warring angels that are surrounding us, protecting us from all hurt, harm, or danger of the enemy. I take my authority and I attack from the third Heaven, and I bind the strongman over my mind, will, emotions, and over my home, in JESUS' mighty name. I command you to leave this area right now in JESUS' name. I bind up every demon that was sent to me, transferred to me, or followed me, and I command you to come out of my conscious, subconscious, unconscious mind, all parts of my body, will, emotions, and personality, in JESUS' name.

Now you are ready to engage fully into spiritual warfare with all of the rights and authority that Jesus gladly gave us to win the war. I will go further with spiritual warfare in the chapter entitled Spiritual Warfare. One thing that I want to leave you with in this chapter is that we cannot be in sin and expect these spiritual principles to cover you. Make sure your fellowship with God is secure.

1 John 1:7

7But if we walk in the light, as he is in the light, we have fellowship one with another, and the blood of Jesus Christ his Son cleanseth us from all sin.

Your fellowship or lack of fellowship determines how clean you are in the eyes of God. Your relationship with God is what the spirit world evaluates before they decide to interact with you. Which leads me to the last point for this particular chapter regarding exousia, using the name of Jesus and applying the blood of Jesus. In **1 Corinthians 5:7b** Paul says *For Christ, our Passover lamb, has been sacrificed.* Which gives us the spiritual awareness that Jesus' blood is to be applied in the same way that the Passover lambs were sacrificed of old in Exodus and the way that it was still being applied before the New Testament and the church age.

In Exodus 12 we see that God told the Hebrew people to mix hyssop with the blood. We see this "hyssop" being utilized spiritually by David in Psalms 51 where he asked God to cleanse him with hyssop in his repentance prayer to God after his affair with Bathsheba was exposed.

Psalms 51:7

[7] *Cleanse me with hyssop, and I will be clean; wash me, and I will be whiter than snow.*

Why did David ask God to purge him with hyssop? Because hyssop was used as a cleansing agent, an aromatherapy, and a mint based leaf that was used in purification ceremonies and more. The hyssop was to represent the testimony of the Hebrew people. The blood of the Passover lambs wasn't good enough to be presented alone. Why? Because the Passover lambs weren't perfect like Jesus, our Passover Lamb, was. So, the hyssop was to take away the pungent smell and make it acceptable in God's sight. The smell reminded God why He was showing them mercy. That's why we have to keep reminding God of our testimony, that we love Him, that we have accepted Him into our hearts and will always worship Him. David was reminding God that God You saved me! God, you chose me! God don't forget that you wish above all that I would prosper and be in good health! Give God your testimony!

Lastly, I want you to remember that this is not a magical incantation. The name of Jesus is the only name that Hell responds too, so use His name. The blood of Jesus is the currency that God has approved and received, so apply it. However, it only works and covers the obedient. Heaven doesn't respond to Hell, because a King never comes off of his throne to intermingle with peasants. However, Hell does respond to Heaven, it has no choice. Heaven only responds to faith. Heaven only responds to holiness. Heaven only responds to righteousness. And in the eyes of God, obedience is better than sacrifice. To end this chapter, I will leave you with the words of John, the disciple that Jesus loved, and Peter, the Apostle that Jesus left to build His church:

1 John 1:7

But if we walk in the light as He is in the light, we have fellowship with one another, and the blood of Jesus Christ His Son cleanses us from all sin.

1 Peter 1:2

[2] *Elect according to the foreknowledge of God the Father, in sanctification of the Spirit, for obedience and sprinkling of the blood of Jesus Christ: Grace to you and peace be multiplied.*

Taking Dominion

Prayers should be your key in the morning and your lock at night.

Apostle Dr. Larry Birchett, Jr.

Ephesians 6:10-17 (KJV)

10 Finally, be strong in the Lord and in his mighty power. 11 Put on
the full armor of God, so that you can take your stand against the
devil's schemes. 12 For our struggle is not against flesh and blood,
but against the rulers, against the authorities, against the powers
of this dark world and against the spiritual forces of evil in the
heavenly realms. 13 Therefore put on the full armor of God, so that
when the day of evil comes, you may be able to stand your ground,
and after you have done everything, to stand. 14 Stand firm then,
with the belt of truth buckled around your waist, with the
breastplate of righteousness in place, 15 and with your feet fitted
with the readiness that comes from the gospel of peace. 16 In
addition to all this, take up the shield of faith, with which you can
extinguish all the flaming arrows of the evil one. 17 Take the helmet
of salvation and the sword of the Spirit, which is the word of God.

We're in a battle in this world. We may not see it, we might forget it's there. But let me tell you this morning that the battle is raging, and a war is going on. But the enemy would love nothing more than to make you think that nothing is going on #1 and #2 fill you with discouragement and defeat, bringing fear and stress. I say to you on today beloved, don't let him fool you and don't let him win.

One writer said this, "Life is like an onion, the more you peel it, the more it will make you cry." But hopefully, by the end of this book you won't be crying you will be decreeing and declaring rebuking and then rejoicing!

The truth is that if you're a TRUE believer who is living like salt and light in a dark world, you won't go for long without encountering spiritual warfare. If you're a true believer who is living like salt and light in this dark world the enemy will hurl obstacles and attacks in your direction. God reminds us in His word to stay aware of Satan's schemes, to live alert in this world, and to stay close to Him. *He says it like this in **1 Peter 5:8-9** - "Be self-controlled and alert. Your enemy the devil prowls around like a roaring lion looking for someone to devour. Resist him, standing firm in the faith."*

He arms us with the sword, the Word of God, to stand against the enemy's lies. **He equips us with strength, wisdom, and discernment through His own Spirit to stay strong in the spiritual warfare battle.** He invites us to spend time in His Presence, through prayer and worship, pressing in to know Him more.

Do you know that if you have Wisdom you will have Well-Being? The problem is that we would rather rely on our own wisdom versus the wisdom of God!

Proverbs 3:7-20 (NIV)

7Do not be wise in your own eyes; fear the Lord and shun evil.
8This will bring health to your body and nourishment to your bones.
9Honor the Lord with your wealth, with the firstfruits of all your crops;
10then your barns will be filled to overflowing, and your vats will brim over with new wine.

11My son, do not despise the Lord's discipline, and do not resent his rebuke,
12because the Lord disciplines those he loves, as a father the son he delights in. (The Septuagint uses the word Chastens instead of discipline implying being chastised not just disciplined)
13Blessed are those who find wisdom, those who gain understanding,
14for she is more profitable than silver and yields better returns than gold.
15She is more precious than rubies; nothing you desire can compare with her.
*(**Note**: Wisdom is Priceless)*
16Long life is in her right hand; in her left hand are riches and honor.
(**Note**: If you are living a life of Godly wisdom you will have **long** life, you will be **respected and not hurting for money**. By the way Witches and Warlocks use this scripture to steal years off of your life and your blessings. Don't let people randomly touch your hands, or ever read your palms, etc. You will die early. One Former Satanist said that he would take five years off of the life of every person that he performed this certain incantation on. Never let anyone read your palms or anything else for that matter. They try to steal your life force for theirs and they try to steal your blessings for themselves or their customers. You've been warned.)
17Her ways are pleasant ways, and all her paths are peace.
(**Note**: Wisdom ain't always in contention with other people! Wisdom ain't shady. Wisdom ain't messy Wisdom ain't insecure. And Wisdom ain't jealous! I'm using "ain't" on purpose.)
18She is a tree of life to those who take hold of her; those who hold her fast will be blessed. (**Note**: Once again, Wisdom will keep you alive! When the devil thinks he has you just reach into God's Word for some wisdom beloved and take a bite of the tree of life and live again. Take a bite and be blessed.)
19By wisdom the Lord laid the earth's foundations, by understanding he set the heavens in place;
20by his knowledge the watery depths were divided, and the clouds let drop the dew.

As we grow to know God's Truth and what is real, we also know more what is false, and we are stronger to stand against it in the powerful name of Jesus. He never leaves us to fend for ourselves in a dark world, but reminds us He is constantly with us, fighting for us, even when we cannot see.

1 John 4:4 (KJV)

4You are from God, little children, and have overcome them; because greater is He who is in you than he who is in the world.

I want to encourage you today by letting you know that there is nothing in front of you that is greater than what is inside of you. God gave us, His children, dominion over everything in this world way back in the Garden of Eden. And guess what? Nothing has changed regarding that gift. I don't care if they're threatening to take your car, just remember that there is nothing in front of you that is greater than Who is inside of you. Doctor might be saying Cancer, but there is nothing in front of you that is greater than He who is inside of you. Your spouse might be saying Divorce, but there is nothing in front of you that is greater than what is inside of you.

Now, that we have that established. Let's continue taking dominion. What we have to do is pray God's Word back to Him. Praying God's words back to Him, is a powerful weapon against the forces of evil. It is Truth going out. And when we start applying truth to power, watch out. When we pray like this it reminds us that God knows our way and understands what we face today. It's not to give God a lesson in His Word. It builds our faith and our trust in God. It guards our hearts and focuses our minds back on Him. It wins the battle and realigns our hope. For some of us it resurrects our hope and keeps our hope alive. When we get to the point of total trust and reliance in God, our prayer is being effective, and we have already won. Why? Because the victory is in the trusting not in the trying.

Ephesians 6:17 tells us that the Word of God is the **sword** of the Spirit. When we pray the Word of God a spiritual sword starts to form in the front of our mouths. The sword starts off small. But as we continue to pray it gets bigger and bigger. And when it gets big enough, our Angel picks it up and slays our demons!

Now, our angels will be defeated if we set them up for failure by producing a dagger in prayer when we should be producing a sword. This is why the Bible says that life and death is in the power of the tongue.

Stay around people that knows how to utilize and apply the Word of God. Faith cometh by hearing and hearing by the Word of God. My personal stance is that if you don't come to Church stay away from me! If you don't come to Bible Study, don't you dare try to pour into me! Take your little sword and go sit down somewhere!

Stay with people that are made out of the same fabric/material as you. Iron sharpens iron not wood. Some people are weak and want to pour their weakness into you. If wood actually tried to sharpen iron it would dull the iron and injure itself in the process. So, stop letting "wood people" try to sharpen you "iron".

One more piece of information for you to ponder since we're talking about what our prayers look like. From Revelations 8 we see that our prayers go up to Heaven like incense. One of my Army friends, Captain Patrick Williams, went to Chicago one Summer with his family to attend a wedding, I believe. When he got off of the bus, he was run over by a bus. The bus driver, realizing that he ran over something proceeded to back up, hence running CPT Williams over again. Long story short, CPT Williams should've died, but he lived. He went into a coma and didn't come out for about a month. I couldn't wait to talk to Pat to make sure he was really okay and to ask him about his experience.

Pat, told me that when he was in the coma, he knew everything that was going on in his room at certain times, from conversations and more. He told his family and friends things that they said at his bedside and while they were in his room at certain times. He said that his spirit was out of his body but he saw and heard it all.

He also said that at other times, his spirit was in the air. He was literally in the air with a lot of other spirits. And he said that they would travel in groups to different places in the world where people were praying at. And they tried to help in the sky and on the ground the person that was praying. And all of this is hard to explain for him by the way, because he knows it doesn't make any sense. But I actually video recorded our conversation. He said that at sometimes there would be a dark "force" that would appear in the sky and he and all of the spirits would sometime "war" against this darkness and at other times they would flee and relocate. The end of his story is that he eventually went back in his body and of course, that's how I was able to get the story from him.

But what I found really interesting about his personal testimony is that there was another man, an Evangelist, that has told the world that before he was born his mother and father had dedicated him to satan and he had become a very powerful witch by the age of 10. So much so, that his parents were scared of him and had to ship him away.

He said something interesting about prayer, that relates to this book on interdimensional prayer. He is obviously a Christian these days, but he said that one of his job back then was to astral project his spirit outside of his body and join with other spirits and "demons" in the heavenly realms to stop the prayers of the saints. He would become part of a big mass of dark rock that would cover the skies. He said that this was one of his jobs along with destroying churches and pastors.

Everything that I said about the Evangelist is not that new. However, check this out. He teaches that our prayers take on three forms. The first is smoke. When a Christian first starts to pray, the prayer is in smoke form. The unfortunate thing is that normally the Christian doesn't pray long enough or seriously enough and so the smoke normally fizzles out and disappear in the atmosphere never making it to the Second Heaven.

The other form is smoke that is strong enough to reach the Heavens, however when it reaches the Heavens, it is stopped by the black rock mass of demonic spirits and powers in the air. The people that produces these kinds of prayers are those that try to produce righteousness based on works. You can never produce enough power in your own strength beloved to defeat the forces of darkness. Not by might, nor by power, but by my Spirit saith the Lord. Remember that scripture?

The third form, according to this Evangelist, is a prayer that looks like smoke with lightning and thunder in it. As this person, that has a real prayer life, and adorned with the full armor of God is praying, the prayer takes on a life of its own and begins to look like lava going up to Heaven. The fabric of this kind of fervent and effectual prayer from a righteous man or woman meets up with the black mass in the sky and starts burning and burrowing through the powers and forces in the heavenlies, until it finally breaks through. Once this prayer breaks through, it creates a hole in the ozone layer of this black force and creates an "open Heaven" over this individual that whatever they ask, God grants it to them. This kind of prayer is hot prayer. Intense prayer. Fervent prayer. Persistent prayer. Not a 2 minute, nonchalant, and rehearsed prayer.

One day my family and I visited a really good friend of ours way up in the Hills of Pennsylvania. As we ascended into the hills it got foggier and foggier. My son asked me a question as our atmosphere dramatically changed. He said, "Daddy is the fog like this only in the mountains?" I thought about it and said, "No Son, every once in a while, it will get foggy even in the valley but if you want to experience it all of the time you have to ascend into the mountains." And right their God's Word vibrated through my
spirit wherein it says that 1 *I will lift up mine eyes unto the hills,*
from whence cometh my help. 2 *My help cometh from the LORD,*
which made heaven and earth. 3 *He will not suffer thy foot to be*
moved: he that keepeth thee will not slumber. 4 *Behold, he that*
keepeth Israel shall neither slumber nor sleep. 5 *The LORD is thy*
keeper: the LORD is thy shade upon thy right hand. 6 *The sun shall*
not smite thee by day, nor the moon by night. 7 *The LORD shall*

preserve thee from all evil: he shall preserve thy soul.
[8] *The LORD shall preserve thy going out and thy coming in from*
this time forth, and even for evermore. **Psalms 121:1-8**

God was reminding me that if you want to experience more of His glory you have to go to a higher place of elevation in Him. If you're dry it's because you're hanging with bottom feeders. Come up a little bit higher. The air is better up here anyway.

Make sure you surround yourself with visionaries. God will always show you a big vision because He's a big God! If you can accomplish it on your own, you don't require His help and He doesn't need to show you anything, but if what He has shown you is BIGGER than you can accomplish on your own, beloved, that just might be the Godly assignment that He will accomplish THROUGH you. Trust in God. Wait on God's good timing.

Habakkuk 2:3 (ESV)

For still the vision awaits its appointed time; it hastens to the end—it will not lie. If it seems slow, wait for it; it will surely come; it will not delay.

Hold on to the vision that God showed you. Because delay does not mean denial. I'm reminded of the story of a man that walked into a publishing company and he handed his manuscript to the first person that he saw that was sitting in a seat. He said here sir, tell me what you think about my book. The man took the book seemingly turned it all around rubbing the front of the cover the back of the book. Held the book open so the pages were hanging out. He smelled the book and everything and said, this book in in good order, very nicely put together. The guy said, you didn't even read it! The man said, Oh, you wanted me to read it? I can't do that Sir. I'm blind! But it sure does feel nice!

What's the moral of the story? Stop letting blind people proofread your vision. And stop letting other people feelings shape your decisions. Trust God.

Some of you are getting so frustrated because of what you're seeing other people do. The truth is that, frustration is the symptom of immaturity a lot of times. Because if you're focused on your assignment you don't have time to be watching what somebody else is doing. Plus, the people in the world don't fight the way we do anyway.

2 Corinthians 10:3-5 (NIV)

[3]"For though we live in the world, we do not wage war as the world does. The weapons we fight with are not the weapons of the world. [4] On the contrary, they have divine power to demolish strongholds. [5] We demolish arguments and every pretension that sets itself up against the knowledge of God, and we take captive every thought to make it obedient to Christ."

Therefore, we don't fight with our hands and being emotional like people of the world. We fight in prayer. So, stop talking about the people that God has placed over you. You be the Leader that you expect others to be. See, the Leaders you're criticizing might be flawed but they called by God. How about you? Have you been called? They might be flawed but they've been chosen! How about you? They might be flawed but they're still anointed! Still appointed! Still got Power! Still have authority! And this sentiment is not just about leaders, it is referring to any and everybody.

Plus, some of us have forgotten the mess that God has delivered us from anyway. See, we're very good Lawyers for our own mistakes, and even better Judges for the mistakes of others. We act like we've done no wrong.

But watch this, and only the Prophetic will appreciate this next statement. Don't forget that your past can speak to your future. Meaning, that you should never forget that there are people that knew you way back when. Something that a lot of people that are trying to serve in our current political climate is finding out firsthand. But that's for another book.

You can't get to Heaven by putting other people through Hell. And lastly, on this issue, stop talking about people and start going into the devil's camp and taking back everything that he has stolen from you! I decree to every person that reads this book and accept the wisdom of it, God shall deliver you from the mouth of every wicked liar.

I release the Blood of Jesus like liquid fire to every conspiracy of the devil and his agents! May every Judas choke on their own plot! May every Delilah be blinded by their own schemes! May the intentions of every serpent spirit and shapeshifting spirit be revealed, exposed and turned around to work against them! To every witchcraft worker FIRE right now in the name of Jesus! We call Holy Fire into this home (institution or sanctuary) against any and EVERY demonic force by/in the name of Jesus! May they never be able to stop the work of Christ or pull you down from your position where God has called you to work in Jesus name!

If you just prayed that prayer with conviction you have just taking back your dominion over the enemy and his imps. Change the you and your in the prayer to me and I and make it personal beloved. Sometimes you have to put your crown back on to remind them who they are dealing with.

Finally, your blessing is always on the other side of the storm. The enemy always turns up the heat when he knows you're about to walk into your season of Blessings. Remember the Holocaust? Holocaust means 'burnt offering'. satan tried to use Hitler to exterminate the Jews before their time of Restoration came. satan knew that the time for the Jewish people to reclaim their heritage was coming and he tried to stop it. But isn't if funny that it was his actions that God actually used make the United Nations vote to have the Jews go back into Israel? God will take the thing that looks like it's going to disqualify you to be the very thing that qualifies you. He will prepare a table before you in the presence of your enemies.

So, remember that the devil is always working for God whether he knows it or not and God is just setting you up for the win. Reflect on the next three passages of scriptures and take dominion beloved.

Romans 8:28 (NKJV)

All things work together for the good for them that love the Lord and are CALLED to His purpose.

1 Corinthians 15:57 (NKJV)

But thanks be to God, who gives us the victory through our Lord Jesus Christ.

John 14:1-6 (NKJV)

[1] "Let not your heart be troubled; you believe in God, believe also
in Me. [2] In My Father's house are many [a]mansions; if it were not
so, I would have told you. I go to prepare a place for you. [3] And if I
go and prepare a place for you, I will come again and receive you
to Myself; that where I am, there you may be also. [4] And where I
go you know, and the way you know." [5] Thomas said to Him,
"Lord, we do not know where You are going, and how can we
know the way?" [6] Jesus said to him, "I am the way, the truth, and
the life. No one comes to the Father except through Me.

Hidden Kingdoms

Ignorance allied with power, is the most ferocious enemy that justice can have.

James Baldwin

Matthew 6:33 (KJV)

But seek ye first the kingdom of God, and his righteousness; and all these things shall be added unto you.

The Bible lets us know in Hosea 4:6 that many of God's people perish for the lack of knowledge. Part of the reason that that God prompted me to write this book is for the Kingdom Seekers that are tired of the bondage of ignorance. In Matthew 6 God tells us to seek the Kingdom of God first. Why would God tell us to seek first the Kingdom of God, if there weren't other kingdoms that we could in fact seek?

There are many parallel kingdoms, dimensions, spheres and realms and I will speak about most of them in this chapter. First, we need to understand that lucifer was kicked out of Heaven and fell to this Earth because of pride. The Prophet Isaiah wrote in the fourteenth chapter:

Isaiah 14:12 (ESV)

12 How you are fallen from heaven, O Day Star, son of Dawn! How you are cut down to the ground, you who laid the nations low!

And then we're given even more important information in another account written by the Prophet Ezekiel in chapter 28 regarding the fall of satan:

Ezekiel 28:11-19 (KJV)

11 Moreover the word of the Lord came unto me, saying,

12 Son of man, take up a lamentation upon the king of Tyrus, and say unto him, Thus saith the Lord God; Thou sealest up the sum, full of wisdom, and perfect in beauty.

13 Thou hast been in Eden the garden of God; every precious stone was thy covering, the sardius, topaz, and the diamond, the beryl, the onyx, and the jasper, the sapphire, the emerald, and the carbuncle, and gold: the workmanship of thy tabrets and of thy pipes was prepared in thee in the day that thou wast created.

14 Thou art the anointed cherub that covereth; and I have set thee so: thou wast upon the holy mountain of God; thou hast walked up and down in the midst of the stones of fire.

15 Thou wast perfect in thy ways from the day that thou wast created, till iniquity was found in thee.

16 By the multitude of thy merchandise they have filled the midst of thee with violence, and thou hast sinned: therefore I will cast thee as profane out of the mountain of God: and I will destroy thee, O covering cherub, from the midst of the stones of fire.

17 Thine heart was lifted up because of thy beauty, thou hast corrupted thy wisdom by reason of thy brightness: I will cast thee to the ground, I will lay thee before kings, that they may behold thee.

[18] Thou hast defiled thy sanctuaries by the multitude of thine iniquities, by the iniquity of thy traffick; therefore will I bring forth a fire from the midst of thee, it shall devour thee, and I will bring thee to ashes upon the earth in the sight of all them that behold thee.

[19] All they that know thee among the people shall be astonished at thee: thou shalt be a terror, and never shalt thou be any more.

The thought amongst some theological minds is that one of satan's responsibilities before his fall when he wasn't walking up and down the mountain of God and in the midst of the stones of fire as verse 16 says was to ensure the affairs of the Earth. Remember, the very first scripture of the Bible says that in the beginning God created the Heaven AND the Earth. Notwithstanding that the biblical genealogy of the first man seems to date back to over 6000 years ago, we need to understand that the Earth is millions if not billions of years old and we only know of some of the life forms that have lived out whole eras on the planet Earth, such as the dinosaurs. So, the thought is that after the angelic rebellion and fall, God made man, in His image no less. And not only did He make us, but He gave us dominion, thereby, taking away dominion from satan, further infuriating him. But let's get back to the main teaching because there are some things that we will never know until we have crossed over onto the other side.

The result of the pride that was found in him and the envy that he purported was that he was kicked out of Heaven and thrown So, we have established that he wanted to be just like God and I'm here to inform you that nothing about his initial motivation has changed. He still wants to be just like God. He wants a kingdom just like God's. He wants to be worshipped just like God. He wants a throne just like God's. And he wants to run things just like God, his Creator, ran things.

Verse 14 establishes that Ezekiel is referring to an angel, specifically lucifer, whereas he called him a cherub, which is short for cherubim. Pay attention to verse 12 in this chapter that says that he was in the Garden of Eden. There is a prevailing down to this Earth. The Bible says that he drew a third of the angels, or shall we say it like Revelations 12 says it, he took a third of the Heaven's with him.

Earth Kingdom

He became regulated to everything less than Heaven, meaning the Third Heaven where the Host of God's celestial beings exist, and is now operating in the realms and dimensions of this universe that does not connect or provide him access and influence into the Third Heaven's affairs. He and the rest of the angels set up kingdoms in the air, which we will call the Second Heaven; the water, which we will call the Marine Kingdom; and of course, the Earth, where all of the ground demons are roaming right now. For the purpose of this book, the Earth Kingdom also comprises of everything in the Earth as well such as the Forest and Mountain Kingdoms. Some of us deliverance ministers have also been trained in the African arts as well. One of the things that is prevalent over there is what is called "Bush Demons". Bush demons are human agents that routinely transfers their essence into trees, bushes, and other pieces of the forests at night. They literally sleep in the trees.

If you are in the west this might seem foreign to you, but I implore you to learn a little bit more about demonology and spiritualism before you dismiss what I'm saying. Let's go to the Bible. In Genesis 2:17 God told Adam to not eat from a certain tree. Have you ever asked yourself why are we talking about trees in regard to sin? I'm almost pretty certain that the serpent was hanging out next to a tree when he "beguiled" Eve. By the way, the word beguiled means "to wholly seduce." But that's another topic for another book. However, just understand that the fate of the whole future human race was not predicated on the natural "eating" of an apple, orange, or anything like that. Why would anyone need to be "seduced" to do such a thing?

Someone is saying, that's some Old Testament stuff. Okay let's parous a little bit in the New Testament.

Mark 11:12-14

[12]The next day as they were leaving Bethany, Jesus was hungry. [13]
Seeing in the distance a fig tree in leaf, he went to find out if it had any fruit. When he reached it, he found nothing but leaves, because it was not the season for figs. [14] Then he said to the tree, "May no one ever eat fruit from you again." And his disciples heard him say it.

Jesus cursed the fig with his mouth! Why? Not because the fig tree didn't grow any fruit. Because the scriptures are clear saying that it was not the season for figs! He cursed it because it was cursed. Meaning that it had been made to be a curse to anyone who would eat of it. Witchcraft had been used on it beloved. And Jesus dried it up. He cursed it at its root. Which is a lesson to all of us. Cover everything that you consume with the blood of Jesus, everything that you buy to wear, everything that you put in your body! Everything that you put on your body! Everything that you put in your ear gate and eye gate. Some of this stuff is nothing but a curse.

Fallen angels and demons need a point of contact to connect with the human race so some of them have chosen the things of the woods, mountains, and forests. Which is why some mountains were worshipped in ancient times and so on and so on. Evangelist John Ramirez said that a part of his initiation into the occult involved him going shirtless to the highest mountain where he lived and placing his hands on a huge tree on this mountain for the transfer of power.

Kingdoms

In terms of time there are three kingdoms that has to be established before Jesus returns for His church; the Anti-God Kingdom, the Anti-Christ Kingdom, and the satanic Kingdom. The first set of Kingdoms that I explained are geographical, the latter are based on time. The Anti-God Kingdom was everything before Christ. No one knew about Christ in the way that we do now during the time of Abraham, Isaac, and Jacob. Even though He was clearly prophesied and referred to in Genesis and other places you have to remember that the Torah, or the Law, wasn't even written yet. Why? Because Moses came after Abraham. Which is why Abraham is so important to the history of Judeo-Christian history. God told him to leave out of the midst of his polytheistic nation to go to a land that He had designated for His chosen people. He chose Abraham because he was monotheistic. Abraham believed in the one true God, YVWH, Elohim. And he had such a close relationship with God that he was even going to sacrifice his son, Isaac, simply because God had requested him too. Isaac, of course, was a shadow of the true sacrifice, the Lamb of God, Jesus Christ, that was going to come and be sacrificed on this same mountain thousands of years later. The enemy setup an Anti-God Kingdom and that's what God tried to wipe away with the flood during Noah's day.

When Christ was born, He established His Kingdom in this Earth, then the spirit of Anti-Christ was introduced and hence, the Anti-Christ Kingdom was established. This makes sense if you understand that we couldn't have been ushered into the Anti-Christ era before Christ actually came to live on Earth and changed this Earth forever. There are many scriptures identifying this fact, but I think that John described it the best:

1 John 2:18

18 Little children, it is the last time: and as ye have heard that antichrist shall come, even now are there many antichrists; whereby we know that it is the last time.

This Kingdom in the air, of course can't be seen with the natural eye, it's a spiritual kingdom. A false Heaven. Some call this The Second Heaven. This kingdom is where the principalities of Ephesians 6 reside. This place is basically a cheap counterfeit of God Elohim's Heaven, with a throne room and everything else, except, chief prince fallen angels and demons occupy the thrones therein. Noticed, I said thrones. I said thrones because there is more than one prince in this heaven, which would require more than one throne. Whereas in the Seventh Heaven, notice I didn't say Third Heaven, God's Heaven, there is only one throne and throne room because only God can sit on His throne.

Why did I say Seventh Heaven? I'll explain in a couple of paragraphs. However, remember, God is the Creator. He exists within and outside the realm of His creation, which mean that He exists outside of this whole universe. The Third Heaven is the realm of God, but His actual throne, the place of the Holy Hill, the place where the "stones of fire" as Ezekiel 28:16 describes are, is beyond even that. If you are skeptical about what I just said, just remember that the Bible says that God will one day roll up the Heavens like a scroll. Stop arguing over things that you didn't create because the Creator cannot be contained by His own creation. The Creator is not regulated by or in time either. Time was created for us. God exists outside of time.

Revelations 6:12-17 (KJV)

*12And I beheld when he had opened the sixth seal, and, lo, there
was a great earthquake; and the sun became black as sackcloth of
hair, and the moon became as blood; 13And the stars of heaven fell
unto the earth, even as a fig tree casteth her untimely figs, when
she is shaken of a mighty wind. 14And the heaven departed as a
scroll when it is rolled together; and every mountain and island
were moved out of their places. 15And the kings of the earth, and
the great men, and the rich men, and the chief captains, and the
mighty men, and every bondman, and every free man, hid
themselves in the dens and in the rocks of the mountains; 16And
said to the mountains and rocks, Fall on us, and hide us from the
face of him that sitteth on the throne, and from the wrath of the*

Lamb: [17]*For the great day of his wrath is come; and who shall be able to stand?*

Isaiah 34:4 (KJV)

[4] *And all the host of heaven shall be dissolved, and the heavens shall be rolled together as a scroll: and all their host shall fall down, as the leaf falleth off from the vine, and as a falling fig from the fig tree.*

Matthew 24:29-31 (KJV)

[29]*"Immediately after the distress of those days "'the sun will be darkened, and the moon will not give its light; the stars will fall from the sky, and the heavenly bodies will be shaken.'*

[30]*"Then will appear the sign of the Son of Man in heaven. And then all the peoples of the earth will mourn when they see the Son of Man coming on the clouds of heaven, with power and great glory.*
[31]*And he will send his angels with a loud trumpet call, and they will gather his elect from the four winds, from one end of the heavens to the other.*

Revelation 20:11 (KJV)

[11] *Then I saw a great white throne and him who was seated on it. From his presence earth and sky fled away, and no place was found for them.*

So, let's finish up this point. He chooses to allow His presence to inhabit the throne room of His created Heaven in the same way that His presence was contained in the Ark of the Covenant on Earth during Moses day, however, please understand the difference. God didn't live in the Ark, He just allowed His presence to reside there. No created thing can contain the Creator. He's too big. We serve a BIG God.

According to the Talmud, which is the central text of Rabbinic literature and the primary source of Jewish religious law and theory, the universe is made of seven heavens. The Hebrew word for Heaven is Shamayim. Below are the names of the seven divisions of Heaven according to the Talmud.

Vilon (וילון), Also see (Isa 40:22)
Raki'a (רקיע), Also see (Gen 1:17)
Shehaqim (שחקים), See (Ps 78:23)
Zebul (זבול), See (Isa 63:15, KJV)
Ma'on (מעון), See (Deut 26:15, Ps 42:9)
Machon (מכון), See (1 Kings 7:30, Deut 28:12)
Araboth (ערבות), The seventh Heaven where ofanim, the seraphim, and the hayyoth and the throne of the Lord are located.

Now I know some of you are saying well the Bible only refers to three Heavens and then you're going to go to **2 Corinthians 12:2-4** where Paul says, *"I know a man in Christ" (usually interpreted as: himself) "who fourteen years ago was caught up to the Third Heaven. Whether it was in the body or out of the body I do not know—God knows. And I know that this man—whether in the body or apart from the body I do not know, but God knows—was caught up to paradise. He heard inexpressible things, things that man is not permitted to tell."* However, permit me to explain. When Paul was referring to the Three Heavens, he was referring to the Three-part Cosmos that mankind is aware of, especially during Paul's time.

From Paul's perspective, the First Heaven is the Atmosphere. God referred to this atmosphere in Genesis chapter 1. The word used for Heaven is Ouranos:

Genesis 1:20

20 Then God said, "Let the waters abound with an abundance of living creatures, and let birds fly above the earth across the face of the firmament of the heavens."

The Second Heaven would be considered the "Starry Space". God spoke of this space through His prophet Isaiah in the fiftieth chapter and Moses in the book of Deuteronomy. The word used for heavens is Cosmos in these instances:

Isaiah 50:3

[3] I clothe the heavens with blackness, And I make sackcloth their covering."

Deuteronomy 1:10

[10] The Lord your God has multiplied you, and here you are today, as the stars of heaven in multitude.

The Third Heaven would be everything beyond the stars, God's dwelling place, as it were, as we break the natural creation down into layers of atmosphere. Again, we will use 2 Corinthians 12:2. The word used for heaven was paradeisos, of which we get the word paradise.

2 Corinthians 12:2

[2] I know a man in Christ who fourteen years ago—whether in the body I do not know, or whether out of the body I do not know, God knows—such a one was caught up to the third heaven.

The Seventh Heaven is beyond time and beyond every atmosphere and just beyond. The truth is that none of us will never know anything about the Third to the Seventh Heaven until we pass into the afterlife. However, regarding Heaven, the created Heaven, let me give you a few more scriptures to reference the point that Heaven is upward, northward, and above. Beyond the brightest of all stars, that orients everything, the North Star. All of these scriptures are referenced from the New King James Version.

Acts 2:32-33: *[32] This Jesus God has raised up, of which we are all witnesses. [33] Therefore being exalted to the right hand of God, and having received from the Father the promise of the Holy Spirit, He poured out this which you now see and hear.*

We see here that Jesus went above all of the Heavens where God resides outside of eternity, creation, and time.

Ephesians 4:10: [10] *He who descended is also the One who ascended far above all the heavens, that He might fill all things.*

Again, we see here that Jesus ascended ***higher*** than the heavens, far above all of the heavens to sit on the right hand of the Father after He went to Hell and made an open spectacle of the devil.

Psalms 113:4-5: [4] *The Lord is high above all nations, His glory above the heavens.* [5] *Who is like the Lord our God, Who dwells on high,*

Again, David is aware of the fact that God's glory is far above the ***Heavens***. Would He be God if it wasn't?

Hebrews 11:3: [3] *By faith we understand that the worlds were framed by the word of God, so that the things which are seen were not made of things which are visible.*

So, to sum up what the Apostle Paul was saying in 2 Corinthians 12, he was referring to a distinction among the Jews of "the supreme heaven, the middle heaven, and the lower heaven". Some even say that he was referring to "the supreme world, and the middle world, and the lower world". But we won't get into an in-depth conversation about "worlds" in this book whereas we I am giving you enough information here to pray with knowledge, precision, and power. Your prayers are going to be more effective after reading this entire book.

The knowledge of the Second Heaven is important because many are being deceived because of the ignorance of the knowledge that you're reading in this book. In this last generation, God has allowed many to experience Heaven in a near death or real death experience and then have subsequently been sent back. Everyone that has had a real after death or near-death experience of this this magnitude that testifies about Jesus Christ have come back with the same message, "Tell them that I am coming back soon." However, there are others that are having other strange experiences that we have to discuss as well.

So, of course the enemy has counterfeited some of these experiences to people that have had close calls that were not destined for Heaven at all. For example, there are many that would testify as to having an after-death experience where they were taken to a heaven. I'm saying "a heaven" on purpose. Jesus said that, *"Not everyone who says to me 'Lord, Lord' will enter the Kingdom of Heaven."* **Matthew 7:21**. However, it is convenient for satan to make people think that everyone can and will make it, because if people believe this, they'll think that there is no judgement or consequences to living a sinful life. No matter of how debaucherously they're living, no matter how lustful, sinful, murderous, and downright evil they are, they will believe that they will be ushered into Heaven. And what is worse is that they will spread the kingdom of darkness propaganda. Of course, this is a lie, but what the principalities do is take a spirit that is not going to Heaven, or I should say God's Heaven, and allow them to see their imitation and fake heaven. They'll tell these poor souls things like, "Everyone is accepted here." "Everything that you've heard about Hell is wrong, because God is a God of love and will not let any of His children perish." Of course, this is not true, but this is the message that these fake heavenly encounters are supposed to produce.

These individuals are taken to principalities, dimensions, realms and "worlds" that they've never even heard of, thought existed, or believed in and are being given messages to send back to Earth to deceive many. They'll come back and say that God accepts everyone in the afterlife, homosexuals, fornicators, murderers, adulterers, and everyone. A great Baptist Evangelist, Howard Pittman, has gone all over the world sharing his testimony about almost being deceived in the afterlife by a very powerful demon that tried to imitate Jesus Himself. He believes it was satan himself. Howard Pittman died in the ambulance as the EMT's were trying to save him from an aortic rupture on August 3, 1979. Once he popped into the other dimension. He heard the most melodious voice he had ever heard in his life. He thought that this must be God, calling out to him, soothing him. The demon was telling him to **let himself go**, meaning his physical body, on the operating table, because he, the demon, was waiting for him. Evangelist Pittman was in between two worlds at this point and he was aware that he could still go back into his body. The Holy Spirit finally whispered in his spirit and said that "I would never tell you to let yourself die." When this truth got into Mr. Pittman's spirit, he reversed the course of his body and started wanting to live more than letting himself drift into nothingness. Once this happen, the "tunnel" that he was in lightened up and the demon turned from beautiful to hideous and was surprised that he was exposed. The demon left, and Evangelist Pittman saw a host of mighty angels peering at him as they God gave praise for what had just transpired.

Let me give you some historical context. The very first scriptures in the Bible say this:

Genesis 1:1-2

[1]*In the beginning God created the heaven and the earth.*

[2]*And the earth was without form, and void; and darkness was upon the face of the deep. And the Spirit of God moved upon the face of the waters.*

The Bible lets us know that God doesn't need a place to live. God doesn't need a place to reside. However, He created the Heaven and the Earth because He is a creator and He had creation on His mind. Please note that the scriptures are clear regarding creation though. He created one Heaven and one Earth. Regardless of how many levels of Heaven there are, we can encompass them all into a singular location, to represent anything that is not the planet Earth. Any and every other heaven, meaning fake heavens, at least as it pertains to Humans, are not the intent or will of God. And there is no other Earth in this dimension for us to inhabit.

Heaven can be described as "higher place" or a "holy" and "transcendent" place where God, His Angels, and other Heavenly beings exist. However, the Bible teaches us about Three levels of Heaven.

God has given us (mankind) dominion over the First Heaven, everything contained in the Earth's atmosphere, which is why we are allowed to create planes that can fly in the sky without God or any other demon knocking them out of the sky. And we're even able to build space ships that can reach outside of Earth's atmosphere into the Second Heaven, commonly called "space" without interference even though many astronauts have talked about seeing "things" such as beings and fast-moving vehicles that show up on the radar and then suddenly vanishes.

The second heaven is the actual habitation of the principalities, spiritual wickedness in high places and the rulers of darkness. Let me say this up front, "Hell" as we commonly discuss it, is located in the second dimension. Hell is a world, not a city, notwithstanding. There are seven realms or sub-kingdoms to satan's kingdom. Some mystics or occultist will even describe these seven realms as seven "worlds". Fallen angels, Marine Agents, Demons, and other spiritual entities, inhabit this realm. I will break them down in classical text book style for ease of reading and learning. The order of these worlds that I'm going to use for the purpose of this book was showed to Missionary Benjamin Kikamona, who is from the Republic of Congo. He was poisoned in 2009 by his stepmom, who was a witch, and he spent 11 hours beyond the grave. He died, was even buried, and was raised again by the power of Jesus Christ. I've read many accounts of these occultic or satanic worlds but his is the most concise and accurate with every other piece of information that I've learned and experienced regarding these things over decades of seeking, prayer, and research. Up front, you will probably never read any of this information in another Christian book, unless they are true Deliverance Ministers. The only people who will not argue with this information are again those who specialize in Deliverance, those who have been in the occult or those who have researched and know a whole lot about the mystic arts.

If it is too much, just understand, that there is a whole spiritual world out there that contains mysticism, occult, and spiritualism. There are many realms, dimensions, and spheres.

Before I get to the seven realms of the world of Hell, I want to give a recount of something else that Brother Benjamin mentioned. His testimony is that an angel came and took him after he had died in the hospital room and when he got to Heaven he saw the foundations of Heaven and the gates of Heaven. His account is that the angel told him that not everyone who makes it into Heaven will enter in the same gate. There are 12 gates that surround the actual "city of Heaven" and each gate represent a different virtue or fruit of the believer while on Earth. For example, some saints will arrive at the celestial gate for Soul Winners, another saint will arrive at the gate for Intercessor, others will enter the gates for Pastors and Ministers. Bro. Benjamin did not give an exhaustive list regarding each of these 12 gates.

In his testimony he also talked about the 7 realms of Hell. I added other personal truths and information to these realms so that you will be thoroughly edified. Whether you accept these realms or not just accept that all of these things are really going on in the spirit world. For some of you it's easier to receive it that way. Let's dig in.

First Realm: Anti-Church. They locate and identify real churches in this realm. They look for churches preaching holiness, sanctification, repentance, prayer, fasting, the Rapture, and repentance. The agents of this realm or sub-kingdom are hell bent on destroying the church.

The demon who runs this realm is a large snake with a human upper body and head. On his head he has two horns with fire that flows between it. I will leave out his name, because it's unimportant and he has many.

This realm is accessed from the waters. The agents from this particular sub-kingdom manifest from the cemeteries, graveyards, and even church graveyards, distance yourselves from them. Cemeteries are hallowed ground and are very spiritual places that are even used as portals to the Cemetery Kingdom, for lack of a better word and more. Some people go to certain cemeteries to obtain the dirt from certain graves, dead man bones and skulls, and even ashes, to do certain incantations. Watch out for people that have a propensity for visiting cemeteries. Jesus said, *let the dead bury the dead.* Watch out for people that have rooms in their basements or anywhere in their house under lock and key. How well do you really know them? Many people are living a parallel or double life. Even false prophets and fake pastors and priests. Be very careful.

When you are a real intercessor you will be attacked from this realm. When you get sleepy as soon as you go to pray, it's from this realm. They will send distractions, especially from people that are close to you. Many spouses are being used unknowingly by satan and this kingdom to distract and destroy the believer from being under the hearing of the Word of God. If that don't work, they will send people to come visit you as soon as you're getting ready for church. They will get you fired from your good job and allow you to be hired at a place that will require you to work on Sundays, for example. This realm also sends demons to check the preacher's message for that particular week and will send out attacks to keep the people that will be helped and delivered from making it to service for that particular week.

This book is about prayer, but it is my duty, I believe to inform and educate the serious prayer and intercessor about the things that they (we) can feel but can never explain and probably will never see on this side of life. Don't discount the information that you're reading right now. Learn beloved. For example, if you are dealing with a person from India, who claims to be a Christian, make sure you really get to know them. There are many different subsets of "Cemetery Kingdoms" all over the world and it takes a long time to learn them by their geographical names. But because I know that many Missionaries and Prophetic Apostles will read this book, I'll give you one common one as it regards to the country of India.

One of the names of a particular cemetery goddess in Delhi, India is Maharashatie. She is invoked by calling up the first person buried in the particular cemetery, who happened to be in the occult. His name is Dr. Kaylash Payba. If you hear them talking to you and saying that their doctor told them to do such and such, ask for the doctor's name. Many of them worship many gods, including our Christian God and will play you like a fiddle. If they can't successfully recruit you, they will kill you. If you are not a true man or woman of God, you will be susceptible to their witchcraft. If that fails, they will contaminate you and you will forever be sullied in the occult believing that you're in right standing with God. You will also find yourself cursed physically and your ministry will die. They know that many in the western culture don't really believe in spiritual things and they will give you the real names of the real entities that they deal with thinking that you're ignorant. To my Missionaries and Apostles, you have been warned. Now, when you travel to these areas, your prayers will be different. Why? Because you can now properly bind the right things. **You can't bind what you don't know exist.** Look in their eyes and listen to their every word. The person that is inviting you to their country might be the demon that you need to address.

Another way that these demons manifest is through toilets. This is common knowledge to anyone who practice black magic. The toilet is a prime place to invoke demons and spirits that are connected to the Marine Kingdom, of which we will discuss in this chapter. In short, for now, just understand that all of the information that is needed for demons and spiritual entities to find out about you is contained in your stool. I know that many of you thought it was your blood, however, your stool contains your blood and every other part of you and can actually fertilize and give life. In the same way that humans use animal stool to fertilize our earth is the say way that these demonic entities will utilize your stool. If you throw blood on the ground nothing will happen. However, if you throw stool on the ground it will fertilize it and create growth. All manner of bugs and insects will grow out of your stool if left alone. What we consider waste on Earth is one of the most underused things and substances on the Earth. In short, everyone in your house will have to use your toilet at one point or another so there are spirits there. Many of the new horror movies are now showing the truth of this and it's amazing that satan is showing many of his secrets.

For my deliverance ministers, if you are called to "pray through" a house because of spiritual occurrences, one of the things that you should be doing is anointing the waters of the house. Take your anointed oil and prayerfully place a drop of the anointed oil in all of the toilets of the house and cast out the spirit that is contained in the waters and water system of that house. There are ten names for the deities that lurk or are assigned to this toilet duty. I won't take the time to go any further with those names because they are many and change from culture to culture. Again, just bind the monitoring spirit in the name of Jesus. You don't have to use a name, just speak to the spirit. Bind her works and cast her out of the in the name of Jesus. If that is too deep or too much for you just use the oil to purify every water of the property and send the spirit(s) to where it came from, never to return again in the name of Jesus. It will work. By the way, you don't have to be a deliverance minister, you can pray this over your own house and/or business as well.

Lastly, about this First Realm of the hellish kingdom. Understand that the agents in this kingdom attacks the Pastor, by trying to discourage him and even make him not believe in the truth of the Bible. If you're under a Pastor and he teach that everything in the Bible is just an allegory or story, he is under the influence of this kingdom. Leave him or her because how can they teach you something they think is fairy tales anyway. I don't care how many letters they have behind their name or what seminary they went through, leave them and go to a Bible teaching, Holy Spirit filled church. If these agents can't get the Pastor, they will work on the Department Leaders to start discord and confusion. If that don't work of course, they'll try the members. It is in this kingdom that they will initiate public paper and legal issues in regard to the official status of the church. When this happens, it means you have been identified and need to pray against this kingdom.

Second Realm: This realm is the source of Occultism and Mysticism. I will give you the name of this particular leader in this kingdom. They call him Dr. Solomon. You cannot look upon him twice because he is the ultimate abomination. He has no hands or feet. He, being the source of all occultist and mystic activity on Earth, is the one responsible for talking satan into setting up satanic churches. He is responsible for many counterfeit Christian churches all over the world. I'm being very brief about him and this realm. But I encourage you to watch the language of everyone you come into contact. If they say this name they are in occultism. Many of them have to travel to this realm or world to get and maintain their powers and abilities.

Many are teaching counterfeit Christianity saying things like all you have to do is get "saved" and then you can live any way that you want to after that, because, "Once saved, always saved." This is unbiblical and untrue. But millions have and will go to Hell because of this irresponsible and erroneous teaching. It is taught in the highest institutions of so called Christian learning. Our cemeteries, oh, I mean Seminaries, are teaching this kind of junk theology and everyone will pay for their deception and in some cases ignorance. Isaiah prophesied about this in Isaiah 59:2:

Isaiah 59:1-4 (NIV)

1 *Surely the arm of the Lord is not too short to save, nor his ear too dull to hear.*

2 ***But your iniquities have separated you from your God; your sins have hidden his face from you, so that he will not hear.***

3 *For your hands are stained with blood, your fingers with guilt. Your lips have spoken falsely, and your tongue mutters wicked things.*

4 *No one calls for justice; no one pleads a case with integrity. They rely on empty arguments, they utter lies; they conceive trouble and give birth to evil.* ***God dwells in the north, in the third heaven beyond the stars.*** *The angels that were banished from Heaven were forcefully sent to this Earth.*

The writer of Hebrews makes it even more plain:

Hebrews 10:26-27 (NIV)

[26] If we deliberately keep on sinning after we have received the knowledge of the truth, no sacrifice for sins is left, [27] but only a fearful expectation of judgment and of raging fire that will consume the enemies of God.

How about our good friend, the Apostle Paul:

1 Corinthians 6:9-11

[9] Know ye not that the unrighteous shall not inherit the kingdom of God? Be not deceived: neither fornicators, nor idolaters, nor adulterers, nor effeminate, nor abusers of themselves with mankind,

[10] Nor thieves, nor covetous, nor drunkards, nor revilers, nor extortioners, shall inherit the kingdom of God.

[11] And such were some of you: but ye are washed, but ye are sanctified, but ye are justified in the name of the Lord Jesus, and by the Spirit of our God.

The key is in verse 11 of 1 Corinthians 6. Understand that Jesus is our perfect sacrifice and His blood atones for all of our sins. When we get saved or receive salvation for the theological student, we are forgiven and if we were to die right then, we would see Heaven. However, once we are "washed" as verse 11 says, with the blood of Jesus, we have to then allow ourselves to be sanctified, which means set apart. So that we can't fall back into sin. If we can do this we will be justified in the name of the Lord Jesus, and by the Spirit of our God.

I'm not talking about being saved on our own merits or by our own works, what I'm saying is that you have to live a holy and righteous life before the Lord. When you sin, because we ALL are sinners, we have to be quick to confess it, to receive the bathing of our sins, in the blood of Jesus. Shall we continue in sin, so that God's grace can abound? God forbid, please understand that God can't be played and won't be mocked. I said this because one of you is saying, "But we're no longer under the law." This is true, but don't be deceived:

Romans 6:15 King James Version (KJV)

[15] What then? shall we sin, because we are not under the law, but under grace? God forbid.

You've been warned beloved. Watch out for the "Grace Movement". It's by grace that we get saved, it's by our obedience that we stay saved. Your name CAN be blotted out of the Lambs Book of Life and satan has all of his kingdoms set up to make this happen. You don't believe me? I guarantee you that Judas is not in Heaven, and He was an Apostle in Training, knew Jesus intimately, and talked to Him face to face. You're saying, but he betrayed Jesus. Exactly. When you sin against God and transgress His commandments, it shows that you don't love Him, and you are in fact, betraying His trust. Do not play with your soul. Because the last time I checked, betrayal has not been listed in the Bible as an unforgiveable sin, however, the Bible clearly condemned his act and not to mention that he committed suicide, furthering himself away from the saving grace of God The last time I checked Ananias and Saphira, followers of Christ, died in their sin and did not inherit the eternal grace of God. Instead they inherited the penalty for their blasphemous and lying spirit. I could go on but just ask God for forgiveness right now. REPENT, while you still have a chance. Use the blood of Jesus continuously.

Many Medical Doctors are intertwined in this realm. Many miracle working Evangelists and Pastors are using the powers from this realm. They visit this realm a lot. Many people that are extremely rich, deal with this realm. You might ask why? It is in this realm that many people destinies are stolen. They do this by stealing your star. It is called "Star Stealing."

I know, I know, you're saying what is Star Stealing? Let me explain it this way. satan and many fallen archangels are star hunters and if they can steal your "star" they can steal your purpose and destiny. Let's go straight to the Bible on this one. There is a "host of heaven," described in the Bible as an "innumerable company of angels" (Hebrews 12:22). God asked Job some pointed questions in response to Job's questioning of His sovereignty. One of the questions He responded to Job with was, 'Where were you Job….."

Job 38:7 (NKJV)

[7] When the morning stars sang together,
And all the sons of God shouted for joy?

God was referring to the stars as literal living beings and the sons of God was referring to the Angels. There is a frequent identification of angels with stars in the Bible (note Job 38:7; Revelation 12:4; and many others) is most intriguing, especially in view of the fact that there is no similarity between them whatsoever. In one we have the angels being present at the creation of a group of stars. In the other, we see language in the Bible that would denote that angels are considered stars in the Heavenly Host as well.

Revelations 12:4a (NKJV)

[4] His tail drew a third of the stars of heaven and threw them to the earth.

The same mysterious correlations are found everywhere in ancient mythology, the gods and goddesses (Jupiter, Venus, Orion, etc.) being identified with various stars, planets and constellations and there is a reason for that, not saying that what they're (those who believe in mythology) are right.

The truth is that the devil is out to exchange your destiny to those that have pledged their souls to him. He doesn't have any blessings to give a person, so what he does is steal from the Believers and give to his followers. That's why the Bible says that he comes to **steal**, kill, and destroy. In the Bible we read that the wise men saw the star of Jesus and knew that the king of Israel was born.

Matthew 2:1-2

1 Now when Jesus was born in Bethlehem of Judaea in the days of Herod the king, behold, there came wise men from the east to Jerusalem,

2 Saying, Where is he that is born King of the Jews? for we have seen his star in the east, and are come to worship him.

So, your next train of thought should be how can satan and these angels do this. I'm here to tell you that the duties of the angels are way above our paygrade and they were there when God created this Earth and when God created us and so they know almost everything as it pertains to the human race and the things that God created to guide us. lucifer is described as the shining one, the morning star, and in some translations, the "day star". So, trust me, he knows about stars.

Isaiah 14:12

12 How you have fallen from heaven, morning star, son of the dawn! You have been cast down to the earth, you who once laid low the nations!

In fact, to go a little deeper for you. Ask yourself a question, how does the enemy know who is going to be great, or who has a great destiny in God? There is a literal answer to this. The fallen Archangels, that comprise what we could Principalities, watch our stars before we're ever born and when our spirits are being ushered from Heaven by our Angel, they try to attack the soul that corresponds to the brightest stars that they can see. Or at the very least, they are taking note of the very brightest of the stars to stop their impending greatness in the Earth. We all have a "star" that represents our life and greatness upon this Earth that appears before we are born. Some are very bright, and some are not. This is why satan and these fallen angels were trying to kill all of the male babies when Moses was born and of course, he did it again, when Jesus was born. Yes, go back and read **Mathew 2:1-2** again, because what I'm telling you is all biblical. These same mighty angels are also trying to capture your soul when you're being transported to Heaven after your death as well. If they can't capture you or even deceive you in death, it has been purported that they will follow you to Heaven and try to bring railing accusation against you being permitted into Heaven. It is a huge operation and God has commissioned special Warrior/Transporter Angels to handle these duties. Praise God that Jesus is our Advocate, our Attorney, so to speak and we are covered by the blood. However, the Bible says that we are to make sure that our salvation is secure in God.

2 Peter 1:10 (NLT)

[10] So, dear brothers and sisters, work hard to prove that you really are among those God has called and chosen. Do these things, and you will never fall away.

John 3:3 (KJV)

[3] "Jesus answered and said unto him, Verily, verily, I say unto thee, Except a man be born again, he cannot see the kingdom of God."

Mark 1:15 (KJV)

[15] "And saying, The time is fulfilled, and the kingdom of God is at hand: ***repent ye, and believe the gospel.****" [emphasis added]*

The Greek word for "repent" in Mark 1:15 in the King James Bible is *metanoeo*, which means, "to think differently." It is a change of mind. It DOESN'T mean to "change your hearts and lives," which is what many corrupt and watered-down versions of this scripture states. The changing of your habits and lifestyle, etc. is not the requirement unto Salvation it is the evidence. The actions without the indwelling of the Holy Spirit that produces the transaction will leave you wanting. You will die thinking that Heaven will be your eternal home and the demon that has been following you your whole life making sure that you've been deceived will snatch your soul from the grips of the guardian angel that God has posted right beside you even now.

Nevertheless, when someone receives Jesus Christ as their Lord and Savior, they have the power to reclaim their stars. Because whereas the stars can be stolen and hidden from a person, it can never be destroyed. Once we become "saved" by accepting Jesus, for real, we than have the Holy Spirit indwelling in us. Once we have the indwelling of the Holy Spirit we then need to understand that we are ruling at this very moment in the high places with Jesus. We also need to recognize that we have a higher authority than any demon and any wickedness and we can order these same demons to return everything that has been stolen from us including our purpose. Sometimes we even have to release mighty warring Angels to pillage these evil kingdoms and return everything that the cankerworm and locust have eating.

Joel 2:25 (KJV)

25 And I will restore to you the years that the locust hath eaten, the cankerworm, and the caterpiller, and the palmerworm, my great army which I sent among you.

Decree with me right now: I apply Joel 2:25 to my life and I decree and declare that my prosperity is being restored! My health is being restored! My family is being restored! My power is being restored! My confidence is being restored! My whole life is being restored! In Jesus mighty name, Amen

Lastly, it is from this second realm that many fake pastors are getting their bewitchment for fake deliverance manufactured by Hell itself and the ability to prophesy. This is why the sound of prophecy in this last generation is strange at best. Why do you need someone to play parlor tricks for you to believe that he or she is hearing from God? I don't need you to tell me my birthdate, I need you to tell me what God wants me to do for tomorrow. I don't need you to tell me what color under shirt I'm wearing or what I did last summer. I need you to tell me what God would have for me this time next year. Tell me what the Holy Spirit is saying about my next major decision to forward the Kingdom of God. There is a strange spirit in many of the assembly of the modern-day church and the strangeness is not of God. Please note that the First, Second, and Third Realm of the "world of Hell" works closely and intertwine with the Marine world.

For many of you, the verbiage or even the concept of stealing stars is too new and too much for you, let's just sum this knowledge up with something that we can agree on, satan is always plotting and scheming to steal your destiny and purpose. Is that churchier for you?

Third Realm: Media and Technology. It is in this realm that all of the scientific discoveries that we learn on the Earth comes from. Most of the science that we enjoy on this Earth is esoteric in nature. The technology that we enjoy is spiritual in nature and was introduced from somewhere else. Think about it. How does the internet work? Well, it has always been here. The ultimate internet is being used in the demonic realm, because again angels are not omniscient nor omnipresent. How are we tapping into a "frequency" that is always there, truth be told, no matter where we are even in space? Does it really have something to do with paying your cell phone or internet bill? What exactly are the Routers routing? Most technological inventions have nothing to do with science but with metaphysical and esoteric knowledge. Also, it is a fact that you're not really considered a scientist unless you are a part of the world's Scientific Community, which includes the community of all the occultist scientist as well.

Unfortunately, even some facets of the "church" are in major alignment with what I'm saying. Have you ever asked yourself why the symbol of Apple Incorporated is an apple with a bite out of it? Did you know that Steve Wozniak, the guy who hand made the computer, sold his units for $666.66 at first, in homage to the devil and the demon who gave him the technology? It was Steve Jobs idea to sell these computers, mass develop them and go global. They are co-founders of this company. Wozniak is currently Chief Scientist at the data virtualization company Primary Data and remains an employee of Apple in a ceremonial capacity.

Was this knowledge given to them mystically or esoterically? We won't know until after this life is over. However, in 1981 he had an airplane accident that he survived where he couldn't even remember his name for a while and then everything came back to him. In 1985 he "developed" the technology for the first programmable universal remote control and then in 2001, Wozniak founded Wheels of Zeus (WOZ), to create wireless GPS technology to "help everyday people find everyday things much more easily." Zeus? Yeah, I'll let you put two and two together, as they say, and do the math.

In short, the devil is using technology as a tool to spiritually manipulate, indoctrinate, and infiltrate the spirits and souls of mankind. Internet means "many nets" which means that are many snares waiting for you to lose your anointing beloved. Be careful. I know that I'm not the only one who has checked for something on the internet and seen an ad pop out of nowhere with a minimally covered female in it. Also, there is occultism in Android and Apple technology. There are some functionalities that you should not be engaged in because there are trigger points designed to indoctrinate. Social networking is the seat of satanic power in this generation. There are cults that snatch pictures off of the internet to invoke incantations, curses and spells. This kingdom works hand in hand with the Marine Kingdom, of which I will discuss in a few pages.

Do you know that there is a website that you can go to, to sell your soul to the devil? I won't give you the URL, but it's legit and people are selling their souls for wealth, notoriety, and prosperity by the hundreds. This website is being ran and monitored directly from hell beloved. I'm not going to mention the fact that the technology is laced with soft and hardcore pornography, as well as tons of siren agents. Last warning; don't join every group that you're invited too on social media because again, some of these groups are being ran by demons.

Fourth Realm: The fourth realm is full of many roads. There are many roads that can lead a person to Hell. This dimension is where all of the chief demons exist that are responsible for specific sins. There is a road that leads to every sin. The sign that is hung on every road is the name of a sin. Each road is controlled by a specific demon that is responsible for a different sin. For example, there is a road that the demon of Fornication presides. He is a hermaphrodite demon with both sex organs and he is able to copulate himself for pleasure. He is responsible for providing and promoting sexual immorality on the Earth. Another is the Demon of Lying. He is heavily using mobile phone technology to promote his particular sin. Have you ever noticed that it is easier to lie on the phone? Even simple lies, like I'm right around the corner, when you know that you're really 15 minutes away? How about Valentines Day? Even Christians deliberately lie on "St. Valentines Day". There is a demon of Drunkenness, a demon of Smoking a demon of Gossip, a demon of Pride, a demon of Divorce, a demon of Lust, a demon of Accident, a demon of Abortion and so many more, of course. **Matthew 7:13-14** says,

13 *"Enter through the narrow gate. For wide is the gate and broad is the road that leads to destruction, and many enter through it.* 14 *But small is the gate and narrow the road that leads to life, and only a few find it.*

Wide is the path to Hell, because it comprises of so many paths. The road to Heaven is one road and that road has one name on it. That name is Jesus. Follow the road that leads to Jesus beloved. Remember in **John 14:6&7** He said,

6 *Jesus answered, "I am the way and the truth and the life. No one comes to the Father except through me.* 7 *If you really know*

me, you will know my Father as well. From now on, you do know him and have seen him.

Fifth Realm: Ruled by 3 Powerful demons. One of these demons is the Principalic demon of Music, called Sang Ke (one of his names). He is over the Marine Kingdom demon of music Phopha (one of his names). Every secular artist that becomes global or huge has to go through this demon. And I gave you these names for a reason to the one reading this right now that is in covenant with these individuals. They're not humans. They're not just figures in your dreams. They are real. You know that a person has signed a contract with Sang Ke and not Phopha when they change their name. I know that some of you are thinking about the musicians that have changed their names in our Earth realm, some of them have changed their names more than once. Have you ever really wondered why? It's to appease their god.

The second demon in this realm is the demon of Sickness. This is a chief demon that is used when all else fails. If a man or woman of God is able to persevere through all of the traps of the enemy and succeed to live a holy life, this demon will be deployed to paralyze their impact on the Earth. Sickness can stop anybody, no matter how gifted, no matter how much money, no matter how beautiful the person is. That is why you have to know how to bind this demon off of your life and prevent his dirty works.

The third demon in this realm is Blockage or Blockade. He sits on a throne with a tree behind him that has nothing but chains and padlocks on it. When a believer is able to maneuver through everything, even sickness, this demon will work to block the full extent of their purpose and efforts. The people affected by this will find that as soon as they are about to get that blessing, something will happen to block it. You have to bind this spirit off of your life to gain open access under an open Heaven that God says is the believers right. However, this demon is not afraid of prayer.

One special note about this last demon called Blockage. **He is not affected by just your prayers. The demon of Blockage can**

only be defeated by giving and prayer. The Bible says to give, and it shall be given to you:

Luke 6:38 (NIV)

[38] *Give, and it will be given to you. A good measure, pressed down, shaken together and running over, will be poured into your lap. For with the measure you use, it will be measured to you."*

In the story of the Rich man and Lazarus the Beggar, the beggar was the believer, but he was still poor. The fear of the Lord will lead you to Heaven, but it will not necessarily make you rich. The Principle of Sowing is what makes you blessed beloved, not prayer. As a matter of fact, those that don't tithe or give any kind of offerings are under a curse from this demon and he uses the Bible to enforce it.

Malachi 3:8 (NIV)

[8] *"Will a mere mortal rob God? Yet you rob me. "But you ask, 'How are we robbing you?' "In tithes and offerings.*

Sixth Realm: Realm of Witches, Wizards, and Warlocks. This realm is the strength of lucifer. Many witches from the Earth visit this realm. The ruler of this world's throne is inside or by a lake of fire, but he doesn't get burned. Those who practice witchcraft get their power from this demon which is why they are not afraid of fire. In fact, they get their power through fire.

Many, many years ago. Before my wife, the beautiful, Prophetess Dr. Joanna Birchett, gave her life to Christ. She knew God but was not walking with God in those days and she was robbed of a lot of money. One of her friends told her that she knew someone who could help her figure out who did it. Lo and behold her friend had taken her to a male witch, which we will call a warlock. Joanna didn't realize what was going on, but she did notice that the guy only had one hand. He told her to step in a ring of fire and that's when she finally realized that something was a little weird. She tells me that she's never felt so terrified and she wouldn't do it. Something happened as he was consulting his spirits and his eyes got wide and he said to her friend, "Why did you bring her here? She doesn't belong here!" He kicked her out.

When someone is calling fire down from Heaven and they are not right sometimes they are really calling witches and entities from other realms. Be careful beloved. If you are an intercessor and have discernment sometimes you can even hear the witches coming and feel the atmosphere changing. Not everyone who is praying is praying to our God. Not everyone who is trying to use our most precious commands have been authorized in the spirit realm to do so. There are levels to this thing. Listen to their every word. Watch their every action. Your life might be at stake beloved.

The ruler of this particular realm is the one that gives witches and Black Magic practitioners the power to "transport". By transport, I'm referring to Astral Projecting. Astral Projecting is the ability of a person's spirit to travel all over the world and even in space for some without their bodies. There are even schools that teach this now. The one thing about this practice is that the person has to be back in their bodies before daytime or their body will have to join their spirit. This is why there are so many cases of people falling out of seemingly nowhere. These people were witches' beloved. They stayed out of their bodies too long and their body joined their spirit and fell from where they were.

This is why we pray against astral projectors and why we break silver cords. They try to fly over your houses and spy on you. In short, a silver cord is the cord that keeps your soul connected to your body. In the occult world they concoct "silver cords" as a means of connecting to their host (victim). Some even have the ability to enter your dreams through your silver cord and imitation silver cords. And this is the reason why we insulate ourselves before sleep and break covenants that has occurred in our dreams upon awakening. I will provide these prayers in their own sections and speak a little bit more about this in another section of this book, however, just know that witches also have the ability to "change face". Meaning that they can look like someone else or even an animal or something. And so, when you think that you were fighting with a dog or bear in your dream it was really a witch.

Two more things about witches, warlocks, wizards that operate from this realm. Some of them are adult during the day but turn into children during the night for their own devices and vice versa. A child that is able to do this is normally sickly though and have a terrible attitude because they are really an adult. I know that is too much information for some of you "religious heads" who think they know it all but have never faced not one demon in your life. You know everything but can't even deliver yourself from demonic oppression not withstanding others. You never been anywhere, seen anything, experienced anything, or have done anything in the realms that I'm speaking about in this book. You will call the things that I'm discussing now, spooky, but you're afraid to go to sleep with the lights off at night. Please, if that's you, go have a seat.

The other thing about these witches and wizards is that they have power in their fingers and toes. If you see someone that is getting fidgety when you're talking about your plans and purposes. Meaning that if they start playing with their fingers or even their toes they are recording you or sending messages and doing incantations to prevent your purpose.

There are four departments in the spirit world of witchcraft. The first one is mechanic. They have aircrafts in this realm. Spiritual aircrafts beloved. A real witch can travel to Africa and back within minutes. There are also witch personnel that work on these aircrafts and these people will normally be dirty during the day as well because they're really mechanics in the spirit realm. Watch out for the beggars.

When we pray, especially as a church, these astral aircrafts come under fire. You can pray these aircrafts down men and women of God. As a matter of fact, you should. Any place that prayer is practiced and is always going up to Heaven emits a supernatural fire to these objects and other spiritual entities. This is why we should always pray. Pray without ceasing! Pray! Pray! And then Pray some more! Note: Sometimes these mystical aircrafts and cars are destroyed or disabled by the particular church's Guardian Angel as well. Yes, every real church has their own Angel.

The second department is Pilot or Driver. They are the Drivers or Pilots of these astral aircrafts. Children are targeted to fly these vehicles knowing that these duties attract and keep children.

The third department is that of Chef. These Chef Witches are hell bent on preparing human flesh. They steal children, kill older people, kidnap, and otherwise and change human flesh into animal flesh so that humans can consume human meat. This activity really rises during September and October leading to Halloween which is their highest occult day.

The fourth department is Bewitchment and Spell Casting. These witches, warlocks, or wizards are very arrogant because they don't believe that anyone can withstand their powers. These people are very newsy. They want to know minor details about individuals lives. Watch out for gossipers and busybodies. They might be witches.

These kinds of witches will try to kill you, for example, strangle you in your sleep. Most of the time if they target you, they will try you in the daytime first to see if you are a strong or weak spirit. If you withstand them in the night they will be mad at you the next day for seemingly no reason. Keep your spiritual armor on beloved and look at everything through a spiritual lens. Witches pray too, and they have an agenda they just pray to the wrong god (who is actually not a god at all).

These individuals are very controlling and they're always looking to get promoted. How do they get promoted? They get promoted via human sacrifice. Don't eat from everyone. Stop being so trusting of people that you barely know. Pray over everything.

Seventh Realm: Realm where satan exists. In this realm there are many pregnant demons. In this realm the demons that have molested and have had sex with humans in their sleep are carrying out the births of these pregnancies. Many of the agents in this world arrive from the Marine Kingdom, where succubus and incubus reside. These babies are taken to the second realm, Dr. Solomon, to be distributed to the native witch doctors and others who have prayed for babies from this world when the natural methods of getting pregnant seemingly, isn't working.

Altars, Principalities, and Kingdoms

It is better to be stabbed with the truth than to be tickled with a lie.

Apostle Dr. Larry Birchett, Jr.

Revelation 12:7-12 New King James Version (NKJV)

7 *And war broke out in heaven: Michael and his angels fought with*
the dragon; and the dragon and his angels fought, 8 *but they did*
not prevail, nor was a place found for them in heaven any
longer. 9 *So the great dragon was cast out, that serpent of old,*
called the Devil and Satan, who deceives the whole world; he was
cast to the earth, and his angels were cast out with him.

10 *Then I heard a loud voice saying in heaven, "Now salvation, and*
strength, and the kingdom of our God, and the power of His Christ
have come, for the accuser of our brethren, who accused them
before our God day and night, has been cast down. 11 *And they*
overcame him by the blood of the Lamb and by the word of their
testimony, and they did not love their lives to the
death. 12 *Therefore rejoice, O heavens, and you who dwell in them!*
Woe to the inhabitants of the earth and the sea! For the devil has
come down to you, having great wrath, because he knows that he
has a short time."

No one knows how long the fallen angels inhabited this Earth before God made man, however, what we do know is that they were here before us. And to go further, we know that before God was able to put man on this Earth, He had to do some construction. In Genesis, we get to learn that before God was able to put us here He had to divide the land from the water.

Genesis 1:1-2

[1]In the beginning God created the heavens and the earth. [2] The earth was without form, and void; and darkness was on the face of the deep. And the Spirit of God was hovering over the face of the waters.

Genesis 1:6-10

[6] Then God said, "Let there be a firmament in the midst of the waters, and let it divide the waters from the waters." [7] Thus God made the firmament, and divided the waters which were under the firmament from the waters which were above the firmament; and it was so. [8] And God called the firmament Heaven. So the evening and the morning were the second day.

[9] Then God said, "Let the waters under the heavens be gathered together into one place, and let the dry land appear"; and it was so. [10] And God called the dry land Earth, and the gathering together of the waters He called Seas. And God saw that it was good.

According to verse nine, before the land and the seas were put in their respective places the world obviously was covered by the water. However, the fallen angels were already inhabiting the planet Earth. So where did they reside? In the waters. Remember angels are already in their celestial bodies. They are not regulated by physical fleshly bodies like you and I are. So, don't think that the element of water is something that could drown or kill them. The fallen angels are ethereal beings that seem to almost prefer the water in some instances because for many of them, it was their first habitation when they were kicked out of Heaven.

However, God instructed the land to form together so that humankind can live on the land. For anyone that has at least a six-grade education, we know that at one time all of the land on this planet was at one time all connected. The name commonly given to this one super continent is called Pangaea. There was an "event" that occurred on this planet that fragmented the one big piece of land into the seven big pieces of land that we call continents and into all of the other little pieces of land, that we call islands, all over this globe.

In line with this subject, the breaking apart of the land was not an accidental one as science would have us to believe, but it was spiritual in nature. And just as there are seven continents, there are seven **governing** principalities in satan's realm.

Ephesians 6:12 New King James Version (NKJV)

[12] For we do not wrestle against flesh and blood, but against principalities, against powers, against the rulers of the darkness of this age, against spiritual hosts of wickedness in the heavenly places.

A principality is a state ruled by a Prince. In this case where talking about spiritual states or territory. As stated before these princes reside over regions and/or territories in the sky. In Ephesians 2:6-7, the Apostle Paul calls satan the "Prince of the Power of the Air". The reference to "air" refers to the air surrounding this Earth. It is just another way of saying that he was the prince of the Earth and the air and everything in it. Putting all of these elements together we see that the Apostle Paul is trying to make us understand that satan, the enemy of God, has an empire that he is running as the Absolute Dictator governing the Princes, Powers, Rulers, and other lesser Spirits in every non- Heavenly dimension. The Apostle John also speaks of satan with this title, in other places as well:

John 12:31

31 Now is the judgment of this world: now shall the prince of this world be cast out.

The Apostle John also wrote about the princedom of satan in **John 14:30** and **John 16:11**. Ephesians 6, however, let us know that we're not fighting against physical forces but spiritual forces, and one of those forces are called principalities; which is written in the plural, which would denote that there are more than one. And the truth is that there are many principalities, seven major ones in total. Isn't it ironic that there are seven large pieces of land that is on this Earth? It would be ironic, if it wasn't perfectly synchronous with how many chief principalities there actually are. Just like there are seven spirits of God. Just like God took 6 days to make the Earth and on the seventh day He rested. God has an affinity with certain numbers and those numbers are 3, 7 and 12. Nothing is coincidental in creation beloved, nothing. Everything, every little piece of information is spiritually significant, everything. By most standards, the prevailing thought is that there is a maximum of seven continents - Africa, Antarctica, Asia, Australia/Oceania, Europe, North America, and South America. Many geographers and scientists now refer to six continents, where Europe and Asia are combined, because they're one solid landmass, but this is an attempt to throw those that are aware and those that would become aware off; there are seven.

In the world of the occult this is common knowledge. We see that this was even understood way back in the Old Testament of the Bible. In Numbers 23 we see that Balaam, an evil prophet, was asked to come and curse the nation of Israel. I'm always careful to describe Balaam as a good prophet that was swayed to become an evil prophet, not a false prophet, because he actually did hear from God. But Balaam held out for a long time because God had told him that he didn't want him to go. But after multiple attempts, King Balak had sweetened the "pot", so to speak, so much that Balaam, pulling on the perfect will of God, did in fact go to King Balak with the intent of cursing Israel. Balak promised him riches and notoriety.

How many of you know that if the enemy can't get you one way, he'll try to get you another way? This is why you always want to pray that God's will be done in your life no matter what situation you're believing God for. King Balak had tapped into Balaam's pride of life issue. He tapped into his vanity, his greed. He was offered so much money, resources and stature that Balaam went from resisting Balak's requests to packing his donkey and going to him. I have to stop right here and give you this disclaimer, which is this, don't allow any trick of the enemy to cause you to sabotage your relationship with the Lord. Many of us start out good, but we end up crashing and burning. Many of you women say that I would never cheat on my husband, until big daddy long pockets, with the brand-new Benz show up and offer you the life that you thought you would never have. Many of you men make the same oath until your once hot wife gets older, puffier, and flabby and the equivalent of your Halle Berry or Meagan Goode shows up and start showing you an excessive amount of interest. Or you're all good until tax season comes up and your unethical tax accountant can get you an extra ten thousand on your return as long as you're willing to look the other way. How much is your love to the Lord worth? Can the devil buy you out? Can your loyalty be bought? Does your righteousness and obedience to the Lord come with a price tag, like Judas?

Anyway, let's move on. This is where we get to the story of the donkey being abused by Balaam because he wouldn't move because of the angel that Balaam couldn't see. God opened the eyes of Balaam after he abused the donkey for the third time and then God allowed the donkey to speak, and he turned to Balaam and said, "Why are you striking me?" And then Balaam saw an angel with a flaming sword not too far in front of him and the donkey. The donkey wouldn't go forward because if he did, he feared that he would've died as well as Balaam. He saved Balaam's life. And likewise, when we get mad at our car for not starting or something else, seemingly unfortunate happens, pray to God that He will open your eyes to see the real reason of why He is allowing this unusual event in your life. However, after this demonstration of God's true heart regarding what Balaam was being summoned to do to the children of Israel, God allowed Balaam to go, with the stipulation of, that he had to do and say exactly what He told him to do once he got there. All of this can be found in Numbers 22.

Numbers 22:31-35

31 Then the LORD opened the eyes of Balaam, and he saw
the angel of the LORD standing in the way, and his sword drawn
in his hand: and he bowed down his head, and fell flat on his face.
32 And the angel of the LORD said unto him, Wherefore hast thou
smitten thine ass these three times? behold, I went out to withstand
thee, because thy way is perverse before me: 33 And the ass saw
me, and turned from me these three times: unless she had turned
from me, surely now also I had slain thee, and saved her alive.
34 And Balaam said unto the angel of the LORD, I have
sinned; for I knew not that thou stoodest in the way against me:
now therefore, if it displease thee, I will get me back again.
35 And the angel of the LORD said unto Balaam, Go with
the men: but only the word that I shall speak unto thee, that thou
shalt speak. So Balaam went with the princes of Balak.

When Balaam arrived in Moab, Balak again reiterated his request to have Balaam curse Israel. We see here, that Balaam, being in tune with Balak's heathen ways, told him to build **seven altars**. Balak had a reputation of hiring diviners and occultists and the like to curse and send witchcraft on any enemy that opposed him and his nation. Basically, he would hire the hottest psychic, witch, wizard, or warlock there was at the particular moment, and unfortunately, he had learned about Balak. From his perspective it was a smart move because he knew that it was by the same God that Balaam supposedly worshipped and was empowered by, that the nation of Israel was crushing their opponents. Balaam told Balak to build seven altars to appease the seven principalities, based off of the fact that there were only seven known planets at that time, and the early Nephilim named themselves the name of the planets such as Venus and Neptune. This was in fact, already out of the realm of what God required, because He only requires only one altar to be built in situations like this, because He alone is God.

Numbers 23:1-3 (KJV)

[1]And Balaam said unto Balak, Build me here seven altars, and prepare me here seven oxen and seven rams. [2] And Balak did as Balaam had spoken; and Balak and Balaam offered on every altar a bullock and a ram. [3] And Balaam said unto Balak, Stand by thy burnt offering, and I will go: peradventure the LORD will come to meet me: and whatsoever he sheweth me I will tell thee. And he went to an high place.

The altars of Balaam are erected to stop the progress of a person. These strange altars are still being erected today and when they are, just know that they are being erected to impede or destroy any progress that you would normally experience in your life. The resistance was to stop the progress of the Israelites. In the same way, today there are altars that are raised by the enemy purposely to stop progress in your life, your career and your business and if you do not conquer altars against your progress others will progress and you will remain where you are. Have you ever noticed that there are some people who cannot go beyond a certain level in their life? There are some individuals and maybe even you yourself that seems to take a drastic loss as soon as there is about to be a breakthrough. If this is common in your life or their life, it could be that someone has erected an evil altar against you or them. It could mean that the enemy is fighting against the progress of that person. Hence, let it be established that the altars of Balaam are raised to make someone lose his/her original value or purpose.

These altars are dangerous because they are erected to dominate a person. You become dominated because your spiritual authority is taken away to ensure that you are controlled demonically. If you are under the control of demons, you better believe that you will never manifest in your area of gifting and your qualifications basically becomes irrelevant. The altars of Balaam even make people backslide and become bankrupt. When the altars of Balaam are erected against you, if you don't take authority over them with the spiritual authority contained in the name of Jesus, you will start well but finish badly. If you are dealing with any of these symptoms you should pray this way:

Father God, there is none like you in all of the earth. You are God alone, seated on your throne and there is none like you. I confess that I am not perfect and in fact have sinned. Please forgive me for all of my sins. I repent of every evil work and of every evil way that I have ever sinned against thee, according to 1 John 1:9. I also release and ask that you release anyone of any consequence regarding their sin and transgression towards me. Because you said that you are just and able to forgive me for my sins, I take you at your Word and believe that I am forgiven. Lord God, according to Mark 16:17 I have the authority to cast out demons. Lord Jesus, I cover myself with the blood of Jesus. I cover my spouse and family with the blood of Jesus and I apply the blood of Jesus between me and any altar that has been erected against me. According to Ephesians 6:17, I have the authority to use the Sword of the Spirit. I take my authority and attack from the Third Heaven with the sword of the Spirit, my weapon of choice, and I strike and break the Altars of Balaam off of my life in Jesus name. I strike and break the Altars of Poverty off of my life in Jesus name. I strike and break the Altars of Infirmity off of my life in Jesus name. I renounce, rebuke, and rescind any covenant and/or allegiance to any altar, especially the Altar of Balaam. Break Altar in the name of Jesus! Break Altar by the power of the blood of Jesus! Break Altar by the finish work of the Cross! I bind every witchcraft in every form that has been launched against me with the blood of Jesus. I apply the blood of Jesus between me and any anti-progress spirit in the name of Jesus. And I bind any kind of witchcraft that has been sent to me or my family, transferred to me and my family, or that has followed me and anyone in my family, in the name of Jesus. I rebuke every delay, I destroy every denial by the Holy Ghost fire that Elijah used against false prophets on Mt. Carmel. I return every spell, incantation,

judgment, and/or witchcraft that has been sent to me or anyone in my family. I bind it to them by the blood of Jesus and decree and declare that their evil works shall not and cannot work! In Jesus name, I pray Amen.

If you just prayed that prayer with sincerity, Father God, I ask you to cover the reader with your blood and put Mighty Warring Angels at the entrance of every departing demon right now in the name of Jesus.

Let's go deeper. Balak tried to get Balaam to curse the nation of Israel four times. Each time Balaam told him to build the seven altars and wait for him as went to seek the heart of God in response to the sacrifices on the altars. Every time, God told Balaam to go back and pronounce a curse on the nation of Israel. This infuriated King Balak, but Balaam, surprisingly rightly said to him, "Can I curse what God has not cursed? I cannot curse what God has declared is blessed!" And I deliver this message to you beloved right now, that no matter what any witch, wizard, or warlock try it will not work. I don't care what any of your enemies or frienemies are trying to send your way, it will not work because God has declared you blessed.

We send back any judgement, any condemnation right now in the name of Jesus, binding Isaiah 54:17 to our spirit, declaring that no weapon formed against us shall prosper. Every tongue that has risen against me in judgement, I use the authority of this scripture and condemn every word to be burned by Heavenly fire right now, in Jesus mighty name. Amen.

Unseen Naval and Subterranean Forces

Your experience is not equal to the mind of God.

Apostle Dr. Larry Birchett, Jr.

Marine Kingdom

Now back to creation. We've already established that the fallen angels were already here on Earth way before man was ever put here. The earth was covered with water, it was basically one big Sea. The non - principalic angels set up their kingdom on the Earth in the waters. This is why we here so many stories of the old sailors seeing what the earth has named as Mermaids, which are really Sirens, which are actually demons who are literally living in this subterranean kingdom.

The reason why you see movie after movie accounts of old powerful kings offering one or more of their children to a water demon for power, such as in movies like Beowolf and others is because it's historically true, not myths. In the same way that the giants of old and people with mythical powers like Hercules is true, because they were the children of human and angels that had sex with each other that created a race of people that the Bible calls the Nephilim. But this book is not about that, but refer to **Genesis 6** for this information, biblically and let's stay on topic. Many people have been taken to this Subterranean kingdom and God has delivered them from their allegiances. This information is relative to be an effective intercessor and prayer warrior, especially if you ever want to be effective in deliverance ministry. You cannot bind or lose what you don't know exist. You can't cast out something that you don't believe in.

The strongholds of the marine kingdoms are in the Indian Ocean, Atlantic Ocean and Africa. According to the testimony of one ex-witch, in particular, the terrestrial headquarters of these marine kingdoms are in Delhi, India (the main marine headquarters of the world), California, USA (the second major marine headquarters) and Nigeria (Lagos). And these areas are where many people are getting initiated into the marine kingdom.

Many world leaders are being physically taken and some are astrally projecting their spirit to these kingdoms to receive power. They do this by way of the entities that comprise many sea lodges, to receive more powers. Many of the very rich and powerful people of the Earth know about this kingdom and the entities that lie therein and will just nod and change the subject if you approach them about it. Because they and their ancestors have made numerous contracts with many of these pseudo gods and entities for many generations. And their lust for wealth, power, importance, and prestige has their souls' captive to these secret things.

If you pay attention, the world is slowly revealing more and more about this kingdom. In the 2018 Oscars, The Shape of Water, from Guillermo del Toro, won the Oscar for the Best Picture of the Year in 2018. The movie is about an entity, a fish man, that came out of the sea and had a love affair with a woman that was lured to the sea to continue the relationship. The next day on national television, Jimmy Kimmel, on his late-night show, said publicly that, "There is a reason why this movie won." People that desire more power and money, such as fake pastors, politicians and actors all are welcome to make contracts in certain sea lodges to acquire their worldly desires. Unfortunately, there are many fake prosperity and miracle healings pastors that are attracting millions to their mega-churches due to the contracts that they have made at these sea lodges. They are prominent members and they regularly must sleep with women to steal their blessings in order to enlarge their own.

Somebody just asked the question in their spirit, “Steal my blessings?” Yes, those possessed by marine spirits steal people’s blessings and good destinies through having sex with them. That’s not the only way, but it’s the most common way. After sleeping with them those victims’ destinies and purpose get buried under the sea or hidden someplace else, and life just seems to turn negative for them after these events. Even born-again Christians can get their purpose and destiny stolen from them, if they sleep with such possessed people.

Also, watch shaking people hands. Don’t let anybody come off of the street and just randomly shake your hands, some people are using obia to steal your blessings and leave you empty. There is more than one occultic system that uses this method. This book is not entirely about the occult, it’s about prayer, but I feel the burden to leave all of this information in your hands so that you don’t perish. Unfortunately, no one is teaching this kind of stuff in “church”. So, if a person comes up to you and just say, “Can I shake your hand?” Say, “Sorry, my hands are covered with the Blood of Jesus right now.”

Let me connect this to the Word of God for you even more, because for most of you, I know this is a revelation. **Hosea 4:6** lets us know that many of God’s people are perishing for lack of knowledge and this is one of satan’s biggest tactics. Most of your pastors have never taught this, either because their ignorant due to heavily marine kingdom influenced seminaries, they have dismissed and/or rejected any part of this knowledge or are afraid of speaking the truth and losing members. However, I’m more afraid of losing Heaven than losing members. **In the very last days there will be a revival on the Earth and there will be more pastors that will be more afraid of losing Heaven than losing members.** Get ready, because we’re getting ready to go way deeper.

Mark 5:7-13

7 And cried with a loud voice, and said, What have I to do with thee, Jesus, thou Son of the most high God? I adjure thee by God, that thou torment me not.

8 For he said unto him, Come out of the man, thou unclean spirit.

9 And he asked him, What is thy name? And he answered, saying, My name is Legion: for we are many.

10 And he besought him much that he would not send them away out of the country.

11 Now there was there nigh unto the mountains a great herd of swine feeding.

12 And all the devils besought him, saying, Send us into the swine, that we may enter into them.

13 And forthwith Jesus gave them leave. And the unclean spirits went out, and entered into the swine: and the herd ran violently down a steep place into the sea, (they were about two thousand;) and were choked in the sea.

The biggest reason why the demons of Mark 5 asked to be sent into the pigs that was nearby is because demons in the spirit realm are territorial. They didn't want Jesus to send them to another demonic territory or even more severe for them, the Abyss. And because they had already been operating in this region under certain principalic rule they wanted to be released to the kingdom that was nearest to them. So being released into the sea after killing the pigs wasn't a bad option for them, knowing that they would be released into the water kingdom that was nearest. The Sirens, that some call Mermaids or Mermen have ranks depending on the body of water that their particular kingdom is surrounded by. For example, an oceanic Siren is stronger than a sea Siren which is stronger than a river Siren which is stronger than a lake siren and so on and so on. Many people who lives around any body of water have encountered these beings, but the problem is that only the family or the inhabitants that live there believe, because of personal encounters and experiences.

This is common knowledge for anyone who lives near a body of water, such as the Caribbean Islands. Many of the inhabitants of Jamaica, for example, has reported of running into these creatures or having mistakenly made contact with these creatures.

One of the elders of my church, Rev. Dr. Ingrid Reid, told me that when she was growing up in Jamaica she was on her way to see her father. She said that anyone from Jamaica knows that to get to where her father lived, which was in Sunnyside Spanish Town, St. Catherine, they would have to get there on foot.

One day while she was making the trek, she had to go to the bathroom to relieve herself. She decided to go down the ravine to a place called the Examination Depot, which was the bottom of a bridge that had an underpass that surrounded a narrow river. As she was making her way there she saw a figure protruding out of the water. It had a female upper body with no clothes on and as she looked down on the body she noticed that the lower body was different. It was a long tail that went into the river and protruded way out on the other side. She said, what drew her attention to the figure was because the creature was splashing her tail loudly before she noticed that she, Dr. Reid, was there. Dr. Reid said they locked eyes and she says that the creature started making this loud squealing noise, as if it was scared or surprised. She said the female had breasts, sandy brown hair, and blue eyes. Her skin was "tannish white", her words. I asked her what it "tannish white" she said the skin tone and color is similar to Pamela Anderson, the actress. Her tail was beautifully made of a myriad of colors. When I pressed Dr. Reid about the colors of the tail, she said that the best way that she can describe it is sequence and it was as if the sun was directly hitting on the tail, so all of the colors were blending and shimmering very beautifully in the sunlight, so it was many colors. The Siren saw her, squealed, and scurried away into the water, while Dr. Reid, pretty much broke her neck to make it back up the hill. Needless to say, that she didn't need to go to the bathroom anymore.

Dr. Reid said that when she made it to her father's house she told him what happened. She said that she'll never forget his response, because his response was, "You too?" As if this wasn't the first time he's heard of this and that he himself, probably has experienced something like this as well.

Now, do you know that the best hiding spot for something is in plain sight? The Bible has already literally told us that the beast, is literally going to come from the Sea, or as I am describing to you in this literature, the Marine Kingdom:

Revelations 13:1-7

[1]And I stood upon the sand of the sea, and saw a beast rise up out of the sea, having seven heads and ten horns, and upon his horns ten crowns, and upon his heads the name of blasphemy.

[2] And the beast which I saw was like unto a leopard, and his feet were as the feet of a bear, and his mouth as the mouth of a lion: and the dragon gave him his power, and his seat, and great authority.

[3] And I saw one of his heads as it were wounded to death; and his deadly wound was healed: and all the world wondered after the beast.

[4] And they worshipped the dragon which gave power unto the beast: and they worshipped the beast, saying, Who is like unto the beast? who is able to make war with him?

[5] And there was given unto him a mouth speaking great things and blasphemies; and power was given unto him to continue forty and two months.

[6] And he opened his mouth in blasphemy against God, to blaspheme his name, and his tabernacle, and them that dwell in heaven.

[7] And it was given unto him to make war with the saints, and to overcome them: and power was given him over all kindreds, and tongues, and nations.

Yes, I know what you're saying. It's been right there the whole time? Yes beloved, it has, and now your eyes are opened. Bible scholars, not knowing how to take this text (Rev. 13:1) have mistakenly tried to ascribe a different interpretation to the scriptures. Many theological minds will tell you that the water represents multitudes of people, for example, which doesn't make any sense. I would always question this and ask the teacher, "So you're saying that the beast is going to arise from the people?" I always knew that it was homiletically, theologically, and exegetically wrong. There is nothing deep about that and God wouldn't have to tell us that because us as normal human beings would probably think that first. However, nothing from the spirit world can come to this world in the regular way because of divine laws that have been imbedded in the matrix of creation itself. That's why the sign of Christ was important, being born of a virgin. Something that no one could miss. And also, I always knew this interpretation was wrong because God would not show Apostle John the Divine, as we call him, something that could be interpreted wrongly earlier and later in this same book. Let's look at **Revelations 10** where God showed John the event of when God will call out the Principalities in the air also known as the Kingdoms of the Air and the Marine Kingdom.

Revelations 10:1-11 (KJV)

[1]And I saw another mighty angel come down from heaven, clothed
with a cloud: and a rainbow was upon his head, and his face was
as it were the sun, and his feet as pillars of fire: ***[2]And he had in***
his hand a little book open: and he set his right foot upon the sea,
and his left foot on the earth, *[3]And cried with a loud voice, as*

when a lion roareth: and when he had cried, seven thunders uttered their voices. ***[4]And when the seven thunders had uttered their voices, I was about to write: and I heard a voice from heaven saying unto me, Seal up those things which the seven thunders uttered, and write them not.*** *[5]And the angel which I saw stand upon the sea and upon the earth lifted up his hand to heaven,* ***[6]And sware by him that liveth for ever and ever, who created heaven, and the things that therein are, and the earth, and the things that therein are, and the sea, and the things which are therein, that there should be time no longer: [7]But in the days of the voice of the seventh angel, when he shall begin to sound, the mystery of God should be finished, as he hath declared to his servants the prophets.***

[8]And the voice which I heard from heaven spake unto me again, and said, Go and take the little book which is open in the hand of the angel which standeth upon the sea and upon the earth. [9]And I went unto the angel, and said unto him, Give me the little book. And he said unto me, Take it, and eat it up; and it shall make thy belly bitter, but it shall be in thy mouth sweet as honey. [10]And I took the little book out of the angel's hand, and ate it up; and it was in my mouth sweet as honey: and as soon as I had eaten it, my belly was bitter. [11]And he said unto me, Thou must prophesy again before many peoples, and nations, and tongues, and kings.

The mighty angel that came down from Heaven set his right foot on the Sea and his left foot on the Earth. When he spoke the Seven Thunders spoke. Who are these Seven Thunders? That's right, you guessed it, they are the Seven Princes or Chief Principalities. Whatever they said, God deemed that we, meaning this earth age, wasn't ready yet. I sure would've loved to hear what these fallen angels had to say, wouldn't you? Probably something like God please forgive us! Anyway, one thing to note before I move on, is that there are many witches, wizards, and warlocks, that can produce lightning and fire, as it were from heaven; heaven with a little h. They can accomplish this because they are asking for power from these principalities for a sign of power to converts and as a weapon to kill strategic targets and threats against satan's kingdom.

During the writing of this book, on March 12, 2018, they say that rain began to pour down on a mountainous Rwandan village Saturday afternoon just as the preacher stepped to the pulpit.

Adventists celebrate the sabbath on Saturdays and in the congregation were hundreds of people, all gathered for a service at the Gihemvu Seventh-day Adventist Church, an old church with no electricity in the southern district of Nyaruguru. The church did not have a lightning rod, because it had no way to pay for one to be installed, according to Jacqueline Benhirwe, the District's Disaster Management Officer. A visiting choir had just got finished singing, the pastor stepped up to the pulpit and bam, a huge lightning strike hit the church knocking everyone out and down to the ground. Seventeen people died as a result of the unusual lightning strike and the villagers believe that occultic power was at play.

According to the report of Pastor Emmanuel Amos, who used to be an agent of the Marine Kingdom, from Congo, Africa, he once was going to kill a Nigerian pastor in Abuta Meta because the pastor was creating to much trouble for them. The pastor was having early morning services where he preached the Word of God and then started binding and rebuking evil spirits. This pastor would post up outside on a certain street every day and start preaching and then started binding principalities and other satanic agents. It was his job to kill him. He said that this pastor walked with two pillars of clouds with him every day, which of course was only seeable in the spirit realm and it was hard to choose an opportunity to slay him. One day, he didn't see the pillars of clouds and thought it was a good opportunity. He summoned the rain to fall and the storm spirits and it became cloudy and windy and ready to strike lightning, however, they heard the man singing. The mas was singing, "In Jesus name every knee shall bow." This passage is from **Philippians 2**:

Philippians 2:9-11 (KJV)

[9]Therefore God exalted him to the highest place and gave him the name that is above every name,

[10]that at the name of Jesus every knee should bow, in heaven and on earth and under the earth,

[11]and every tongue acknowledge that Jesus Christ is Lord, to the glory of God the Father.

When he heard these words that the pastor was singing, immediately after he had finished his chorus, the winds stopped, and the rain had ceased. Pastor Amos saw two Angels come down beside the Congolese pastor, one on each side. They had eyes like fire and flaming swords. Then a strong wind carried him away and he found himself in another town. He was baffled. But he was so hardened that Pastor Amos said, who was an agent of the devil of that time, "He has escaped us again." Let me stop and explain something right here. Praise is a weapon. Let me say it again, PRAISE IS A WEAPON! Praise Him when things are going well and beloved PRAISE HIM when they're seemingly not, because your praise just might save your life. Thank you, Jesus! Hallelujah! Glory to God! Lord You're worthy of all my praise!

Okay, let me get it back together. But I will never apologize for praising my God. He's been better to me than I could ever be to myself. When we speak or sing the Word of God, there is much spiritual activity going on. For one, when a Christian gives a command utilizing the Word of God, the Bible says that fire proceeds out of their mouths. Learn the Word. Speak the Word.

Jeremiah 23:29 (KJV)

[29]"Is not my word like fire," declares the Lord, "and like a hammer that breaks a rock in pieces?

Preach the Word beloved. Be instant in season and out of season but keep on speaking the Word. The Bible tells us to pray without ceasing. What do we pray? His Word. Pray it back to Him. This is the reason why many of us can only pray for about three minutes. Because we don't know how to pray. We don't have to memorize all of these fancy prayers. Just pray naturally in the beginning telling Him how much you love Him and how awesome He is, because He is. We serve a mighty big God, that nothing in creation can contend with. And we need to have that in mind when we go before His presence. Then we should make our requests known unto God, all while remaining thankful for living and grateful for His giving. Ask for forgiveness and repent if you have too. Then our supplications should be for the things related to His will concerning us, others, the ministry, and the world. And then once we finish that we should simply bring His law, meaning His Word, before Him and pray them concerning our particular assignments and giftings. Pray His Word back to Him.

The more fervent the prayer, the stronger and brighter the fire that is ascending up to Heaven. Our prayer and our praise are weapons that can tear the devil's kingdom down by themselves. Remember Jericho in **Judges 6**? All they had to do was march, pray, and shout. And it was all over. It was a wrap. If we would just take the model that God has already laid out for us and we'd be alright.

Isaiah 66:16

16 For by fire and by his sword will the Lord plead with all flesh: and the slain of the Lord shall be many.

The fire is produced by our praises, the words that comes out of our mouths. The sword is the Word of God. The Bible says the Word of God is sharper than any two-edged sword, dividing to the asunder of soul and spirit. In the book of Jeremiah, God got mad at the false prophets and changed their fire into strange fire that consumed the hearers:

Jeremiah 5:14

14 Wherefore thus saith the Lord God of hosts, Because ye speak this word, behold, I will make my words in thy mouth fire, and this people wood, and it shall devour them.

See, I know that you're constantly being told that life and death is in the power of the tongue (Proverbs 18:21), which is true. However, we need to know that this means more than just speak positive things at all times, we need to know that everything that we encounter in this life is because of or affected by our words. This is one of the main attacks that satan has launched against the church, our own words.

The demons report to satan every time we sin and every time we say something that can be used against us. They do something called, "Word capture." For example, if you say something like, "I want to get married, but I'm only marrying someone that is this and this and this." Guess what? The enemy will capture your words and has a legal right to keep you single for the rest of your life because of your very own decree. So, instead of saying something so restrictive, learn how to say that I'd like to get married someday to the guy or girl that God has in store for me. Don't worry, God knows your preferences and will give you someone that you will love and probably more importantly, will love you back.

Word capture is important, because the enemy will try to use all of our words against us not only in this life, but when we die. The words that he'll use against us will be the ones that show that we're not saved. If you're truly saved at the point of death, you will have the blood of Jesus to wipe away every stain of sin in our lives. However, if he catches you in sin, before you have a chance to repent, well you already know the rest.

There are demons that follow us for long period of times just to capture our words. For example, when we get angry we normally don't think about what we say and will say anything to hurt whoever we're mad at. Everything that you say during these moments are captured and are being used against you in the spirit realm. Words like "I hate you." Or "I hope you die." Or "I can't do this anymore." Or "I wish this never happened." Or "If I could do this all over again, I would've never married you." Or how about this one, "I wish you were never born."

Let's take the last one, "I wish you were never born." The enemy will take the death that you spoke spiritually, because your words are power, they are life and death, and they employ angels; the heavenly ones and the fallen ones. He'll take your words and manifest it in real life and you'll lose the child that you've directed those bullets too. Or take the marriage comment. He'll take your words and before you know it, you will be heading for the divorce court. That's why the Bible said that we should never go to sleep angry. If you go to sleep without correcting whatever you created in the spirit realm with your words, it will be established. So, stay up all night if you have too, until you get it right with yourself, your spouse, and most importantly God.

Another little secret I want to leave with you before we continue, because the Bible says in Proverbs 18:21, that the power of life and death is in the tongue. Do you know that your words employ and un-employ angels? For example, if you say something like, "You are my angel" to your mate or your spouse, your guardian angel has to leave you and you're left to fend for yourself. Hopefully that person can ward off the host of demons that will come and start systematically destroying your life if they can't kill you right away.

Back to fire breathing, because the Bible tells us literally that our tongue is a fire:

James 3:5-7 King James Version (KJV)

[5] *Even so the tongue is a little member, and boasteth great things. Behold, how great a matter a little fire kindleth!*

[6] ***And the tongue is a fire**, a world of iniquity: so is the tongue among our members, that it defileth the whole body, and setteth on fire the course of nature; and it is set on fire of hell.*

[7] *For every kind of beasts, and of birds, and of serpents, and of*

things in the sea, is tamed, and hath been tamed of mankind:

Watch your words. If you don't have anything good to say, don't say anything. If you're about to comment on something that you don't understand, stop, and wait until you get an understanding. Don't allow the fires of hell to enter your lips as James 3:6 describes due to ignorance. Speaking of ignorance, let us finish my cursory introduction of the marine kingdom to you at this time.

When you speak or sing praises directly to the Lord, there is a fire that is produced from your lips to Heaven and it creates havoc in the spirit world. When you say Hallelujah, for example, fire leaves your lips and go directly to Heaven and it displaces demons because they can't stand in the proximity of true and authentic praise. Your words alone produce energy. The Word of God is a supernatural energy that can literally be seen in the spirit world when read or spoken. Pastors, you should always have a time just for scripture reading in your church, even before the Word comes forth. Yes, look at your programs and revamp them if you have too. That's why God lets us know that anyone who ministers in His name are to do so as His oracles.

1 Peter 4:11 (KJV)

[11] *If any man speak, let him speak as the oracles of God; if any man minister, let him do it as of the ability which God giveth: that God in all things may be glorified through Jesus Christ, to whom be praise and dominion for ever and ever. Amen.*

"If anyone speaks, let it be as it were the very words of God …." (HNV)

I can keep going on with scripture after scripture letting you know how powerful the Word of God is, especially in the unseen dimensions, however, remember that your praise and prayer are pillars of fire especially when they are infused with the Holy Word of God. Let's remember what the prophet Jeremiah had to say about the Word that was placed within him:

Jeremiah 20:9 King James Version (KJV)

[9] Then I said, I will not make mention of him, nor speak any more in his name. ***But his word was in mine heart as a burning fire shut up in my bones****, and I was weary with forbearing, and I could not stay.*

Therefore, let us start using the Word more in our speech, in our daily confessions, in our prayers and in our praise to the King of Kings, Lord of Lords.

In Zimbabwe the marine spirit is called mweya wenjuzu, and it is found in seas, rivers and oceans. It has been reported that there are many marine agents that has formed their own churches. These churches are there to bring confusion and unnecessary arguments among people. If you want to tell a person attending these churches that they are being deceived into worshipping the wrong god you will never reach an agreement because this person has already been affected by the spirit of discord and unnecessary arguments.

These churches will always have themes revolving around water. You'll see a tree in the midst of water inside of the church for example. I guarantee you that the tree is demonic, and the water is directly from the water kingdom. You'll see a prominent waterfall but no sign of the Cross anywhere. However, it'll be hard to believe because of course because the enemy has access to the things of this world, namely money and resources. They can give you a big church, they can give you a big business and make you think that they are coming from God. Beloved, not all blessings are blessings. Some things that we call blessings are really curses because they come from the enemy. You must make it up in your mind that you will never allow the devil to bless you. Somebody say with me, "devil, you cannot bless me!"

I'm saying this declaration for a reason because this spirit is confusing. Remember that the enemy always tries to imitate the light. In 1962 this spirit decided to establish churches in Zimbabwe and the first church was in Mutoko. From my research I learned that there was a man named Sixpence. He was possessed by one of these spirits and one day he tore off all his clothes and ran into the hills and had many followers. They followed him, and he made them wear all white and they confused his actions with being moved by the Holy Spirit.

You should understand that whenever this sect wants to set up a church they will look for a place close to a river. If there is no water around they will make a set-up of stones from the river and clay pots full of water from big rivers and oceans to make their shrine which they call a krawa. They do this to transport the spirits from their particular kingdom into the church. If you are entering their shrine one of the first instruction that they'll give you will be to remove your shoes. The reason behind this is homage to the marine kingdom. No one in their right mind would enter the river with their shoes on, right? They will ask you to remove all your valuables like watches, chains, necklaces and you will also have to roll up your pants to your knees.

I'm going to finish this little portion on the Marine Kingdom by explaining some hard things to believe, but it is true. Many of the people that are missing on this earth are not really missing, they have been taken to this part of the world and they are serving there. All of the fashion that we see on earth was originated first in the marine kingdom. That's why the clothes are getting more and more seductive. Even clergy clothes are becoming tighter and more revealing. We laugh at holiness churches because of their strictness regarding earrings and makeup and the sort, but I'm here to tell you that there is some merit to the line of thought. Calm down, because I'm not saying that there is anything wrong with a little jewelry or a little make up, however, when you do a biblical study of these things you see that God was never a big fan of any of this stuff. In fact, the people who wore these things were idol worshippers and people of the occult.

Did you know that earrings were first used to identify which Gods a person worshipped? They literally wore their god on their ears whereas to attract their supposed "god" and publicly identify themselves and their beliefs. Unfortunately, when the nation of Israel left Egypt the Bible tells us that they took much of their former captor's jewelry as well. And after 400 years of slavery, we all must understand that those born in slavery were probably dreaming about the day when they too would be able to wear all of the jewelry that the Egyptian would've wore during those days. We know that they adopted these methods quickly because when Moses went up the mountain to receive the Ten Commandments, they demanded of Aaron, for him to make them an idol and he told them to take off all of their earrings and the rest of their jewelry and give it to him so that he could melt it down and make the idol. The earrings in their ears were in the forms of Egyptian gods beloved. Read your Bibles.

Also, much of the make-up that women use all over the world has been scientifically developed in the marine kingdom. The substance is demonically engineered and transfers demons to the individuals that are using it. They are also transmitting diseases, like skin cancer, and premature aging with these drugs. In the West Indies and Africa there have been cosmetics brought from there that contain ingredients not known from anything known on this earth. Lipsticks, blushes, eyeliners, fake lashes, hair attachments, weaves, etc. all of these things are being circulated all around the earth. And they have either been demonically tampered and/or cursed or they are actually from the marine world itself. Many ex witches and wizards confess to using certain demonically tampered facial and body products before they'd leave their houses to gain spiritual sight for example. One, even said that she was a star hunter, and would be transported to a place under the sea to get all of the products that she needed to apply to her eyes so that when she was around a newly impregnated woman, she would know before them and go and talk to the person and do incantations and steal the soul right from the mother's womb.

The entertainment industry is also being ran from the marine kingdom. The movies that we see here on earth, many of the ideas were directly fed from the agents from this kingdom. Bill Wiese, the author of "23 Minutes in Hell" said that when he came back to

Earth, one day someone was watching the movie Hellraiser. He stopped them because he noticed that most of the demons that were in the movie, he had seen while he was in Hell. Of course, this is not a coincidence. Just like most of the popular secular music here on Earth. Do you not know that most of it was fed directly from Hell?

Leviathan is the representative of satan in the Marine Kingdom. Better said it is the form that satan takes when he shows himself in the Marine Kingdom. The reason that satan was kicked out of Heaven was because of pride. His form when he fully manifested in this pride is Leviathan. He is about 6 meters tall, which is about 20 feet and he is a hybrid demon of a crocodile and a snake. I know that you thought that the scriptures in the Bible was just representing some ancient fish or sea monster, however, the Bible is telling us all of the information that we need to know. The Bible is referring to this demon, the actual manifestation of satan when pride was fully manifested. Which is why God punished the serpent and dragon that was in the Garden from the beginning to go on its belly from that point on.

His head is that of a crocodile, his body is that of a snake, and he has the tail of the crocodile. When you understand that the things that happened in the sea in the Bible are literal, it will free your mind. For example, Jonah in the belly of the whale. Do you think it is a parable or an analogy? No, it actually happened, in the way that the Bible said it did. And just like the Bible said, Jonah went to Sheol, and then was vomited up on the shores of Nineveh. Jonah, saw the Marine Kingdom, and all of the activities going on there, but God delivered him from there and gave him another chance to be obedient. Let's look at Jonah's prayer, shall we?

Jonah 2 King James Version (KJV)

1 Then Jonah prayed unto the Lord his God out of the fish's belly,

2 And said, I cried by reason of mine affliction unto the Lord, and he heard me; out of the belly of hell cried I, and thou heardest my voice.

3 For thou hadst cast me into the deep, in the midst of the seas; and the floods compassed me about: all thy billows and thy waves passed over me.

4 Then I said, I am cast out of thy sight; yet I will look again toward thy holy temple.
5 The waters compassed me about, even to the soul: the depth closed me round about, the weeds were wrapped about my head.
6 I went down to the bottoms of the mountains; the earth with her bars was about me forever: yet hast thou brought up my life from corruption, O Lord my God.
7 When my soul fainted within me I remembered the Lord: and my prayer came in unto thee, into thine holy temple.
8 They that observe lying vanities forsake their own mercy.
9 But I will sacrifice unto thee with the voice of thanksgiving; I will pay that that I have vowed. Salvation is of the Lord.
10 And the Lord spake unto the fish, and it vomited out Jonah upon the dry land.

Jonah had died and went to Hell in his words, Sheol in some translations, and guess what? He didn't like it. Even though he was a prophet of God, he was disobedient and apparently bias or racist and didn't want to deliver the message of salvation to God's children of Nineveh. God used a fish that was big enough to swallow him whole, he died, and his spirit saw things that changed him and made him do the right thing. Beloved, may God never have to show you why He wants you to heed his message of Hell. Hell, and all of the variants thereof is real. You don't have to look for it or try to experience it, take His word for it. Take Jonah's word for it. We'll leave the Marine Kingdom for now, but just know that we know about Mars than we do the deepest waters on Earth.

Music Domain

Colossians 2:15 (KJV)

And having spoiled principalities and powers, he made a show of them openly, triumphing over them in it.

Music is lucifer's domain. He didn't create it. But God created him to be a specialist regarding it. He was a cherub in Heaven that was responsible for the music and worship of Heaven. So, one must understand that music was originally made for worship and praise to God. Anything else can be manipulated by satan and is not in accordance with the original intent of what music was created for. God kicked our mutual enemy out of Heaven because of the pride found within him (Isaiah 14; Ezekiel 28) and because the music had changed. Pride can change the most beautiful things into the evilest things. Music is so strong that it can get into your spirit without your permission. Therefore, because of this, God kicked satan and all of his followers out, because secular music is unholy, and God is holy. Nothing unholy can enter into Heaven. I'm going to give you a few confessions by the artists that admit that their music came from Hell itself.

Elvis Presley, believed he had a twin that communicated with him spiritually. In the Angel Times magazine, (Oct. issue), a childhood friend of Elvis states that Elvis communicated with beings as a child. These beings had showed Elvis a vision of dancing, and of people "dressed in white with colors all around."

In Smash Hits magazine, Bon Jovi says: ". . . I'd kill my mother for rock and roll. I would sell my soul." Robert Plant and Jimmy Page of LED ZEPPELIN both claim that they don't know who wrote their occultic song, "Stairway to Heaven." Roger Plant testified truthfully: "Pagey had written the chords and played them for me. I was holding the paper and pencil, and for some reason, I was in a very bad mood. Then all of a sudden, my hand was writing out words. … I just sat there and looked at the words and then I almost leaped out of my seat" (Davin Seay, Stairway to Heaven, p. 249).

"We receive our songs by inspiration, like at a séance" (Keith Richards of the ROLLING STONES, Rolling Stone, May 5, 1977, p. 55).

"I felt like a hollow temple filled with many spirits, each one passing through me, each inhabiting me for a little time and then leaving to be replaced by another" (John Lennon, People, Aug. 22, 1988, p. 70).

"The music to 'Yesterday' came in a dream. The tune just came complete. You have to believe in magic. I can't read or write music" (PAUL MCCARTNEY, interview on Larry King Live, CNN, June 12, 2001).

"Rock has always been the devil's music, you can't convince me that it isn't. I honestly believe everything I've said—I believe rock and roll is dangerous. … I feel that we're only heralding something even darker than ourselves" (DAVID BOWIE, Rolling Stone, February 12, 1976, p. 83).

"It happens subliminally. It's the music that compels me to do it. You don't think about it, it just happens. I'm slave to the rhythm' (Michael Jackson, explaining the reason for some of the filthy sexual gestures during his concerts, during a 1993 Oprah Winfrey interview, The Evening Star, Feb. 11, 1993, p. A10).

"I wake up from dreams and go 'Wow, put this down on paper,' the whole thing is strange. You hear the words, everything is right there in front of your face. I feel that somewhere, someplace it's been done and I'm just a courier bringing it into the world" (MICHAEL JACKSON, Rolling Stone, Feb. 17, 1983).

"I was directed and commanded by another power. The power of darkness ... that a lot of people don't believe exists. The power of the Devil. Satan" (LITTLE RICHARD, cited by Charles White, The Life and Times of Little Richard, p. 206).

I can go on and on. Do you know that Kanye West sold his soul to the devil? And then he got mad and publicly wanted to sue the devil because it seemed to him that satan didn't honor his part of the contract. The next two paragraphs are from the International Times.

"He was promised exceptional musical skills after signing his soul away for eternity and that, obviously, up to now he has received absolutely nothing in return."

"Mr West mumbled unintelligibly from behind a mixing desk in an LA recording studio, 'I thought me and the Chief had an understanding, Know wha' I'm sayin'? Everybody do it these days. Know wha' I'm sayin'? Only a fool who don't want no Grammy don't sell his soul to the Devil. Know wha' I'm sayin'? I ain't no fool. Know wha' I'm sayin'? Uh uh. No way. Know wha' I'm sayin'?'"

Some of you are saying really? Well I can go on and on about the artists of our time that claims to have sold their soul. Snoop Dogg sold his soul when he got shot and was about to die when he was young. The devil came to him in the form of a dog and told him that he would make him a household name for his soul. He did it. He recovered and now he is a household name.
Jay Z, not only sold his soul, but he made a song to pay homage. It is called, "lucifer, son of the morning." Yeah, I know. Some of you used to bump this track in your cars, thinking it was harmless. Beyonce, admits that she is taken over by an entity named Sasha Fierce, when she is collaborating and performing her music, yet some of you still big her up and support the shenanigans.

Songs that promote fornication, rebellion, drugs, drinking, violence, rape, murder, fighting, lust, anarchy, false religion, the new age, etc. are obviously satanic, and are spreading openly the message of lucifer. Pastors, watch the kind of music that you're allowing to be played in your churches.

To the reader that is reading this right now and is being ministered by a deceptive spirit telling you that the music can't be bad if people are seemingly getting saved. Music is not for winning souls, but for singing praises to God! Preaching is the tool given by God to win souls for the kingdom.

Romans 10:14

[14] How then shall they call on him in whom they have not believed? and how shall they believe in him of whom they have not heard? and how shall they hear without a preacher?

Some may ask, “Why can’t a Christian enjoy "worldly" music also?” Know this beloved. Everything we do should be to the glory of God. Can anything secular or worldly give glory to God? If it can than you’re free to have at it. However, know that the things of this world are carnal and brings enmity between you and the Holy Spirit.

1 Corinthians 10:31

[31] Whether therefore ye eat, or drink, or whatsoever ye do, do all to the glory of God.

The devilish secular music on Earth is generated from this particular part of satan’s kingdom. The name of the demon that controls this realm is called Phopha, which means sound. He is the god of Secular Music. He has a male top with an antelope bottom. Some musicians have visited his realm, this place under the Earth. This is part of the Ground Kingdom. You enter it by descending into a huge pit. It is one of the many underground kingdoms that satan made when he fell to the earth.

Isaiah 14:12-16

[12] How art thou fallen from heaven, O Lucifer, son of the morning! how art thou cut down to the ground, which didst weaken the nations!

[13] For thou hast said in thine heart, I will ascend into heaven, I will exalt my throne above the stars of God: I will sit also upon the mount of the congregation, in the sides of the north:

[14] I will ascend above the heights of the clouds; I will be like the most High.

15 Yet thou shalt be brought down to hell, to the sides of the pit.

16 They that see thee shall narrowly look upon thee, and consider thee, saying, Is this the man that made the earth to tremble, that did shake kingdoms;

When satan fell to the Earth, he fell deep in the Earth. And he excavated and made many kingdoms, this place being one of them. It has no sun or stars. The color of this place is red. Or a red hue, with loud music. Some name this place, Pandemonium. There are plenty of sirens there always dancing and partying to the rhythms that are produced there. They are humanoid in their appearance, not with fish tails, they have wings, but they are not fully human. Let me explain something right here about these demonic creatures and a host more. Most people are clear with understanding that according to Genesis 6 the angels slept with the woman of this Earth and produced hybrid children. Half angel and half human. The same way that satan initiated this practice, in the garden beloved, is the same way that he made an innumerable number of many other extra-terrestrial creatures. The only difference is that he did it with the animals of this planet. So, there are hybrid bear demons, hybrid lion demons, hybrid crocodile demons, hybrid snake demons, hybrid spider demons, and on and on and on. satan's whole intent is to pervert God's creation and make it his own and grow his kingdom, to wield his influence in this Earth. It's easier than you think for them to do this, because the animals of this Earth realm don't have the complex body, spirit, and soul makeup that we humans do. Let's go back to the music.

When artists descend to this place to make a deal with Phopha to bless their next record, cd, or release, he always has a couple of sirens to "tend to" these artists to appease their flesh. Normally, he tells these artists to offer a number of souls to "seal the deal" for the blessing of their music as well. One well known Congolese musician had to kill thirteen people in some way as a payment for his success. To all of you groupies out there that would do anything to spend "some time" with these well-known secular artists, you are literally playing with your life.

Another thing that I want to tell you before I sort of transition to another subject based on hidden kingdoms and hidden knowledge is that our guardian angels cannot stay in the presence of secular music. Yes, you do have an angel that is assigned to you beloved. Some of us may have more than one depending on our purpose and particular assignment in this life. Secular music makes them flee or withdraw themselves from us. The reason is that the essence of the music is so strong, howbeit unholy, that it can make them a fallen angel as well. So, this means that you can't play both sides of the fence and act like you're a Holy Ghost filled man or woman of God while saturating your atmosphere with Lil Kim, Jay Z, Lil Wayne, Def Leopard, Pearl Jam, Rolling Stones, and a host of other debaucherously sin laced lyrically and rhythmically music. You are deceiving yourself. And the truth of the matter is that you're unprotected during these times and the kingdom of darkness knows it. This is why an incident will happen in a night club and only the people that are not the normal club goers get killed. The Christian that just went out under pressure to fit in is the one that will get shot or left in a burning building, etc. Because Hell knows that they're uncovered and unprotected and will step up their methods from stealing and destroying to killing.

The other thing is that whenever secular music is played in a house an alarm goes off in this part of the underworld and Phopha and his sirens comes to you and tries to claim your house for satan. After a while you'll feel the seduction of the sirens in your room and if you're not careful you'll be lusting as well as worshipping Phopha and indirectly worshipping satan, the ultimate musician, himself. Be careful because demons are attached to all kinds of music, even Gospel music. Music is the only thing that can be created on this Earth and the heart and spirit of the one who is creating determines what spirits are attached to the product. The test regarding which music is Godly is simple. Ask them, "Who is this song for?" If it's for lovers, that's not the same thing as praise and worship and most of the people that made these "love songs" ain't right. Do your homework. If they say, "I just wanted to make some music that makes people move and get on the dance floor." That's not the same thing as praise and worship. Not everything that makes you want to move is good. As a matter of fact, a lot of the beats and rhythms that we're hearing in these last days are directly from Hell anyway. This is why you have to watch the cultural festivals.

Many cultural festivals are just occultic ceremonies anyway. You have to be very careful because much of the clothes are demonically touched and the dance moves and gyrations, if you do your research, are being done to specific entities that are not the one and true God. Many people are possessed at these festivals and at the very least have demons transferred to them. Never take any items given to you. Never buy or accept any art from these festivals and if you find yourself with any of this stuff get rid of it immediately.

In the same way we have to be very prayerful about the foods we eat. Daniel got in trouble with Nebuchadnezzar because he knew that he wasn't supposed to be eating foods that was sacrificed to idols and also he wasn't supposed to eat the foods of unclean animals. Daniel 1:8 *But Daniel resolved not to defile himself with the royal food and wine, and he asked the chief official for permission not to defile himself this way.* Some of us think to ourselves, well this is one sin that we will never engage in or be accused of. But do you know that many of the foods that we eat from other countries are blessed and offered to their specific gods? Did you think that all of the Buddhist calendars on the wall in your favorite Chinese Restaurant was just for decoration? Don't you know that the Halal meats from the Islamic restaurant are ceremonially blessed even in preparation?

The word "halal" means "permissible" in Arabic, and when it comes to food, it means nourishment that follows Islamic law. It is the opposite of "haram," which means forbidden.

Under Islamic law, meat must come from an animal that was killed according to specific practices. The animal must have been alive and healthy when it was slaughtered, and the kill must come from a cut to the jugular, carotid artery and the windpipe. Also, a dedication known as a tasmiya or shahada to honour Allah is also spoken during the kill.

Always bless your food and cover it with the blood of Jesus. The next thing I will tell you to bring this point home even more is that not every meat you eat is what it seems. One of the things that occultist must do when they are making covenants with spirits from other dimensions such as fallen angels, sirens, or otherwise, is that they have to drink human blood and sometimes they even have to eat human flesh. Now one of the powers that they are normally given is to turn themselves into another creature, such as a rat, cat, bird, or snake. They become shape shifters, and this is common knowledge amongst occultist. However, what is not known is that one of the punishments that is sometimes used on an individual that is disobedient to one of these demonic entities is to make them remain in their transferred state. For example, they will force you to turn into a rat, and then take away your powers and cause you to live out the rest of your life as a rat. What they do to those that come to the saving knowledge of Jesus Christ, is make them turn into a lamb or a goat, thereby mocking Jesus, the Lamb of God, that was slain before the foundations of the Earth.

So, what is happening, is that they are systematically substituting natural animal meat for human meat, however, it is in animal form. Only those that can see in the spirit realm will be able to determine which meat is really human. So, you think that the goat meat that you've bought at the local market is good meat to prepare your Curry Goat dish. Or that the lamb that you've purchased is good to go for that perfect lamb dish. My question to you is did you pray over it at all? Did you thank God for your food and ask God to bless it?

1 Timothy 4:1-5 Authorized (King James) Version (AKJV)

1 Now the Spirit speaketh expressly, that in the latter times some shall depart from the faith, giving heed to seducing spirits, and doctrines of devils; 2 speaking lies in hypocrisy; having their conscience seared with a hot iron; 3 forbidding to marry, and commanding to abstain from meats, which God hath created to be received with thanksgiving of them which believe and know the truth. [4] For every creature of God is good, and nothing to be refused, if it be received with thanksgiving: [5] for it is sanctified by the word of God and prayer.

In the English Standard Version, the fourth and fifth verse is stated that we're to pray for over our food to first give God thanks, and secondly, to change it from natural to holy; *"[5] for it is made holy by the Word of God and prayer."* And this means that much of the food that we eat, especially meat, is unholy and thereby dangerous to our spiritual DNA, notwithstanding our physical bodies. Pray this way:

Father God, thank you for this food that you have once again provided for me. Bless this food for the nourishment of my body. Please remove anything harmful from it even right now in the name of Jesus. I apply the Blood of Jesus over this meal right now in the name of Jesus. Thank you for the hands that have prepared this meal. Thank you for the finances that could afford this meal. In Jesus name, I pray, Amen.

Since I'm on this subject you should know that all of us that have come into covenant with Jesus Christ through our verbal confession of belief in Him through the shedding of His blood for us and by being baptized in water. In the spirit realm we all have a garment of white that we are walking around with. This garment is white in the spirit realm and is shining and glistening. The garment that we wear is the garment of Christ's righteousness.

Isaiah 61:10 (KJV)

[10] I will rejoice greatly in the Lord, My soul will exult in my God, For He has clothed me with garments of salvation, He has wrapped me with a robe of righteousness, As a bridegroom decks himself with a garland, And as a bride adorns herself with her jewels.

Before we're giving this shining garment as being lights on this Earth, we are observed as having on filthy garments. Also, it is important to know that even after we're giving this garment we can soil them via sin and disobedience, and in consequence, lose our shine.

Isaiah 64:6 (KJV)

[6] For all of us have become like one who is unclean, And all our righteous deeds are like a filthy garment; And all of us wither like a leaf, And our iniquities, like the wind, take us away.

I gave you this information because we are always being monitored in the spirit realm. Every spirit knows exactly what state that we are in at all times. We have lights on or above our heads in the spirit realm, which is really fire. This is why the scriptures say, "Let your light so shine before men….". We have these Godly shining garments and we also have the name of Jesus written on our forehead. When we are in compromise, let's just say sin, the name on our head gets blurred. Even though we have made a contract with Jesus, if we die in that state we would be taken to hell for judgement. They know when the name of Jesus is smeared, they know when our fire is shut off, and they know when our garments are soiled. Make your salvation sure beloved.

Now, let me address something here, because I know that someone is saying in their spirit, "But aren't we saved by grace?". The answer is yes. I'm going to give you a litany of scriptures to prove this:

Ephesians 2:8-9 (KJV)

For it is by grace that we are saved, not by works lest any man should boast.

Hebrews 10:14 (KJV)

[14] For by one offering he hath perfected forever them that are sanctified.

Romans 3:21-26 (KJV)

21 But now the righteousness of God without the law is manifested,
being witnessed by the law and the prophets; 22 Even the
righteousness of God which is by faith of Jesus Christ unto all and
upon all them that believe: for there is no difference: 23 For all
have sinned, and come short of the glory of God; 24 Being justified
freely by his grace through the redemption that is in Christ Jesus:
25 Whom God hath set forth to be a propitiation through faith in his
blood, to declare his righteousness for the remission of sins that
are past, through the forbearance of God; 26 To declare, I say , at
this time his righteousness: that he might be just, and the justifier
of him which believeth in Jesus.

However, let's be clear. Sin is not okay with God. Don't be fooled by the whole "Grace Movement" of this end time generation where you can be a practicing homosexual and be a Pastor or Priest at the same time. Or you can be a practicing whoremonger or adulterer and still expect Heaven. Let me be clear. God says that He will not be mocked. Any pastor or spiritual leader teaching this may be from the Marine Kingdom or in some way is an agent of the devil. Let me tell you what Paul said about this issue in his letter to Galatia. He told them straight up:

Galatians 5:20-21 (KJV)

20 Idolatry, witchcraft, hatred, variance, emulations, wrath, strife,
seditions, heresies, 21 Envyings, murders, drunkenness, revellings,
and such like: of the which I tell you before, as I have also told you
in time past, that they which do such things shall not inherit the
kingdom of God.

Notice that verse 21 says that those who does those such things shall NOT inherit the Kingdom of God. So don't come to the altar and cry and spit in front of your mom to make her get off of your case and then go out and sell drugs and poison to your community and kill and steal and cuss and listen to the devil's music, and shack up and watch porn, and masturbate, and talk about people, and hinder the work of churches, and on and on and on and think that God is going to say, "Good job my child." I don't think He's up there waiting to say, "Well done my good and faithful servant."

1 John 3:22-23 (KJV)

22 And whatsoever we ask, we receive of him, because we keep his commandments, and do those things that are pleasing in his sight.
23 And this is his commandment, That we should believe on the name of his Son Jesus Christ, and love one another, as he gave us commandment.

Galatians 2:16 (KJV)

16 Knowing that a man is not justified by the works of the law, but by the faith of Jesus Christ, even we have believed in Jesus Christ, that we might be justified by the faith of Christ, and not by the works of the law: for by the works of the law shall no flesh be justified.

Jesus said that He did not come to destroy the Law and The Prophets, but to fulfil. He did not destroy The Law. I am going to say that one more time: HE DID NOT DESTROY THE LAW. You got it? He FULFILLED the Law. Look up the word fulfil. God would not and could not have set aside His Law. That would have been unjust. He fulfilled the Law's requirements. He did this morally, ceremonially and civilly. When He paid the price for our sins and satisfied the justice of God. He established a New Covenant. When this happened, it required a change of Priesthood and Law.

The offering of souls in payment for power, prestige, wealth, and fame, is a norm in the kingdom of darkness. To be a Voodoo Incarnate, you will have to offer at least eighty souls. To be blunter, to be a Voodoo Incarnate you will have to kill at least eighty people for whatever powers that you're asking for to be granted unto you. What is a Voodoo Incarnate? It is a person that obviously practices the voodoo religion, and that has done the necessary incantations, studies, spells, and killing necessary to be possessed full time by a network of demons that will give them "powers" to dominate others and do other dark spiritual things on the Earth. For example, turning into animals to sneak into houses. Or the ability to kill a person that is not covered by the blood of Jesus for money. And many other sinful and debased things.

In the nation of Haiti, slaves from many different parts of Africa fused all of their beliefs into yet another dark and occultic religion called Voodoo. Haitians not only blended different African beliefs, but also added other influences into their religious mix, including Native American traditions and the Catholicism of their conquerors.

The results are unique though in comparison to other devil worshipping religions. Catholic saints, for example, play a part in voodoo but represent quite different figures. St. Peter, for example, is recognized by Haitian vodounists as Papa Legba, the gatekeeper of the spirit world. So, missionaries when you travel to Haiti and you're speaking with a so-called pastor or priest, watch his language, because he might actually be a Voodoo priest that will kill you when he gets the chance and cut your body into pieces to offer to certain demonic deities for more power. He'll use your skull for other spiritual witchcraft curses, drink your blood and will use your organs to harvest demons on earth. I know, it's freaky stuff, but you need to know it, because everything that I'm saying, along with more that I know I can't write, is true. Do you see why you need to pray beloved? And not just any old kind of prayer, prayers that rout demons, glorify Heaven, and horrify Hell.

Lastly about Voodoo, because I don't want you to be deceived. People who practice Voodoo believe in one god, however, not the God, and they communicate with their "divine" through thousands of spirits, or "Loa," which have power over nature and human existence. The souls of the deceased act as intermediaries between god and the living. Notice that I keep using the little g for God because they're not worshipping the true God, Elohim, YVWH. Do not allow yourselves to be deceived. In the USA voodoo is heavily used in Miami and in New Orleans.

When I was active duty for the United States Army, I was Active Guard Reserve for the PA Army National Guard in 2005 when Hurricane Katrina hit Louisiana and some parts of Mississippi. When we made our way into the heart of New Orleans around Bourbon street, everything was closed due to the floods and the water hadn't yet receded in many places. However, when I looked around there were only two business still operating. They were the Strip Clubs and the Fortune Teller businesses. I was shocked. At one point I had to call an emergency formation because many of my Soldiers were missing. And I realized that some of them were sneaking into the strip clubs. I had to have a "come back to Jesus" moment with them and make them think. I asked them, "Where do you think these strippers are washing up at, since we, the military, know that there is no running water in any of these facilities? How many men and women have they grinded on? How much bacteria and disease do you think are in the facilities?" This was really a wakeup call for a lot of my young men and most of them didn't inhabit those places again, at least while I was out on that patrol with them. Notice I said, most of them.

Many people go to the voodoo priests for healing, love, false protection, and to cause harm on other people. Isn't this sad? Isn't God Jehovah Rappha, our Healer? Isn't God Jehovah Shammah, always Present? Isn't God Jehovah Nissi, Our Banner? Why would you go to the devil for love when there is no love in him? Beloved, if the devil ever tells you he loves you, know that this is a lie because he is incapable of love. **The devil can't love you because you are made in the image of God.**

Kingdoms of the Air/Principalities

Ephesians 6:12 New King James Version (NKJV)

12 For we do not wrestle against flesh and blood, but against principalities, against powers, against the rulers of the darkness of this age, against spiritual hosts of wickedness in the heavenly places.

Let me digress and give you the basics as we dive into this portion of talking about the Heavens and how things are really situated in the atmospheric heavens and dimensions that is undiscernible with our human eyes. I'm going to use a portion of scriptures to start the discussion:

Genesis 6:1-7

[1] And it came to pass, when men began to multiply on the face of
the earth, and daughters were born unto them, [2] That the sons of
God saw the daughters of men that they were fair; and they took
them wives of all which they chose. [3] And the LORD said, My spirit
shall not always strive with man, for that he also is flesh: yet his*
days shall be an hundred and twenty years. [4] There were giants in
the earth in those days; and also after that, when the sons of God
came in unto the daughters of men, and they bare children to them,
the same became mighty men which were of old, men of renown. [5]
And GOD saw that the wickedness of man was great in the earth,
and that every imagination of the thoughts of his heart was only
evil continually. [6] And it repented the LORD that he had made man
on the earth, and it grieved him at his heart. [7] And the LORD said,
I will destroy man whom I have created from the face of the earth;
both man, and beast, and the creeping thing, and the fowls of the
air; for it repenteth me that I have made them.

Now, I chose to start here on this one for a reason. The Bible is clear about something. That something is that the angels themselves looked upon the beauty of the women of the Earth and desired them. The angels are sometimes referred to as the "Sons of God" in the Bible. The Sons of God in the Hebrew is translated as **Bene Elohim**. And we could read it as the **Bene Elohim** saw the daughters of men that they were fair. This is an important distinction because when Jesus walked the Earth, he referred to other humans and Himself, as the "Sons of men" or "Son of man", meaning that we were all born from Adam, the first human being.

Verse four told us that the giants not only came into the daughters of men, meaning had sex with them, but they bore children. These children are called Nephilim. Nephilim means fallen. The root of the word Nephiliim is Nephil which means "he fell". Verse four also tells us that the mighty men of old that were renown were actually these Nephiliim, the hybrid, half angel, half human species. So therefore, the Hercules that we hear about as mythology now days actually wasn't a myth; he was real. He was real, and he did many marvelous feats which is why his story is as old as anything biblical. That means that at least some of the "monsters" that we hear about were real too. We have to understand that these were different times and the things that we think that are now only for movies and fantasy were actually happening in those days. The fallen angels not only tried to taint the human race, but they also tampered with the animals, fruit, and vegetation. We know this because when Joshua and Caleb came back from spying out the lands they were carrying grapes that were so big that two people had to hold them.

In the same way that there were thousands of years before rain ever hit the Earth. In the same way that when Abraham, Isaac, Jacob and Elijah would build altars to God and He would send actual fire down to the Earth to burn up the sacrifice in response. In the same way that the Bible speaks about a Leviathan that was in the waters and the Phoenix bird that was still living during those days. Oh wait, you never heard about the Phoenix bird? You thought that was a myth too? The phoenix bird, also known as the firebird, does not show up by name in the KJV Bible translation, however, it does show up in a Jewish translation of the Old Testament. It also shows up in the Septuagint (a Greek version of the Old Testament dated to the third century B.C.), Vulgate (Latin version of Scripture compiled by Jerome in the fourth century), and some Bible commentaries for **Job 29:18**.

The Hebrew word khole (Strong's Concordance #H2344), translated as 'sand' in the KJV, is interpreted as referring to the phoenix bird in the Jewish Publication Society Bible and other sources.

Job 29:18

Then I said: 'I shall die with my nest, and I shall multiply my days as the phoenix;'

(Jewish Publication Society Bible of 1917)

Lastly, about the Phoenix. The life span of the Phoenix was 500 years. It could live for 500 years and then it would build a cocoon of frankincense, myrrh, cinnamon and some other substances. The story goes that he would get in that cocoon it would burn with fire and from the ashes he would be reborn. He was given the abilities because supposedly, he was the only bird that did not eat from a certain tree in the Garden of Eden and so God blessed him with immortality.

Open your minds beloved, the truth is better than any fantasy book, movie, or fable that you've ever heard. And the truth is that most of the fables that you've heard of was taken from true things, facts, and events. **Many of us talk about the Holy Spirit, but we don't believe in spiritual things.** In the same way that there were giants named Venus, Jupiter, Mars, etc. The Nephilim that were born by the "daughters of men" were named by their angelic fathers who knew the names of the planets and so they literally reigned on the Earth. Literally beloved. The Prince or King of Persia, like you saw portrayed in the movie "300", was based off of a real person. Yes, possibly, the same Prince of Persia that withstood the angel Gabriel when he was trying to respond to Daniel's prayer in Daniel 10. I'm going to show you how I could even make a claim like this at all in a few more pages.

You might be saying woah, wait a minute brother! How can this be? Well let me explain. Fallen angels are just that, fallen angels. They don't need a body because they can appear in human form anytime they want. Just like the Godly angels in Genesis 18.

Genesis 18 Authorized (King James) Version (AKJV)

[1] And the Lord appeared unto him in the plains of Mamre: and he
sat in the tent door in the heat of the day; [2] and he lift up his eyes
and looked, and, lo, three men stood by him: and when he saw
them, he ran to meet them from the tent door, and bowed himself
toward the ground, [3] and said, My Lord, if now I have found favour
in thy sight, pass not away, I pray thee, from thy servant: [4] let a
little water, I pray you, be fetched, and wash your feet, and rest

yourselves under the tree: [5] and I will fetch a morsel of bread, and comfort ye your hearts; after that ye shall pass on: for therefore are ye come to your servant. And they said, So do, as thou hast said.

Notice that when Abraham went to the three individuals he bowed himself to the ground and said, "My Lord." Nowhere in the text do we see them saying get up or don't say that term as angels later said to other human beings. So, we would count this as a Theophany, a God appearance on Earth. Or better yet, a Christophany, an appearance of Christ before He was placed into Mary's womb and came into the world as a human being because the Bible says that no one has seen God and lived. We also know that one of those three beings were something greater than the other two because of Genesis 18:22:

Genesis 18:22 (KJV)

[22] Then the men turned away from there and went toward Sodom, while Abraham was still standing before the Lord,

Again, the scriptures say that the Lord stayed back to talk to Abraham while the other two went on to Sodom. And after the Lord spoke to Abraham personally and privately, He went back to Heaven and the other two angels still was carrying out the mission. The early Jewish writers depict these three individuals as three angels, not the Lord and two angels. And one must understand that this would be consistent with their beliefs because they don't believe that the Messiah has showed up yet. I should say, Orthodox Jews, are still waiting on the Messiah.

The Judaic version of the story according to their Talmud is that the three individuals were Raphael, Michael, and Gabriel. Raphael, is the Archangel that is responsible for healing. They say that it was he that asked Sarah, "Why did you laugh?" Because he was the one responsible for doing the healing in her so that she can give birth. However, even though he is the angel that is responsible for providing healing to men and women that is in the Earth, that third person wasn't an angel. It was the Lord.

While we're at it, ancient Hebrew Scholars point to the fact that there are Seven Archangels. However, there are Fifteen Archangels that has been recorded over the whole spectrum of Judaic-Christian works. Before I list them along with the common knowledge and traits of each of them, I'd just like to say that **you should never pray to angels**. And never pray to the image of any angel. Pray to God in the name of Jesus, for whatever it is that you're in need of from God and allow God to dispatch His angels anyway that He sees fit. They work for Him and hopefully as you're reading this book, you'll start to understand that your prayers employ them to more and more works within their scope.

To bring this point home in a brief way, remember John when he bowed to an angel in the book of Revelation? The angel told him to get up.

Revelations 22:8 (ESV)

[8] I, John, am the one who heard and saw these things. And when I heard and saw them, I fell down to worship at the feet of the angel who showed them to me, 9 but he said to me, "You must not do that! I am a fellow servant with you and your brothers the prophets, and with those

Another point regarding why we should not pray to angels is that when we pray we're actually engaged in worship to God and if we direct this to anyone or anything else, we are in fact, worshipping that person or thing. Don't get yourself in trouble beloved. God is jealous. Not to mention that when Jesus was teaching us how to pray in **Matthew 6**, He said, "Our Father…".

When Jesus was praying in **John 17** on behalf of His followers, He was asking God for their sanctification, glorification and preservation. An angel cannot sanctify, glorify, or preserve anyone, especially not for an indefinite period of time. Remember, an angel can choose to be in a fallen state as well. So, in that area, they're just like us.

Okay, back to listing the angels. Keep in mind that I will be listing the angel's name along with additional knowledge about them along with the respective body of work that the information was derived or possibly, revealed to us from. This is in no way my co-signing for the authenticity of the source and in some cases different forms of thinking. I am a Christian, one who professes Christ. I am not a Jew, neither a Catholic, nor a Kabbalist, not a Muslim, not a Mystic, definitely not an Occultist, satanist, or otherwise. But, I believe that you're not really praying dimension breaching, effective prayers if you don't know what's out there and what truly comprises these dimensions that Eph. 6:12 refers too. Before I list them, let me warn you again. NEVER pray to angels. I know that Catholics and some other "religious" sects do; however, you must know that this is demonic and you are engaged in witchcraft when you are doing so. Let's get on with it.

Archangel Michael, whose name means 'he who is as God' or 'he who looks like God', is most often thought of as the angel of protection and the most powerful of all the angels. He is considered a leader within the angelic realm and a patron angel of righteousness, mercy and justice. He is the protector of Israel and is a Commander under Jesus of course, of all of the angels in Heaven.

Archangel Michael is probably the most famous of all the archangels. He's been sainted by the Catholic church of course, because they have sainted everybody. However, churches are named for him, and he features prominently in the Bible and other sacred texts. Ancient and modern artwork portray Michael as a muscular, athletic archangel with intensely powerful facial expressions and body language. One notable Ex-Marine Kingdom agent said that they encountered the Archangel Michael twice, when God sent Michael to protect him from a direct attack from lucifer. One notable note about his testimony, is that he said that Michael is at least 10 Meters tall, which would be over 32.8 feet. The only reason why I include this information is because it is consistent with every other credible testimony of privileged men and women of God that has encountered this special angel as to his huge appearance and height. Usually he's painted with his sword poised above a pinned-down demon. This is to signify Michael's primary purpose of being a warrior angel and as well as slaying the ego and fear. Michael is a protector and a pride slayer. And of course, sacred texts and countless men are named after him.

Archangel Raphael, whose name means 'God heals', is the archangel designated for physical and emotional healing. In Hebrew the word "rophe" means 'to heal'. Archangel Raphael not only helps in healing individuals but also helps healers in their healing practice. He can help reduce addictions and cravings and is powerful in healing other injuries and illnesses, with cures often occurring immediately. Archangel Raphael aids in restoring and maintaining harmony and peace.

Again, don't pray to Raphael or any angel. But if your prayers are effective, who's to say that God won't dispatch Raphael regarding your particular petition?

Archangel Gabriel's name means 'God is my strength'. One of the two archangels specifically named in the Bible in both the Old and New Testament, he is often portrayed holding a trumpet and it should be known that some Catholics portray Gabriel as the only female archangel. However, I don't believe that there is any basis for this.

Again, Gabriel is one of two archangels specifically named in the Bible (the other being Michael). In the Old Testament's Book of Daniel, Gabriel appears to Daniel to help him understand his visions of the future. In the New Testament's Gospels, Gabriel appears in the Book of Luke in famous scenes called the Annunciation, because the archangel announces the forthcoming births of John the Baptist and Jesus Christ. Scriptural roles underscore Gabriel's mission as the supreme messenger of God.

Archangel Jophiel's name means 'beauty of God'. Jophiel is listed as one of the seven principal archangels in Pseudo-Dionysius's De Coelesti Hierarchia ("Celestial Hierarchy"), a 5th-century work on angelology that has been influential in Christian theology. It's said that this work influenced Thomas Aquinas's writings about the nine choirs of angels.

It is said that he helps us to see and maintain beauty in life and supports us in thinking beautiful thoughts and in staying positive as well as in creating and manifesting beauty in our surroundings and hearts. Archangel Jophiel watches over artists supporting in creating beautiful art, assists us in slowing down and bringing calm to our lives, and heals negativity and chaos, helps to tame your ego, and to bring organization to a place or situation.

Archangel Ariel's name means 'lion or lioness of God'. His role is to protect the earth, its natural resources, ecosystems, and all wild life and is always available with support and guidance for any activities that involve environmentalism and protecting, healing, rejuvenating, and/or maintaining our environment. Archangel Ariel assists in healing injured animals working closely with Archangel Raphael in these endeavors. It is believed that he also works to oversee the order of the physical universe including all planets, the sun, the moon and the stars.

Archangel Azrael's name means 'whom God helps'. However, he is often referred to as the 'Angel of Death'. Azrael meets souls and helps them in the transition of death, in addition to helping newly crossed over souls adjust. He also helps loved ones who are still on the earth plane in dealing with their grief and processing the loss. My discrepancy with the description of this angel is that it is said that Archangel Azrael helps ministers and spiritual teachers from all belief systems and religions in their spiritual counseling and assists grief counselors to shield themselves from absorbing their clients' pain and to guide their words and actions. My question is that if this is true, can he really be one of God's angels? I mean does he also assist the Satanist and Buddhist that are not going to what we know as Heaven? Again, it is purported that the Archangel Azrael assists in all types of transitions and endings, not just those involving loss and death. He also helps with transitions related to relationships, career, addictions, etc., helping us to navigate as smoothly as possible through life.

Archangel Chamuel's name means 'he who sees God'. This

archangel has been called by many names throughout history and therefore is sometimes confused with other angels. His mission is to bring peace to the world and as such he protects the world from fear and lower vibrations, negative energies. He is believed to have all knowing vision seeing the interconnectedness between all things. Archangel Chamuel assists us in finding the strength and courage to face adversity when it seems we have none left. He can also help to find items that are lost, to find important parts of our lives such as life purpose, a love relationship, a new job, and supportive friendships, and to find solutions to problems. Lastly, Archangel Chamuel also helps to heal anxiety, bring peace, and to repair relationships.

Archangel Uriel's name means 'the fire of God'. He is the angel of thunder and earthquake, and is, moreover, the divine messenger who warns the son of Lamech of the end of the world, and bids him hide (Enoch, x. 1-2); he appears in a like capacity in II Esd. iv., where he propounds three difficult problems to Ezra and instructs him. Of these problems the first was, "Weigh me the weight of the fire," a demand closely connected in concept with the name "Uriel" which means the fire of God.

ArchAngel Jeremiel means "mercy of God". Archangel Jeremiel helps newly crossed over souls review their life, Jeremiel can also help the living review their lives. Jeremiel delivers mercy to everyone, while guiding people to act in merciful ways.

Archangel Jeremiel is recognized by Eastern Orthodox tradition and in several noncanonical and Coptic books such as 2 Esdras, which outlines conversations between him and Ezra, and then later Zephaniah. Jeremiel explains that he watches over the departed souls from the great Flood. In the Ethiopian Book of Enoch, **Jeremiel is listed as one of the seven archangels and is frequently referred to as Ramiel**. In this sacred text, as well as the non-canonical 2 Baruch, Jeremiel (Ramiel) is the angel of hope who inspires Divine visions and ministers to the souls who are set to ascend to Heaven.

ArchAngel Zadkiel means the "righteousness of God". Archangel

Zadkiel helps release unforgiveness towards our own selves and other people. Zadkiel sweeps and clears away emotional toxins from the heart, activating deep emotional healing. Zadkiel acts as a spiritual professor, accessing knowledge and offering kind patient guidance. Some say that this angel helps restore our memory.

ArchAngel Raguel means "friend of God". He overseas Archangels and angels ensuring harmony and cooperation, while keeping order in all relationships. It is said that Raguel helps sort out your feelings, allowing you to sort and follow their guidance. Raguel is often referred to as the relationship angel, because he is an excellent mediator. It is said that he feels like a warm gentle breeze steering you in the right direction.

ArchAngel Raziel means "the secret of God". Raziel (as Ratziel) is the archangel of the Chokmah, second Sephirah (aspect of God) of the Kabbalah's Tree of Life. There Raziel presides over the action of turning knowledge into practical wisdom. Raziel helps us humans ply our knowledge until it becomes spiritualized and second nature to us. In the Chokmah sphere, we learn how to stay focused and avoid tempting distractions. This requires attuning to our higher self, which is the connection to Divine wisdom.

ArchAngel Metatron - Unlike the other Archangels it is purported that Metatron and Sandolphon have lived lives on earth. Mctatron was the prophet and scribe Enoch.

Metatron is one of two archangels whose names don't end in the -el suffix, which means "of God." That's because the story goes that Metatron and Sandalphon were both human prophets who lived such pious lives that they were rewarded with ascension into the archangel realm.

There's no consensus on the origin of the name Metatron, nor are there records of him being called anything else. Thc Talmud, the Zohar, and the apocryphal Book of Enoch do refer to Metatron as the "Lesser YHVH" (YHVH are the Hebrew letters for God) and make reference to Metatron sitting as ascribe next to God. Some rabbis believe that in Exodus when God says to obey the angel who is leading the mass departure “since my Name is in him,” this refers to Metatron.

It is said that this angel loves children and spends a lot of time with them. He helps with natural talents and gifts and is very close to children who are sensitive to the spirit realm.

Archangel Metatron is also utilized in record keeping and organization.

ArchAngel Sandolphon – It is said that Sandolphon was once the prophet Elijah. Like Metatron, Sandalphon’s name ends in -on instead of -el, signifying his origin as a human prophet. Sandalphon was the biblical prophet Elijah, who ascended at the end of his human life, just as Metratron did. Interestingly, Metatron presides over the entrance to the spheres of the Kabbalah’s Tree of Life, and Sandalphon presides over its exit. In Sandalphon’s human existence, Elijah was the one Jesus was compared to when he asked his disciples, “Who do the people say I am?” This may be because Elijah was said to be a precursor of the coming Messiah.

The alleged functions associated with Sandalphon include being an intercessor for prayers between humans and God, helping determine the gender of a coming child, and acting as a patron to musicians. The Talmud and the Kabbalah describe Sandalphon as a deliverer of prayers from Earth to Heaven. This may be because of his legendary height, which is said to span from Heaven to Earth. Whereas, this is a book about prayer, I would like you to remember this next tidbit of information regarding this angel. Sandolphon delivers and answers prayers, making sure that every prayer is heard, as the all are of equal importance.

Archangel Haniel, means “glory of God”. In the Kabbalah, Haniel presides over the seventh, or Netzach, Sephirah (emanation of God’s will). This sphere is related to victory and represents our inner world of intuition, imagination, and emotions.

ArchAngel Michael. "he who looks like god" The Angel of protection. ...
ArchAngel Raziel. "The secret of God" ...
ArchAngel Ariel. "lioness of God" ...
ArchAngel Haniel. "glory of God" ...
Archangel Uriel. "the light of God" ...
ArchAngel Jeremiel. "mercy of God" ...
ArchAngel Zadkiel. "righteousness of God" ...
ArchAngel Raguel. "friend of God"

So, the whole point of writing about this part of the Bible is to bring home the point that angels already have a body and can show up at any time which is why the Bible says in the Book of Hebrews:

Hebrews 13:2

2 Be not forgetful to entertain strangers: for thereby some have entertained angels unawares.

Now I know that some of that information was new to many of you. But since we're talking about things that will shape our paradigm concerning the things unseen, past, present and future. Let me continue to blow but educate and inform your minds. Because I just got finished talking to you about giants on the Earth from hybrid beings from the consummation of Angels and Humans. I also just told you about a 32-foot angel and the possibility of an angel that spans from the Earth to the Heavens as well. I know that some of you are skeptical about things like that. But we have to understand that according to Cecil Dougherty, author of Valley of the Giants (Valley of the Giants Publishers, first edition, 1971), Adam, the first man, was 16 feet tall! Did you know that? See, the truth will set you free beloved. There was a reason why satan stayed away from Adam huh? Notwithstanding the spiritual dominion and authority that he possessed. **But we underachieve and under believe because we don't know who's image we were made in.** We were made in God's image and we serve a big and mighty God.

So, if Adam was about 16 feet tall, it's not really hard to believe that there were 25-foot giants, and monsters, and leviathans, and whale's big enough to consume a man and on and on and on. Let me give you more Bible about this subject though, because there is plenty to talk about just in the canonical Bible. Did you know that Moses had to contend with the giants as well? Well he did, in Deuteronomy 3 he had to go to God and ask if he and the Israelites would prevail over King Og and his people. God said he would. So, Moses and the Hebrews became giant slayers. I know that only a few of you knew that. Now, if you're smart, this information should make you rethink the images of the Sphinx and other huge beings that Egypt is known for in their art, but I won't go there for the sake of the length of this book.

However, two points and I'll leave this subject alone. When you think about the proposed height of Adam, the first man, it's not hard to understand that lions were like kittens to him and bears were like little cute cubs to him and so on and such. He really had dominion over all things and was the prototype of the man that God had in mind to have dominion on this Earth. I believe that Adam before the fall was special, sort of like a Superman, if you will. He had to name everything, but the birds were in the sky, so he probably had the capacity to fly or float. The whales and the sharks are in the sea, so he probably could walk on water just like the second Adam, Jesus, did. You get my drift? Open up your mind men and women of God so that you can possess the true power that God said is ours. If you choose not to accept any of this, it doesn't change a thing about the Gospel message, so let's carry on.

King Og, whose bed according to the Bible was 14 ft. by 6 ft. was 14 feet tall. According to the same book, Valley of the Giants, Noah was 12 feet tall, Goliath was over 9 feet tall, and over time, it seems as though we've been getting shorter and shorter. The modern man is approximately 6 feet tall, so of course, this is hard to believe. However, if you do the research you will find that everything that I'm saying to you is true. These are blessed revelations that make us understand who we are.

In **2 Corinthians 12:2** Paul says he knew a man who went to the "third heaven." Most theologians believe that he was referring to himself, talking in the third person. The third heaven here simply means the spiritual dwelling of God, as opposed to the other two "heavens," the atmosphere and outer space. The three "heavens" implied in **2 Corinthians 12:2** would be the three different realms that we call the sky, outer space, and the spiritual heaven, where God dwells.

The Ancient Jewish writings believed in Seven Heavens. In Judaism, they teach seven heavens. Seven Heavens is a part of religious cosmology found in many major religions such as Islam, Judaism and Hinduism and in some minor religions such as Hermeticism and Gnosticism. It is said that the Throne of God is said to be above the seventh heaven in the Abrahamic religions.

The word heaven itself has several meanings. The Hebrew for "heaven," shamayim, only appears in the plural form and can mean "sky" refer to **Genesis 1:8–9**. It means "outer space" in **Genesis 22:17**, and then it means "the place where God dwells" in **Joshua 2:11**. Let's look at the New Testament. In the New Testament, the Greek ouranos can mean "the dwelling place of God" as we see this in **Matthew 12:50**. This same word can be translated as "the sky" as we see it in **Acts 10:11**. And paradeisos ("paradise" or "garden") is used in three ways in the New Testament. It can refer to the place where dead believers await resurrection, as we see **in Luke 23:43**. It can also refer to where God dwells now as we read in **2 Corinthians 12:4**. And finally, it can refer to our eternal home as we read in **Revelation 2:7**.

Now, I told you that I would explain, my Prince of Persia comment and how many of the other names that we hear about in the spirit realm are still here. Here we go. First, understand that when the Nephilim existed on Earth, the Bible says that it got to a point that the corruption that they had brought to the world vexed God. He was sorry that He made us, humankind, in our mortality.

Genesis 6:1-8

[1]When human beings began to increase in number on the earth and daughters were born to them, [2]the sons of God saw that the daughters of humans were beautiful, and they married any of them they chose. [3]Then the Lord said, "My Spirit will not contend with humans forever, for they are mortal; their days will be a hundred and twenty years."

[4]The Nephilim were on the earth in those days—and also afterward—when the sons of God went to the daughters of humans and had children by them. They were the heroes of old, men of renown.

[5]The Lord saw how great the wickedness of the human race had become on the earth, and that every inclination of the thoughts of the human heart was only evil all the time. [6]The Lord regretted that he had made human beings on the earth, and his heart was deeply troubled. [7]So the Lord said, "I will wipe from the face of the earth the human race I have created—and with them the animals, the birds and the creatures that move along the ground—for I regret that I have made them." [8]But Noah found favor in the eyes of the Lord.

Now, you know the old story, God wiped out humanity with the flood. Noah, found favor in the eyes of the Lord because they believed in Him, the one and only God, and in addition, he and his family were pure blooded humans. He found favor in the eyes of God and God decided to begin again with Noah and his family. Here comes the important part that many people miss.

During the flood, all of these giant and mythical creatures were drowned, for the most part in the flood. The question is what happened to them? Good question. The answer is that their spirits which were unauthorized and demonic in nature left their mortal bodies but continued to exist in the dimensions of the spirit world. I didn't say dimension, I said dimensions. Hell, for all intents and purposes and from the human perspective, is not just one place, it is a world of its own. It consists of seven kingdoms or to explain what I'm saying better, it consists of seven realms or dimensions. There are three Heavens to be broad. The Third Heaven is where God, Elohim exists. However, the first two Heavens consists of seven dimensions/kingdoms/realms, of which satan resides in the seventh. I will break this down in its own chapter, so I won't go any further with it for the moment. But some of these newly freed spirits took their residence as princes and imps in the Marine Kingdom which had already existed. Some took their places on the ground in the forests and mountains and became the foot soldiers of satan's army. And then, some took their residence in the air, the Second Heaven, with the Principalities and Powers, and Rulers of darkness in High Places. That's why when, Daniel's prayer was being thwarted by the Prince of Persia, it is possible that we are really discussing the same person. The mythical Prince of Persia was drowned, and his spirit took up residence in the air apparently. The power of the demon or entity really depended on the angel that impregnated the human woman. The greater the angel, the greater the Nephilim.

All of these spirits will be judged one day just like it says in Revelations, chapter 20:

Revelations 20:13 (KJV)

13 And the sea gave up the dead which were in it, and death and hell delivered up the dead which were in them, and they were judged every man according to their works.

But, until then they are on a timetable that they know will soon expire. That's why when Jesus approached them in Mark 5, they said, "Have you come to torment us before our time?" If you notice, we don't read anything about demons in the Bible until Deuteronomy 32:17.

Deuteronomy 32:16-17 (NLT)

16 They stirred up his jealousy by worshiping foreign gods; they provoked his fury with detestable deeds.

[17] They offered sacrifices to demons, which are not God, to gods they had not known before, to new gods only recently arrived, to gods their ancestors had never feared.

Deuteronomy 32:16-17 (KJV)

[16] They provoked him to jealousy with strange gods, with abominations provoked they him to anger.
[17] They sacrificed unto devils, not to God; to gods whom they knew not, to new gods that came newly up, whom your fathers feared not.

Again, the reason why you don't hear about them that much is because they were actually on the Earth in the forms of humans and other creatures that God wiped out with the flood. For example, **2 Chronicles 11:15** refers to goat demons. But let's move on. When they lost their bodies, they became disembodied spirits that will do anything to inhabit a nice warm body. However, some of them don't and they choose to be ethereal. Another point to reiterate is that the word "demon" is almost never mentioned in the Old Testament because it is a Greek word and the Old Testament was written in Hebrew. The Greek word for demon is demonia for singular and daemones for plural. Another word that is also used for demon is daimon.

Another thing to keep in mind is that even after the flood, these giants or Nephilim, were still seen and living on the Earth. Refer to **Genesis 6:1-8**. They were just very few in number at that point but started growing in number. However, they lasted on the Earth about 1200 years after the flood. Which is easy to establish even without the prior scripture because we know that Nimrod, the guy that was in charge of building the Tower of Babbel, was a renown Giant Hunter.

Genesis 10:8,9 (KJV)

And Cush begat Nimrod: he began to be a mighty one in the earth. He was a mighty hunter before the LORD: wherefore it is said, Even as Nimrod the mighty hunter before the LORD.

According to the book of Jasher, Nimrod became a mighty hunter by wearing the dress brought by Adam from heaven. It was an animal skin. This skin was in custody of Seth after Adam then Noah, and was then stolen by Ham from the Ark.

Nimrod, which was undoubtedly a giant himself, built many cities, and introduced many different pagan gods for people to worship. He promoted mixing amongst the races back then and promoted a knowledge that was allegedly above God. Of course, we know the end of the story. Because God smacked his tower down and then scattered the people all over the Earth, as well as confounding their language.

Now, I know that I just introduced something else that you've never heard of; the book of Jasher. I'm not going to go deep into it, but this is another book that was quoted from a couple of times in our canonized Bible. For example, the Book of Jasher is mentioned in **Joshua 10:12-13** when the Lord stopped the sun in the middle of the day during the battle of Beth Horon. It is also mentioned in **2 Samuel 1:18-27** as containing the Song or Lament of the Bow, that mournful funeral song which David composed at the time of the death of Saul and Jonathan. However, let's move on.

Also, I want you to remember that we see at a certain point in the Old Testament where evil spirits vexed certain people. Remember that whenever Saul was vexed by a "spirit" David had to come and play his harp to get the spirit to leave.

And all the way up to David we see these giants being an opposition for the nation of God. David and the Israelites were still fighting them in his time, which was way after Noah. After David slew Goliath, he had to go after the five other giant brothers of Goliath, and he was successful.

Last thing, I'll say about this subject, is that this is the reason why there are so many things on the Earth that is unexplainable to the population of humans that exist today. There were actually 36-

foot giants and creatures back then. And when you think of these things, it's not hard to believe that they could build a Stone Hedge and even the Pyramids, with no problem.

Within and without the principalities that I'm explaining in this book we have an organization of enemies called the Powers. Powers are those that hold power within a principality, kingdom, or even an empire. In the spirit realm there are local powers, national powers, and international powers. The Powers deals with the witchcraft, black magic, psychics, and sorcerers of the world. For example, the Powers empower the Voodoo practitioner. They empower the Santeria practitioner and so on and so on.

The Second Heaven, again is populated by very strong angelic forces, howbeit, that they are of a fallen nature. It is said that amongst these principalities, of course is satan's throne. Because he wants to be like God, with a heaven and all of that. Now, I want to introduce to some of you and just reiterate to others because you're already worshipping falsely, some of the other things that are in the Second Heaven.

There is an entity called the Queen of Heaven. It is a real entity. She has been worshipped over the years in many different capacities. She has been worshipped under the name of Isis, Inanna, Anat, Astarte, Aphrodite, Asherah, Hera, Diana, and even in the Catholic Church, she is being worshipped as the Virgin Mary, the Immaculate, Our Lady. Do you know that it is sacrilegious and an abomination to pray at the foot of any idol? Yes, even the image of Mary, which is not her image. The image that you're bowing down too is that of the Queen of Heaven. Is she really a queen? Of course not, but know this, whatever you worship is your god. So satan has set her up for those in the occult who believe as such. She is a Siren demon.

I should note that Asherah, was and is considered to be the Queen in Heaven by those who worshipped the female deity in the Old Testament. She was represented by a pole that would always be situated right next to the image of Baal. So, in their warped minds, Baal was the husband and Asherah or Astarte, was the wife.

I know it doesn't make any sense, nevertheless, this is historically accurate. So, it's not hard to believe that of course there is a reason for this belief. The reason is because satan presented this knowledge to those that would worship him from the beginning, because it suited him.

The image of Mary holding the baby Jesus is not really Mary, it is the Queen of Heaven and the Queen of Issachar who is supposedly sitting on the right hand of lucifer.

In reality, the Queen of Heaven is the most powerful next to lucifer because the concept of her and the worship of her (in the Catholic Church and otherwise) probably even trumps satan worship itself. Many Catholics have talked about having life changing experiences meeting "Mary". Many, of course, don't even believe that they are involved in a luciferian religion, but satan is the one that is being glorified whenever glory is being given to any other person or entity than God Himself. She is not an angel; however, she is the most elevated Siren in the parallel world. She is one of the governing principalities of course, set up by lucifer himself. So, when you're praying your Hail Mary, full of grace prayers, just know that this is who you are praying too, and you will go to Hell for this transgression beloved unless you repent right now.

Revelation 21:7-8

[7] Everyone who wins the victory will inherit these things. I will be their God, and they will be my children.
[8] But cowardly, unfaithful, and detestable people, murderers, sexual sinners, sorcerers, ***idolaters****, and all liars will find themselves in the fiery lake of burning sulfur. This is the second death."*

Have you ever wondered who that image of Mary is that you're bowing down too? It is the image of the demonic Queen of Heaven, who of course, is not a real queen. Just like the image that you're wearing on your crucifix. Do you know whose image that is? It is the image of lucifer around your neck. Take it off! Jesus is no longer on the cross!

satan is very crafty, and I know you thought that you were doing a good thing, but remember that he is the one that is going to deceive the whole world:

2 Corinthians 11:14

14 And no wonder, for even Satan disguises himself as an angel of light.

Now, before you Bible thumping, seminary trained, western culture theologically trained, men and women immediately start saying, "I've never heard of a Queen of Heaven." I implore you to stop trying to learn how to exegete a text and make people shout about becoming rich and famous and learn the truths of the Word of God. Read your Bibles, because Jeremiah knew who the "queen of heaven" was and God knows who the "queen of heaven" is, and He is very angry about the whole thing:

Jeremiah 7:18-25

18 The children gather wood, and the fathers kindle the fire, and the women knead their dough, to make cakes to the ***queen of heaven****, and to pour out drink offerings unto other gods, that they may provoke me to anger.*

19 Do they provoke me to anger? saith the Lord: do they not provoke themselves to the confusion of their own faces?

20 Therefore thus saith the Lord God; Behold, mine anger and my fury shall be poured out upon this place, upon man, and upon beast, and upon the trees of the field, and upon the fruit of the ground; and it shall burn, and shall not be quenched.

21 Thus saith the Lord of hosts, the God of Israel; Put your burnt offerings unto your sacrifices, and eat flesh.

[22] For I spake not unto your fathers, nor commanded them in the day that I brought them out of the land of Egypt, concerning burnt offerings or sacrifices:

[23] But this thing commanded I them, saying, Obey my voice, and I will be your God, and ye shall be my people: and walk ye in all the ways that I have commanded you, that it may be well unto you.

[24] But they hearkened not, nor inclined their ear, but walked in the counsels and in the imagination of their evil heart, and went backward, and not forward.

So, the prophet Jeremiah knew who the Queen of Heaven was, even before the Virgin Mary was on the scene. Is this hitting home yet? Stop bowing down to idols. The Bible told us not to make an image of anything in Heaven, under the Earth or the Sea. This means that we shouldn't be bowing down to images of the Sun, Angels, Stars or anything else. Yes, get rid of your Michael, the Archangel statues because it is not him, it's a replica of a demon. **Idolatry is attributing divine power to a human object. You will go to Hell for this sin beloved unless you throw this stuff away and repent of your sins.**

Lastly, on this Queen of Heaven topic, the biggest idol of her can be found right here in America. That's right, you guessed it, our very own Statue of Liberty is really an idol representing a Roman goddess called Libertas (yet another name for her). The goddess Libertas is also depicted on the Great Seal of France, created in 1848. This is the image which later influenced French sculptor Frederic-Auguste Bartholdi, a well-known Freemason, in the creation of his statue of Liberty Enlightening the World. It was built by French Engineer, Gustave Eiffel, another well-known Freemason. The statue initially was not created for us, it was created initially by Bartholdi for the opening of the Suez Canal in Egypt in 1867.

To reiterate, the Statue of Liberty in New York Harbor was presented in 1884 as a gift from the French Grand Orient Temple

Masons to the Masons of America in celebration of the centenary of the first Masonic Republic.

Bartholdi, like many French Freemasons of his time, was deeply steeped in 'Egyptian' rituals, and it has often been said that he conceived the original statue as an effigy of the goddess Isis, and only later converted it to a 'Statue of Liberty' for the New York Harbor when it was rejected for the Suez Canal." The goddess Isis is known by many names, including Juno, whose appearance made it on a Vatican coin in 1963 when the then Pope, was an alleged Mason as well.

"Lady Liberty" is holding the Masonic "Torch of Enlightenment". Also referred to back in the 1700's by the Illuminati Masons as the "Flaming Torch of Reason". The Torch represents the "Sun" in the sky. Yes, lending to Sun worship. The Statue of Liberty's official title is, "Liberty Enlightening the World". So, we have the Masons, goddesses, illuminati, and not to mention the fact that some link America's idol to the appearance of the woman in Revelations 17. However, I don't espouse to the literal application of that one entirely because "Lady Liberty" has 7 horns, not 10 horns like the Bible says, but it's interesting. You woke yet? Wouldn't you love to pick the minds of our top governmental officials to see what they really know? Why do I bring all of these things up? Am I exalting the enemy? No, I'm exposing everything. All of these forces are out there fighting against our prayers and the angels that transport them and God's responses to them.

Romans 1:18-23 (KJV)

18 For the wrath of God is revealed from heaven against all ungodliness and unrighteousness of men, who hold the truth in unrighteousness;

19 Because that which may be known of God is manifest in them; for God hath shewed it unto them.

[20] For the invisible things of him from the creation of the world are clearly seen, being understood by the things that are made, even his eternal power and Godhead; so that they are without excuse:

[21] Because that, when they knew God, they glorified him not as God, neither were thankful; but became vain in their imaginations, and their foolish heart was darkened.

[22] Professing themselves to be wise, they became fools,

[23] And changed the glory of the uncorruptible God into an image made like to corruptible man, and to birds, and fourfooted beasts, and creeping things.

Be aware that idolatry is also spiritual adultery. Refer to (Jeremiah 3:8-10). However, let's move on because I want to tell you something that is important. I'm kind of splitting the lines between the Air Kingdom and the Marine Kingdom with this one but it's important.

The Internet, as we know it, was created by demons in the Marine Kingdom. It has always existed. They have a network that is way beyond our primitive internet that we're using on Earth. As a matter of fact, it was their world that introduced this technology to our world. In their world they have monitors of every person that is living on the Earth. And this system knows our preferences, regarding our actions, activities, and proclivities. This angelic technology is in Heaven as well and we must remember that the same angels that were in Heaven are now in Hell and in the many demonic Kingdoms set up by satan. It has been reported that at the entrance gate of Heaven, every thought that you have comes up on a monitor. If you have any sinful thought you will not be allowed into Heaven. That's why the scripture says:

Philippians 2:5 (KJV)

[5] Let this mind be in you, which was also in Christ Jesus

Watch your thoughts beloved. Remember, **Philippians 4:8-9 says that:**

[8] Finally, brethren, whatsoever things are true, whatsoever things are honest, whatsoever things are just, whatsoever things are pure, whatsoever things are lovely, whatsoever things are of good report; if there be any virtue, and if there be any praise, think on these things.

[9] Those things, which ye have both learned, and received, and heard, and seen in me, do: and the God of peace shall be with you.

But back to the internet. This piece of information is important for a lot of reasons. For example, whenever a person looks at pornography, for example, your face shows up in Hell, more specifically the Marine Kingdom, and demons, also known as Sirens, are sent to you. That's why many computers will get a virus from the amount of spirits that will try to contact you right at that moment. Man or woman of God. I'm here to let you know that some of the women and men on the other end of the computer screen are not human. They are literal demons.

Now why did I go back to the Marine Kingdom to talk about this? Because, this technology broaches over to something else that I want to warn you about. I already told you that Leviathan is the marine kingdom representative of satan, the designated figure head, so to speak. satan, is using Leviathan in tandem with another demon called Halloween, to spread his mark. Yes, do you think it is a coincidence that the greatest demonic day on the Earth is called Halloween? Nothing is what it seems beloved and there are no accidents in the spirit realm. The Bible talks about the mark of the beast. I'm here to let you know that his mark is already in the Earth. His mark is being spread through the cell phone and cell phone technology.

Every time you make a call, it goes through the servers of the Marine Kingdom first before your call gets connected and therefore they're monitoring every conversation that you're having beloved. What we need to realize is that there are many kingdoms and in all of them we are being monitored. Satan's modus operandi is to always counterfeit and mimic God. He wants to be just like God and he's not omniscient, so he has to be very organized.

This is why we, as those who profess Christ, have to be organized. This is not a time to be scattered. This is not a time to be lukewarm. And this is not a time to be offended. Unseasoned Prophets/Prophetess are some of the most offendable servants in the body of Christ. Because they haven't yet figured out the difference between the Heavenly forms of communications (which assists our God given discernment) and the "scrambling" spirit, which will always try to distort the message and cause paranoia. Immature Prophets will terminate God ordained relationships based on the something that was never said and that never happened and call it prophetic discernment. When this starts to become the way that you operate, you are a double agent, easily usable by the other kingdom, so that God's great purpose will never be manifested on the Earth. Pray that God will develop your gift to the level that exemplifies His character.

The shed blood of Jesus has made us free from Sin, sickness and disease, depression and oppression. He has broken every chain of bondage and loosed every fetter He has torn down walls of isolation and separation. He has made us FREE and whom the Son sets free is free indeed!

The Power Behind Your Praise

If you only pray when you're in trouble, you're in trouble.

Apostle Dr. Larry Birchett, Jr.

Psalms 34:1-3 (KJV)

1I will bless the LORD at all times: his praise shall continually be in my mouth. 2 My soul shall make her boast in the LORD: the humble shall hear thereof, and be glad. 3 O magnify the LORD with me, and let us exalt his name together.

When Adam sinned in the Garden of Eden the world became fractured. We are living in a shadow of what God's perfect intent for mankind was. Consequently, ever since then we've been living and operating in multi worlds to please God and include God in our affairs. For example, the early fathers of the faith would build altars to God and God would show that He has received and honored the offering by sending fire or lightning down from Heaven and burning the offering up. This is an example of two worlds colliding and intertwining.

God told His people to build the Ark of the Covenant so that His presence could dwell there. Again, this is the colliding and intertwining of two worlds and multiple dimensions because of the fractured relationship that sin had caused. Those that practice occultic religions such as Santeria would readily tell you that there are 21 realms to the dark side and that the number one number of satan's kingdom is in fact, 21. This is why it took 21 days for Daniel's prayer to be answered.

In light of this from my two examples above we understand that the only things that can penetrate through these various realms, dimensions, and worlds is prayer and praise.

Our five greatest weapons are:

1. The name of Jesus – Col. 1:14; **Col. 3:17** – [17] *And whatsoever ye do in word or deed, do all in the name of the Lord Jesus, giving thanks to God and the Father by him.* **Prov. 18:10** – [10] *The name of the Lord is a strong tower: the righteous runneth into it and is safe.*
2. The Blood of Jesus - **Col. 1:13-14** - [13] *Who hath delivered us from the power of darkness, and hath translated us into the kingdom of his dear Son:*[14] *In whom we have redemption through his blood, even the forgiveness of sins:*
3. The Word of God - **Proverbs 28:9** – [9] *He that turneth away his ear from hearing the law, even his prayer shall be abomination.* Not being under the hearing of the word of god, causes a curse on your prayer life. You might as well stop praying because god doesn't want to hear them. Psalms 138:2; Col. 3:16
4. The Praises of the Saints – **2 Chronicles 20:21** - [21] *And when he had consulted with the people, he appointed those who should sing to the Lord, and who should praise the beauty of holiness, as they went out before the army and were saying: "Praise the Lord, For His mercy endures forever."*
5. Obedience – **1 Sam. 15:22** – [22] *And Samuel said, Hath the Lord as great delight in burnt offerings and sacrifices, as in obeying the voice of the Lord? Behold, to obey is better than sacrifice, and to hearken than the fat of rams.*

All throughout this book I am teaching about the power that is contained in the name of Jesus, I have also extensively covered the power contained in applying the blood of Jesus. So, for a minute, right here, I really want to elaborate more on point #4, the praises of the saints, because it is so overlooked. Every time that you apply one of the weaponry that God gives us to be victorious in this life we have to learn to give God praise for His favorable actions toward us. In essence, we're thanking and praising God for

His yes. I break this down for my congregation by simply declaring that we need to **"put a praise on it"** after I am sure that God has released some of His power and virtue to us.

Just as the Bible tells us to pray without ceasing we also need to understand that we should praise without ceasing as well. I'm about to show you how the praise amplifies your prayer. God inhabits the praises of His people and whenever or wherever there is an atmosphere of true genuine praise you can be sure that an extra measure of God's Spirit is present. This is why you should include praise in your prayers. Remember Jesus prayed, "Our Father, who art in Heaven, Hallowed be Thy name….". What was Jesus doing by saying Hallowed be thy name? He was praising and showing adoration to His Father. "Bigging Him up" as some say on the street. He was showing adoration and holy reverence. Therefore, praise before, during, and after your prayers men and women of God. Praise during the good times and the bad times in your life as well beloved. I don't care what's going on in your life, never lose your praise. I have made a covenant with God that my very first word every morning of every day will be Hallelujah, which is the highest praise that an individual can verbally give God while they are here on Earth. Let's look at one story in the Bible concerning this principle. If you have a Bible I would like you to read **2 Chronicles 20:1-13**. I won't print it all out here for the sake of space, but I will highlight a few key verses to set up the teaching. Basically, the Moabites and the Ammonites were coming against Jehosophat and then we get to verse 2.

2 Chronicles 20:2

> [2]*Then some came and told Jehoshaphat, saying, "A great multitude is coming against you from beyond the sea, from Syria; and they are in Hazazon Tamar" (which is En Gedi).*

Be thankful when others can see the attacks that you haven't had to endure yet. Please understand this; not everyone is hating on you. Sometimes God really allow other people to have insight into battles and sometimes wars that are on the horizon. We are required to warn others regarding what God is showing us. And the Bible says that we should do good especially to those that are in the household of faith. If we don't the Bible is clear in underscoring the fact that if we don't their blood will be on our hands.

Ezekiel Chapter 3

[20] Again, when a righteous [man] doth turn from his righteousness, and commit iniquity, and I lay a stumblingblock before him, he shall die: because thou hast not given him warning, he shall die in his sin, and his righteousness which he hath done shall not be remembered; but his blood will I require at thine hand.
[21] Nevertheless if thou warn the righteous [man], that the righteous sin not, and he doth not sin, he shall surely live, because he is warned; also thou hast delivered thy soul.

So, if we expect our souls to be delivered than we are required to help one another. However, our response to the warning is what is very critical.

Proverbs 12:1 (NIV)
Whoever loves discipline loves knowledge, but whoever hates correction is stupid.

Proverbs 12:1 (NLT)
To learn, you must love discipline; it is stupid to hate correction.

Therefore, stop fighting correction because correction could be the only thing standing between you and the condemnation of God. Let's look at the next verse in Proverbs 12:

[2] Good people obtain favor from the LORD, but he condemns those who devise wicked schemes.

Again, your response to the warning is very critical. We see that Jehosophat feared because of what he had heard **(2 Chronicles 20:3-4)**. And we need to understand that this is one of the tactics of the enemy. He uses threats, intimidation, innuendos, and ultimatums. Praise God, that even though that is true God hasn't given us a spirit of fear but of power, love and a sound mind.

There are some things that start to occur in our lives that we can definitely chalk it up to the fact that God is **allowing** and, in some ways, even **directing** these events. At these times a Godly fear should arise in us to get God's attention.

Proverbs 9:10 (KJV)

The fear of the LORD is the beginning of wisdom, and knowledge of the Holy One is understanding.

Watch Jehosophat's response though:

4 *So Judah gathered together to ask help from the Lord; and from all the cities of Judah they came to seek the Lord.*

He called the people together to pray. The response of any genuine spiritual leader that has really been called by God is their propensity to pray and to get others to pray. A person that hasn't been called by God will try to figure the issue out on their own. A person that God has called will go to Him about everything.

Why do we NOT ask God for help when we are in need? Why are we not going to God in prayer to solve our issues? We try EVERYTHING else except God when we first get in trouble and wonder why our troubles don't turn. The Bible says that we have not because we ask not.

The real reason why we don't go to God in these situations is because we really don't think that He can solve them! We don't believe in the power of prayer! We don't believe that there is really a God that is concerned about our needs.

Prayer for many of us is just an act of Shakespeare. It's almost as if we're just making positive affirmations (like the world says). And this is one of the reasons why our prayers are not being answered.

Let's look at what the scriptures have to say about this issue:

1 John 5:14-15 (KJV)

And this is the confidence that we have in him, that, if we ask any thing according to his will, he heareth us: And if we know that he hear us, whatsoever we ask, we know that we have the petitions that we desired of him.

Prayer is a lifestyle. Don't just be excited about the call, be excited about the lifestyle. Many of us love it when someone seeks us to pray publicly but we're not so excited about the private sacrifice that's necessary to have the relationship with God that produces the power and subsequent results. When is the last time you fasted without anybody knowing? Or does every time you do something of this nature the whole world has to know? How many hours a day do you spend in communication with our God? Or does your prayer time only consist of your public prayers in church? How are you an intercessor, yet when you pray, you're only praying for yourself? How many chapters do you read per day of God's Holy Word?

Now let's look at how Jehosophat prayed in **2 Chronicles 20**. He did three things:

1) Affirmed God's mighty power and greatness.

6 And said, O Lord God of our fathers, art not thou God in heaven? and rulest not thou over all the kingdoms of the heathen? and in thine hand is there not power and might, so that none is able to withstand thee?

7 Art not thou our God, who didst drive out the inhabitants of this land before thy people Israel, and gavest it to the seed of Abraham thy friend for ever?

2) He reminded God of how much favor they seemed to have with Him in the past.

[9] If, when evil cometh upon us, as the sword, judgment, or pestilence, or famine, we stand before this house, and in thy presence, (for thy name is in this house,) and cry unto thee in our affliction, then thou wilt hear and help.

[10] And now, behold, the children of Ammon and Moab and mount Seir, whom thou wouldest not let Israel invade, when they came out of the land of Egypt, but they turned from them, and destroyed them not;

[11] Behold, I say, how they reward us, to come to cast us out of thy possession, which thou hast given us to inherit.

3) He appealed to the Righteousness and Justice side of God concerning the current issue that he was dealing with. Ending it up with Lord we just don't know what to do. Our eyes are on you. (vs. 12)

[12] O our God, wilt thou not judge them? for we have no might against this great company that cometh against us; neither know we what to do: but our eyes are upon thee.

Let me tell you a secret about prayer, as long as you act like you can handle it all. Like you have all of the answers. Like you can figure it out on your own. God is not going to do nothing anything. Remember, prayer is an act of submission. When we pray, we're inviting God into our situations admitting that we can't achieve whatever we're asking Him for on our own. Jehososphat did that and we get to read about his victorious results in the Bible today.

Now, watch God's response in verses 14-17, because it is key. The king's posture of prayer pulled on the power of God so much that the spirit of prophecy was sent to the people. Prophecy was sent to the house of the prophet, specifically, the son of Zechariah the prophet, and said that because my people that are called by my name have humbled themselves, sought my face, turned from their wicked ways, I have heard your prayers, I have forgiven your sins, and baby, now I'm about to heal your land!

To go even further, God said, in fact, you won't even have to fight in this battle! You won't even have to sweat in this battle! You won't even have to worry about this battle! You won't even have to argue about this battle! You won't even have to stress about this battle! You won't even have to stay up at night about this battle! You won't even have to throw a punch in this battle! You won't even have to defend yourself in this battle! You won't even have to belittle yourself in this battle! You won't even have to come out of character in this battle! You won't even have to try in this battle! Because your prayers have ushered you under an open heaven! I have heard you and now watch out here I come! It's on like popcorn and I'm about to wipe out your enemies! Scream Hallelujah somebody! Again, I won't apologize for getting excited about God's Word and His promises.

God was saying to his people, 'I got you!' And if you're reading this right now God has impressed on my heart just to tell you this same message, that, He's got you. Praise God because we serve a God that gives us the answers to the test. Prayer is the prerequisite to Prophecy and when the fountains of the prophetic are pouring God will reveal things that will help us in life before they even happen. He does this through His Intercessors and through His Prophets. Let's look at what the Prophet Amos had to say about this:

Amos 3:7

Surely the Lord GOD will do nothing, but he revealeth his secret unto his servants the prophets.

What is Amos saying? He's saying that God gives us the answers to the test. Isn't that wonderful? However, again, Prayer is the lever that turns on the faucet. Prayer literally pulls on Heaven to reveal and help the Saints. This is why we have to pray and pray and then pray some more beloved. Prayer delivers, prayer maintains, and prayer will cause God and His angels to fight for you.

Watch God's response, He told them that they won't have to fight. But at the same time God told them to go out against them. Beloved, just because God has guaranteed you a victorious outcome doesn't mean that your actions are not important. It doesn't mean that you're not supposed to show up on the battlefield. It doesn't mean that you can just stop praying, stop believing, and stop pressing into Him. Remember that it took 21 days for the answer to Daniel's prayer to make it to him. One of the biggest secrets out of the whole sequence of events is that Daniel was still praying when the angel Gabriel showed up with the answer. Your position determines your condition. If you receive a Word from God, it is based on God being pleased with your actions. You can still make that word null and of no-effect just like Saul did over his own life. Keep on going until you receive the manifestation. And then after that make sure that you incorporate whatever you've done to get God's attention into your lifestyle.

Another important point to point out is that God spoke to Jehosophat. You need to understand that God will give the instructions to the one that speaks his language. That's why you have to be full of the Holy Spirit. An amateur would've said okay God is just saying that we're going to win, get your swords ready everybody and let's go to battle in the way that we normally do. But Jehosophat was a man of wisdom and he prepared his Levites (verses 18-21).

The Levites stem from the priestly lineage of Aaron. God told Jehosophat to place them in the front to sing praises unto Him. I'm sure we would all agree that this is the farthest thing from what a seasoned General would've prescribed for this moment and particular situation. But God's ways are not our ways and His thoughts are not our thoughts. God fights in the spirit realm beloved. Stop fighting back in your own strength. (*For the weapons of our warfare is not carnal but it is mighty through to god to the pulling down of strongholds*).

Stop sending your pain in front of you and start sending your praise.

2 Chronicles 20:21

> 21 *And when he had consulted with the people, he appointed those who should sing to the Lord, and who should praise the beauty of holiness, as they went out before the army and were saying:* ***"Praise the Lord, For His mercy endures forever."***

Listen, I know that the bills are due but praise the Lord for his mercy endureth forever! I know that you're not working at your dream job but praise the Lord for his mercy endureth forever! I know that your spouse ain't saved and your children ain't saved but praise the Lord for his mercy endureth forever! I know that your car is giving you issues praise God because His mercy endureth forever. For some of you, at least you still have a car. For the others praise God that He will not allow anything to fall in your life in Jesus name. So what that there are people talking about you. Don't you know that if they don't say these things directly to you that it is really none of your business? It doesn't matter what they say, all that matters is what God says because you can't control what other people think about you anyway. Praise God for His mercy endureth forever because other people thoughts do not change who you are in God! I keep using exclamation points because I am yelling right now beloved. Now, I'm laughing because I feel a wave of joy and the joy of the Lord is my strength. Just know that there is power in your praise. Give God a loud and heartfelt praise because His grace and mercy in unceasing and last forever.

The power is in your praise. Jehosophat knew that way before we had mega churches and multimillion dollar Gospel Artists and everything else. I can show you that Moses knew this. Joshua knew this. Even Gideon knew this. However, even though praise in itself is powerful there are ways that we can make it even more powerful. **Ephesians 3:20** says it like this, *Our God is able to do exceedingly and abundantly according to the power that worketh within us.* What power is working in you? His name is Jesus! We do nothing in our name, all prayer is to be prayed in the name of Jesus because He said that as long as we prayed in His name our prayers would be acknowledged. In **John 14:13**, Jesus said to His disciples, *"Whatever you ask in My name, that I will do, that the Father may be glorified in the Son."* And in **John 16:24**: *"Until now, you have asked nothing in my name. Ask and you will receive that your joy may be full."* From these two passages of Scripture, we find the two overarching basic purposes of prayer: one, to glorify God; and two, that the joy of the Lord that is our strength, might be full.

Stay with me here because I'm going somewhere with this point. We can do exceedingly and abundantly according to the power that is working within us. Watch the progression here:

2 Chronicles 20:18-19

18 And Jehoshaphat bowed his head with his face to the ground,
and all Judah and the inhabitants of Jerusalem bowed before the
Lord, worshiping the Lord. 19 Then the Levites of the children of
the Kohathites and of the children of the Korahites stood up to
praise the Lord God of Israel with voices loud and high.

After Jehosophat humbled himself in front of all of the people and bowed his knee to God in prayer, the people followed suit. Then the Levites, which are the people designated to the priestly order, starting all the way back from Aaron, stood up and started praising God loudly, the scriptures says. God told Jehosophat to assemble the praise and worship team to go first on the battlefield. And they weren't there to look pretty. They were instructed to **sing** praises unto the Lord. Sing the praise unto the Lord! When you sing your praises to God they are amplified. It pushes your praise to heaven. This is a lost secret I'm telling you right now.

In the same way, that singing pushes your prayer as a way of amplifying them, singing pushes your prayers. Have you ever wondered why you hear Catholic Priests start singing their prayers in certain masses? It is because the Catholic church knows this secret. They get a lot wrong, and some of them are not even "saved" as they would think that they are, but they hold on to some of the most ancient secrets and methods that comprise the church.

I hear you in the Spirit. You're saying it don't take all that. All of this praising and singing makes you uncomfortable. The truth is that we find comfort in being around people who agree with us however, we can only grow around people who disagrees with us. God sent me to grow you, so let me help you. Music is one of the most underused weapons in the church. It's the reason that satan got so prideful that he thought he could rule in Heaven. He evidently could create an atmosphere like no other.

People like Benny Hinn has tapped into this secret. If you ever go to a Benny Hinn healing crusade, he will instruct and even lead a certain litany of songs every time before he even allows himself to transition into healing mode. The praise and the worship are what causes the barriers between dimensions to evaporate so that whatever you pray becomes more effective. Praise and prayer equals prayer to the highest power.

Praise and worship is a lifestyle not just one day a week thing. And we also see in verse 23 and 24 of this same chapter that praise confuses the enemy. So, praise him in spite of. When things are going wrong, learn how to say Hallelujah anyhow. This is how you can tell a true praiser because circumstance does not hinder or change their praise. Why? Because a true praiser actually derives enjoyment out of giving God praise.

Praise creates room for you. Proverbs 18:16 says, *A man's gift maketh room for him, and bringeth him before great men.* The gift of Judah is their praise! The gift of the Levite is in their praise! Your Praise will make room for you!

A good friend of my wife and I, Prophetess Chantell Ellis Poole, who is also a Pastor, has a very good saying. She says that your atmosphere will tell on you. Therefore, make sure that your happiness and relationship with the Lord is showing through today beloved. It is your job to create and maintain a heavenly atmosphere.

I rebuke the thieving spirit that will try to steal your praise. I send fire to every python spirit around your necks that would keep you from praising our God. While everybody else is singing or are you singing along or is your mouth shut? Loose yourselves from that spirit and sing praises to the Lord!

Get rid of pessimistic conversations and negative thoughts because these kinds of things will hinder your praise. And watch out for those that say you're weak for praising God. That you're weak for not needing them and their pity parties anymore.

Some people are only upset you're in a better place because your last place made them feel better about their current place. They don't want to hear the truth because truth sounds like hate to those that hate the truth. But nevertheless, the end of the story in verses 25-30 is that after God gave them the victory they praise God like there was no tomorrow. Are you getting the memo here about the importance of praise?

29 And the fear of God was on all the kingdoms of those countries when they heard that the Lord had fought against the enemies of Israel. 30 Then the realm of Jehoshaphat was quiet, for his God gave him rest all around.

I prophesy that to those who will make praise a Lifestyle, God will deal with all of your enemies and when other enemies hear how God has dealt with them, He will make all of the rest of your enemies fear you. So, let it be written. So, let it be done.

Full Body Prayer

I want to give you a technique in this chapter that will help you. It is called Full Body Prayer. In the secular world, if you want to make sure that your whole body is being worked out and you can only go about twice a week, you would have to do a full body workout, to hit everything on the days that you're able to get to the gym. This full body workout will allow your whole body to get to toned, strengthened and conditioned. Athletes that do full body workouts are always more beautiful and conditioned than bodybuilders who do one body part a day. The body builder might have huge muscles but could never run 10 or 15 miles. The runner can. The swimmer can. The boxer can. The US Army Soldier, CIA agent, or FBI agent can. And on and on because these kinds of athletes are always doing full body workouts and have a deeper strength that is usable in the real world.

This is what full body prayer kind of looks like in the spirit realm. There are layers to reality and you can pull them away to see through, but you have to go pass the physical and beyond what your mind it is telling you. Your very movements are spiritual beloved. Did you know that? Clapping your hands, raising your hands, walking around, even kneeling add something different to your prayers. As I already told you, your position determines your condition. This is why Yoga is so huge, because the movements of Yoga open you up so that spirits can come in. A lot of people don't understand that. A lot of people have gotten possessed unknowingly because of their practice of these demonic poses in the direction of the Sun. Yeah, some of you are putting it altogether. What I am saying is known by serious martial artists as well. Do you think that breaking boars with your head is something that you can teach? No, it is something that you can do after enough demons have entered into your body.

Sometimes we have to engage in Full Body prayer. Instead of just sitting numbly and praying, it would be better, if we'd clap our hands, put our hands in the air, walk around, shout, stump even. One of the most powerful things that you can do when you're engaged in fervent prayer is to raise your hands. When you raise your hands when you pray they become like antennas, signaling the light that is in or on your head. The fire that is coming from your head is sent into the sky when you raise your hands because your hands pull the fire and send up one big huge light into the Heavens for the purpose of God to answer prayer.

Watch this: When Moses had his hands lifted in the book of Exodus, we see that Israel prevailed. When his hands were being lowered they started to lose.

Exodus 17:11 (KJV)

[11] And it came to pass, when Moses held up his hand, that Israel prevailed: and when he let down his hand, Amalek prevailed.

Now, some of you might be trying to rationalize this with human reasoning saying that the raising of the hands were a spiritual metaphor or symbolic. And I would almost agree if the scriptures weren't clear that his hands had to literally be raised for God's people to get the victory. They had to put a stone under him, because he had gotten tired in his humanity. And then Aaron and Hur had to literally hold up Moses' hands beloved.

Exodus 17:12-13 (KJV)

[12] But Moses' hands were heavy; and they took a stone, and put it under him, and he sat thereon; and Aaron and Hur stayed up his hands, the one on the one side, and the other on the other side; and his hands were steady until the going down of the sun. [13] And Joshua discomfited Amalek and his people with the edge of the sword.

We must understand that there is something about the upraised hands beloved. Our prayers are powerful without the raising of the hands and they ascend from our lips, but our hands act like powerful antenna's that picks up the signal that our prayers create and sends them with more force. It also symbolizes devotion, praise and worship at the same time.

The hand is one of the most important organs or limbs of the body. And the hand in the Bible has great meaning. For example, the expression "Jehovah's hand" signifies the Lord's power (Refer to Isa. 59:1 and Acts 4:28). And then we see in Proverbs 6:17 where it says, "Hands that shed innocent blood". So, in that case it represented murderous people, etc. So, what do we get out of this? We get that when our hands are clean, and our heart is pure, we can ask what we will in holy boldness, with our hands lifted, in praise, in reverence, and in power, as the Lord sends His mighty Angels to go forth in battle on our behalf. Mind you, that Moses was at war, so this is more in line with warfare prayer, because there are many situations where we will not be able to pray this way if you are praying all day without ceasing. However, there are times when we must get physical in our prayers, not as a matter of works, but as a matter of sincerity, fervency, and a difference of posture.

There are times when we must be audible in our prayers, because demons can't read our minds and needs to hear the commands and the Word of God launched against them to take away their legal rights. Another reason that we want to practice these kinds of prayers is because the great Apostle Paul told us to:

1 Timothy 2:8 (KJV)

8 Therefore I want the men everywhere to pray, lifting up holy hands without anger or disputing.

The question is are your hands holy? I can go on and on about being physical, such as with Jacob when he wrestled with God, physically, all night, before God blessed. Get the point beloved? Let's get physical.

The reason why this chapter is a must in a book like this is because when we pray to God we should never just go to God with a laundry list of items to be dealt with. We have to understand that we should go to God first of all because He is God, which means He is royalty, and when you present yourself before any royalty there is always protocol. Your ability to follow protocol a lot of times determines what kind of goodwill you will garner from them. And we should all want the will of God to be enacted in our lives, because His will is the only will that really matters. And right now, I hear someone saying, no just come as you are and it's all good right? Three words for you, Cain and Abel. God rejected Cain for a myriad of reasons, but one of them was protocol. God didn't want grass and vegetables, he wanted the blood (the life force) of certain animals. Cain's offering to God was very lackluster in regard to effort and showed an insincere heart. But we should go to God with a sincere heart, not looking at Him as a Santa Claus or genie, but as King of Kings and Lord of Lords. Therefore, in the same way that you would show the upmost respect and give all of the courtesy related to the throne or stature of a human dignitary, how much more so, should we honor God when we "call his phone" so to speak?

Of course, we should give Him more honor, courtesy, and reverence than anyone or anything else. The way we accomplish this is by giving Him the praise that He deserves and if you can really spend enough time with Him in praise, your praise will transcend into worship and before you know it, God will take over the whole communication process. Try it beloved, you're going to find that your prayer life will be taken to a whole another level. Before you know it, your spirit and God's Spirit will be in communion and you will be speaking in a language that only Heaven can decipher.

The last thing I'll say about this subject in this chapter is that what I am giving you is biblical and it also proven and tried. I know that there are a lot of manuals and now schools that try to intellectualize prayer, but I'd like to submit to you that many of those individuals don't believe in the power of prayer and approach it as a useless religious exercise.

Education does not breed experience. And anti-school does not mean anti-intellectualism. For example, I'd rather take advice from a person that has built 6 churches over 30 years and is currently doing many great things in the Kingdom than a person that has spent 6 or 8 years in school. I don't care what school (seminary) it is, it is NOT the same. In Christendom, we need to understand that just because we have been to school, doesn't mean that we know Jesus.

When I used to train Soldiers in the Army, I always remembered to tell that brand new 2LT to chill and learn from these crusty old sergeants before you say **anything**. The point always was to watch who you're talking too, because you don't know what they've done or the wisdom that they can teach you. And the bottom line is that we're all (supposedly) on the same team, so we should uplift each other, not delineate between who has the "Ivy League" Christian education and who doesn't.

Peter and Paul were both great theologians, with different assignments. The difference between them, is that one had walked with Jesus, lived with Jesus, talked to Jesus, prayed with Jesus, while the other "met" Jesus. So, while one, Peter, walked in His God given authority, given by Jesus Himself (Matt. 16:18), Paul always had to show and purport to everyone that he was in fact, an apostle, as well (1 Cor. 9:1).

He (Paul) was taught by the great Gamaliel, whom a lot of people don't realize, was baptized by Peter. Paul had more time to write because of his jail time, which of course was God ordained, because that was his assignment, not because he knew more than everyone else. Yes, he was very highly educated, even before his conversion, which would make him the right choice for the assignment that God had on his life. While there is many stressing on getting the letters behind their name there are many casting out demons in Jesus name and the like. **Many** seminary students don't know the first thing about these kinds of things because they've never been on the battlefield, and sadly, some don't even believe in this kind of stuff.

I just used one little example there. I, a very educated person, have learned over the years like Solomon, that all of these things are vanity (which is why bringing up your education is unnecessary). God is only impressed by our heart and lives and conduct that would, if we're doing it right, bring Him all of the glory. I rather be like Peter, whereas people got healed in his shadow. I rather be led by Peter, "perfectly flawed" who was there from the beginning and learned from all of his mistakes. He was an ordinary man, that had **been** with Jesus. Have you been with Jesus? No matter what your answer is your ability to invoke His presence via praise and worship will tell on you. I've met many people that claim to have this awesome prayer life that when they are put on the spot couldn't get pass the first sentence let alone create the correct atmosphere that pulls the virtue from the hem of our Lord's garment.

Acts 4:13 (KJV)

13 When they saw the courage of Peter and John and realized that they were unschooled, ordinary men, they were astonished and they took note that these men had been with Jesus.

Much love to you and all of the mighty men and women of God that has a heart to reach the world for Christ. God bless.

Heart Prayers

The most important part of prayer is not what we say to God but what He says to us.

Apostle Dr. Larry Birchett, Jr.

Isaiah 65:24

It shall come to pass That before they call, I will answer; And while they are still speaking, I will hear.

When Jesus went to the Garden of Gethsemane the only people He took with Him were Peter, James and John. Once He got to the garden He told them to wait a little distance away and then He went and prayed by Himself. This spot was known according to the book of John by all of His disciples, to be a place of prayer and solace for Jesus. That's how Judas knew where Jesus would be at when he decided to betray Him. How many of you know that sometimes we have to go to the garden alone so that we can have our private time with God? When you are really praying from your heart, guess what? It can get so raw that you better not have anybody around you. Some of you know what I mean. And these are the prayers that God loves, because He already knows what's in your heart anyway.

Prayer and privacy go together. I would submit to you that you don't really have a prayer life if you don't have a private time where it's just you and the Lord. Public prayer has its place and is very necessary, especially in a corporate setting or a consecrated assembly. But there are some truths and confessions in prayer that can only be communicated between you and God Himself.

Everyone don't need to know that you were tempted to use another person's credit card numbers to pay your bills or purchase something. Everyone don't need to know that you almost gave into your ex-lover that you ran into out of nowhere that offered you "a night: just for nostalgia sake. The general public doesn't need to know that you had a fleeting thought of running away from your family to relieve some of the pressures of life that you're dealing with. And on and on and on I could go making up scenarios that many real people run into and deal with every day. My advice to you is, confess your sins to God.

1 John 1:9 (KJV)

> [9] *If we confess our sins, He is faithful and just to forgive us our sins, and to cleanse us from all unrighteousness.*

We all can't go to the Mount of Olives and steal a few minutes away to pray but what we can do is build an altar where we go to meet with God all by ourselves. If we can't build an altar than what we can do is designate a prayer room where we go to do war with the devil. You could even call it your "War Room". If you can't do that, maybe your car could be your special place that you "get real" before the Lord. It could be the shower. It could be get to your office a half hour before everyone else and "soak" before the Lord. Whatever you have to do to really focus and more importantly, allow your spirit to focus and communicate with THE SPIRIT, do it. It's that critical.

I mentioned the term soak in the prior chapter. There is such a thing called Soaking Prayer. It is relevant in this chapter because most of what we call Heart Prayers or Heart Praying can be one of the initial steps to soaking. Soaking is exactly synonymous to the natural definition of immersion or submerging within water or another substance. Soaking is simply immersing yourself in the presence of God. It is positioning yourself in the love of God and dwelling in His secret place. It is losing yourself in the Holy Spirit via audile prayers, heart prayers, praying in the Spirit, crying, moaning, praising worshipping, singing, even dancing sometimes, and for those of us that has ever soaked overnight, sometimes it can include drifting into a heavenly sleep and reemerging with more praise and worship and prayer. It is tapping into God's love and His love flowing back through you. Refer to Psalms 91:

Psalms 91:1-4

[1]He that dwelleth in the secret place of the most High shall abide under the shadow of the Almighty.

[2]I will say of the LORD, He is my refuge and my fortress: my God; in him will I trust.

[3]Surely he shall deliver thee from the snare of the fowler, and from the noisome pestilence.

[4]He shall cover thee with his feathers, and under his wings shalt thou trust: his truth shall be thy shield and buckler.

A lot of people confuse Intercession or Intercessory Prayer with Soaking but it's not the same thing. Intercessory Prayer in literally interceding on behalf of someone else. It's laying out in the presence of God for someone else's situation. I think that the confusion has arisen from uneducated clerics following the error of other untrained spiritual leaders that has called soaking interceding. I'm not sure how the two can be intertwined or even used as a synonym because the definition of interceding and soaking are nowhere near the same in the natural or the spiritual. Now, can you intercede or engage in Intercessory Prayer in your time of Soaking? Yes, you can. But they are not the same thing. Let me be clear, I'm not referring to the demonic practice of soaking that one would do as a part of cults like Yoga. Practicing Yoga in its purest form is practicing the occult. It comprises of a group of physical, mental, and spiritual practices or disciplines which originated in ancient India. Hinduism, Buddhism, and Jainism all utilize a form of Yoga whose main goal is to make you "free yourself" so that demonic spirits can enter in. They do this under the guise of spiritual and physical wellbeing. The trick that the enemy uses is that the stretches are actually helpful and beneficial, but I have heard one ex-satan worshipper say that some of the moves are moves that one would use to open themselves up for the purpose of summoning spirits into their spirit. If you were ignorant before reading this, now you know the truth. Just stretch beloved without the rhythm and meditative qualities of the demonic practice of Yoga. Okay, let's move on.

In the beginning of Jesus' official ministry, He went into the wilderness and fasted for forty days and nights. Sometimes God will send you into a wilderness like experience just so that He can commune with you. Many times, our daily lives are so full of distractions and so God calls for a wilderness experience or two to get our attention. This may be the reason why everyone is leaving you and you're feeling all alone. Is God trying to commune with you? No matter where you go you must find a time where it is just you and Him. Because most of the times, it's in our alone time with God that we really get to know Him. The track record of Jehovah God is full of instances where He met with great men and women of God when they were by themselves. You can take Moses when He saw the burning bush. Abraham, when He consulted Him about Sodom and Gomorrah. Gideon, when He called him a great man of valor. And how about the time when He showed off for Elijah on the mountain top. I think it's safe to say that God chooses to make private, one on one connections with the individuals that He's trying to reach, because He is a personal God. What God has for you is for you, not your friend or family member.

David Wilkerson wrote, "Some do not come to God's throne because they think prayer must be audibly voiced. There is indeed a time to pray with the uplifted voice, to cry aloud, but I find my most effective praying is silent. IT IS THE VOICE OF THE HEART. This is heart crying, or heart praying."

When I refer to heart crying or praying, I want to take it a little bit further. In the first chapter of this book we started off talking about Philippians chapter 4 where it says that we're not supposed to be anxious for anything, but in everything, with prayer, supplication, and thanksgiving, let your requests be made known unto God and the peace of God that surpasses our understanding will overtake us. Question for you. Do you know what supplication mean? Supplication means to beg or to ask for something in earnest. In simple to request or petition. As it relates to the spiritual realm regarding prayer, it means to go to God in earnest as if you **would** beg Him, if the outcome of what you're petitioning God required it. Of course, we don't have to beg God because He said to come unto His throne of Grace boldly and we'll receive grace and mercy in Hebrews 4:16. But our heart should be so humble that in fact He understands that we understand that only He can grant whatever it is that we're requesting. Even Jesus supplicated when He prayed to His Father, "Give us this day our daily bread…".

Hebrews 4:16 (NKJV)

16 Let us therefore come boldly to the throne of grace, that we may obtain mercy and find grace to help in time of need.

I believe the word supplication was derived from the word supplicatio. In the ancient Roman religion, a supplicatio was a day of public prayer when the men, women, and children of Rome traveled in procession to religious sites around the city praying for divine aid in times of crisis. A supplicatio was also used as a thanksgiving after they had received the aid that they prayed for. Supplication is a formal petition to a superior authority. For instance, if you are pleading for your life or someone else's life, this would reach the level of a supplication. I'll talk a little bit more about supplication later in this chapter, so let's proceed a little bit further in our discussion regarding Heart Praying.

We minimize the effect of our prayers when we speak weakness to power in the form of statements like "It don't take all that" when we see someone going all out whether it's in their praise, worship, or prayer. When we take this stance, we are in fact exhibiting a superior attitude and essentially saying that they should be more like us. The problem with that is who's to say that you're giving God an effective praise, an authentic worship or that your prayers are fervent enough? **The most important part of prayer is not what we say or even how we say it, it is what God**

has to say to us. Therefore, please understand that God will only speak to a heart that is genuine and a spirit that is pure. Don't judge your spirituality against another person's spirituality because this kind of attitude, according to the Prophet Isaiah, is like smoke in God's nostrils.

Isaiah 65:24

Who say, 'Keep to yourself,
Do not come near me,
For I am holier than you!'
These are smoke in My nostrils,
A fire that burns all the day.

Their personality and methods may be different than yours, but it doesn't mean that they are not effective. Make sure that your heart is right before the Lord rather than inspecting someone else's. You never know the distress of someone else's heart. Let's look at David:

Psalms 120:1

In my distress I cried unto the LORD, and he heard me.

David is praying for relief from enemies that falsely accused him. It was a plea to God for help and strength in spite of the circumstances. His heart was in distress and one of David's ways of coping during these times, obviously was in his writings. David's writings were so effective that you and I are still reading them today. He was fervent in his writings, which is why there are many that we can choose from and his relationship with God was so evident that even his recorded prayers are being used by many of us daily, in our day and time. Take Psalms 23 for example:

Psalms 23
1 The LORD is my shepherd;
I shall not want.
2 He makes me to lie down in green pastures;

He leads me beside the still waters.
[3] *He restores my soul;*
He leads me in the paths of righteousness
For His name's sake.
[4] *Yea, though I walk through the valley of the shadow of death,*
I will fear no evil;
For You are with me;
Your rod and Your staff, they comfort me.
[5] *You prepare a table before me in the presence of my enemies;*
You anoint my head with oil;
My cup runs over.
[6] *Surely goodness and mercy shall follow me*
All the days of my life;
And I will dwell in the house of the LORD
Forever.

This psalm has been a psalm of comfort to many ever since he wrote it. David looked at God as his shepherd and he put his trust in God exclusively believing that God loved him so much that he would never be in need and that goodness and mercy would follow him all the days of his life. He believed this in his heart and he communicated this in the written word. The reason why it has lasted through the ages is because he wrote it from his heart.

Whatever we do from our heart will last through an eternity. The messages of the heart are eternal. The Bible says in Proverbs,

Proverbs 23:7

*For as **he thinketh in his heart, so is he**: Eat and drink, saith **he** to thee; but **his heart** is not with thee.*

God taught me a lot about the heart from this scripture and I'll give the revelation to you right now. Basically, we think with our heart and not our brain. Which is why the scripture says as "he thinketh in his heart". Because, our most serious decisions are not made with our brain, it's made from our heart. If you decide to marry someone, it's not a mind decision, because your mind will tell you that more than 50 percent of couples who try marriage end up with divorce, so stay single. But the love that you fill for the other person in your heart will lead you to make a decision that defies the logic of your brain and make a lifelong covenant. You've made a decision with your heart not your mind.

If your little son or daughter was about to get hit by a car and only you could save them by running into traffic and pushing them out of the way or shielding them with your body, would you do it? If you love your children, you have just undoubtedly said yes. This means that you would defy the rationale and logical thinking of the brain whereas you mind as well stay safe and have decided to put your life on the line just so that your child might have a chance to live. You've just made another heart decision beloved.

During your prenatal exam, the doctor informed you that your baby is going to be born with issues and that you should terminate the pregnancy. However, you've already seen the ultrasound pictures with the ten fingers and ten toes and heard the heart beat and everything. You don't even need a day to think about it and your response to the doctor is that you're not going to abort your baby. Your heart is full of compassion and love and you tell him that you would take care of that baby no matter what issues it has because it's a life that didn't ask to be here. The doctor will never understand but you do perfectly because your heart has directed you in this one, not your head.

Bottom line, "As a man thinketh in his heart so is he." We are the product of whatever comprises the totality of our heart. Are you an angry person? I guarantee anger is in your heart. Are you a lustful person? You're going to have to deal with this issue at a heart level. Are you bitter towards someone? This means that unforgiveness and resentment has made its bed within your heart. Do you berate people with your words? Are you still a curser? These are issues of the heart, not a psychologic issue.

Proverbs 4:23

Keep thy heart with all diligence; for out of it are the issues of life

Whatever comes out of our mouths had to first be filtered through the portals of our heart. It may not seem like it, but this is always true. A pure heart will filter every thought to whereas only pure and uplifting content will come forth. Whereas a wretched heart will emit filth and negative things that will tear down, offend, and displease God. One thing to keep in mind is that God is omniscient, meaning all knowing. So, He knows our thoughts even before we speak them or act them out. Again, the Word of the Lord from the Prophet Isaiah:

Isaiah 65:24

It shall come to pass That before they call, I will answer;
And while they are still speaking, I will hear.

Sometimes we can find ourselves in such an overwhelming situation that all we can do is grunt and groan and sometimes we're not able to say anything at all, but yet we are communicating with God. These are what we call heart prayers. I praise God that as Isaiah said, God sometimes send the answer before we even ask, based on the anticipation of our request. The Bible says in Jeremiah 29:11 that God has plans to *prosper us and keep us in good health*. Which means that if we need healing and it's in His will, He has already sent healing, based on the anticipation of our prayer. It means that He already has provision waiting for us, and all we need to do is ask for it, so that it can be released. Remember, Jesus said that *we have not because we ask not.*

A heart prayer is normally rendered when we are in a tough place in life. Heart prayers are silent or almost inaudible. They might be barely intelligible or unintelligible to the human senses, but you better believe that God is hearing the transmission. The Bible gives an example of a heart prayer in Hannah's silent and inaudible petition that we can find in 1 Samuel chapter 1.

1 Samuel 1:10-17

10 In her deep anguish Hannah prayed to the Lord, weeping
bitterly. 11 And she made a vow, saying, "Lord Almighty, if you will
only look on your servant's misery and remember me, and not
forget your servant but give her a son, then I will give him to
the Lord for all the days of his life, and no razor will ever be used
on his head."
12 As she kept on praying to the Lord, Eli observed her
mouth. 13 Hannah was praying in her heart, and her lips were
moving but her voice was not heard. Eli thought she was
drunk 14 and said to her, "How long are you going to stay drunk?
Put away your wine."
15 "Not so, my Lord," Hannah replied, "I am a woman who
is deeply troubled. I have not been drinking wine or beer; I was
pouring out my soul to the Lord. 16 Do not take your servant for a
wicked woman; I have been praying here out of my great anguish
and grief."
17 Eli answered, "Go in peace, and may the God of Israel
grant you what you have asked of him."

Hannah prayed silently, and Eli thought she was drunk or crazy. But the truth of the matter is that she wasn't crazy, she was in her right mind and as focused as she had ever been in her life. Her heart was broken, she was weeping bitterly, and she was doing warfare in her heart. As verse 13 states, she was praying in her heart. Guess what beloved? I believe that Hannah had learned a valuable lesson at this point of her life that I want to relate to you now. The reason why she had been continually defeated is because she had let the enemy know what her intentions were if God would ever allow a baby to be birthed by her. The enemy had kept her barren because he knew that there was a Samuel inside of her.

Just like Joseph when he was younger, Hannah had spoken a little too much into the atmosphere. I believe that she had always wanted to rear a spiritually strong and Godly son. I believe she knew that if she would ever be allowed to give birth that the baby was going to be special and she let her intentions be known about the baby before the baby was ever born. The reason why many of you are spiritually barren is because you let the devil know too much and so he has dispatched his strongest demons against you.

The principalities have your name on their radar and the Prince of Persia has erected delay portals for your prayers. The good thing is that delay don't mean denial, but the plan of the enemy is to wait until you can no longer effectively do what God has placed in your heart. He will fight against you and try his best to keep your womb barren beloved. It's not about you, it's about your seed. It's about your potential. It's about your purpose and indeed it's about what God has promised you.

When this happens, you have to know how to go into another realm. You have to be able to know how to P.U.S.H. **pray until something happens**. And I mean push in the spirit realm. Hannah, the enemy is trying to keep you barren. He doesn't want your prayer to be released until your ninety years old like Sarah. But the devil is a liar because God has ordained that you would read this book on this day at this time to learn how to warfare. The most important person on the battlefield besides the officer in charge is the person carrying the radio. Why? Because, if you can stop the communications between the unit and the rear, you can stop supply from coming in. If you can stop the communications between the unit and its command, you can stop intelligence from being communicated. If you can kill the person that knows how to work the radio you can kill the ability to receive the next set of orders. The enemy is after your words beloved and you have to learn how to not tell him everything. I urge you to ask God for a prayer language that only Heave can understand. We call this the gift of tongues. A spiritual language that only you and God can understand.

You have to know how to push some communications past the opposing forces with an encrypted message. In the spirit realm, our encryption method, can only be taught and given by the Holy Spirit. If you think that speaking in tongues is strange or hocus pocus, I'd have you know that in the occult they do the same thing, because satan is a counterfeiter. They call it demonic tongues. And that's why the Bible warns us to test the spirit by the Spirit. Not everyone who is speaking in an unknown tongue is speaking under the unction of the Holy Spirit. I've literally had to tell someone to shut up, because my spirit was being grieved by the demonic language that a person was trying to pass off as Godly. Right at the altar, I should say.

I want to explain why I keep saying the term push. We live in the natural world. However, God and the spirits, good and bad, live in the supernatural world. There are laws that govern both, but we can push the boundaries therein and accomplish great and mighty things. For example, in the natural world, we have the law of gravity. This means that whatever goes up must come down. This means that we can't fly and nothing that we put in the air should be able to fly if we just were to be regulated to the laws that govern our existence. However, God placed it in the human mind to dream that one day we'd be able to invent some kind of vessel that would be able to fly in the air in spite of the law of gravity.

Beloved, sometimes you just have to push pass the gravitational pull against your destiny! Sometimes you have to PUSH pass the gravitational pull against your purpose! You must be able to PUSH beyond every opposition that the kingdom of darkness tries to throw against you. Push through one dimension after the next, by loving God with all your might, all your heart, and all of your strength. No weapon formed against you shall prosper and the way that you defeat thc formation of those weapons is by our greatest weapon, namely prayer.

Stop telling the devil that if Ricky kiss you on your neck one more time you're going to cave in and give him anything he wants. If you keep telling him that Suzie is your weakness, get ready for a healthy dose of Suzie and every girl that looks like Suzie to walk in your life and suddenly take an interest in you. Stop telling the demons that you're weak towards certain things and that you're about to give up. Stop telling the devil all of your weakness, innermost desires, and plans because when he hears it, it lets him know that you have figured out your purpose. Once he has this information, he'll try to take your job, your family, and even your peace to distract you and cause you to be discouraged from your divine purpose.

This again is why Jesus, spoke in parables. Everything is not meant for everybody and He never cast His pearls before swine. Learn this lesson quickly beloved. It will save you from unnecessary warfare. This applies to mistakes as well. The Bible says that we all sin and fall short of the glory of God. So, when we sin we shouldn't be so surprised, and we must remember that the enemy and all of his imps sometimes don't even know that we've sinned. Again, only God is omniscient and so when we sin in our mind, for example, all we need to do is take it to God. We don't have to cry aloud in the streets so that every demon, principality, power, and ruler of darkness in high places know about it. John 1:9 says that if we confess our sins to God that He is faithful and just to forgive us. So, if you sin in your mind, pray from your heart to God for forgiveness because every thought is originated from your heart.

There are no specific instructions on praying silently or praying from your heart, but it doesn't mean that silent prayer is any less valid than prayers that are spoken aloud. Notwithstanding, that we see that Hannah did it and God answered her. Remember that God can hear our thoughts just as easily as He can hear our words. That's why we should pray like David prayed in Psalms 139:23-24.

Psalms 139:23-24

23 Search me, God, and know my heart;
test me and know my anxious thoughts.
24 See if there is any offensive way in me,
and lead me in the way everlasting.

Again, we see David understanding all of the attributes of our awesome and loving God and praying as such. The best thing about a person that knows how to pray internally so to speak, is that they also know how to hear internally. I want to repeat something that I mentioned earlier, which is, **the most important part of prayer is not what we say, but what God says unto us.** Praying is our vehicle of communicating with God. It is a spiritual transmission from the earth to Heaven and just like we send transmissions up, God sends transmissions back to us. This is the role of those that would consider themselves intercessors. When you are interceding, you are not only basking in the presence of God, you are praying on behalf of another.

And intercessor not only prays, but they dwell so long in God's presence that they start to hear His thoughts. Do you want to know the mind of God? How serious is your prayer life? The methodology of Jesus's prayer in Matthew 6 was **Adoration, Confession, Thanksgiving, and Supplication**. Notwithstanding the first part again was adoration. He adored His Father and spent some time loving on Him even with His words by saying, "Hallowed be Thy Name, Thy Kingdom come, Thy will be done!" How deep do you go? And then do you have the reverence and wisdom to just shut up and let God minister to you? Let's look at what David had to say in a few earlier scriptures in the same chapter.

Psalms 139:17-18

17 How precious to me are your thoughts, God!
How vast is the sum of them!
18 Were I to count them,
they would outnumber the grains of sand—
when I awake, I am still with you.

God knows our thoughts. We see that Jesus knew the evil thoughts of the Pharisees in Matthew 12:24-26 and Luke 11:17. Nothing we do, say, or think is hidden from God and He does not need to hear our words to know our thoughts. Never forget that He has access to all prayers directed to Him, whether spoke or unspoken.

We have an arsenal with God that can get us through any situation. When my wife, Prophetess Dr. Joanna Birchett, was in proceedings for deportation back to her native country of the West Indies, Jamaica, I had to take the stand. The reason why I had to take the stand, is because I had to explain to the judge how her deportation would be a hardship to me, an active duty Commissioned Officer in the US Army at the time, and our children. As I sat on the stand in my uniform, the first thing that the judge said to start the proceedings was, "I don't care who your husband is, but you overstayed your Visa and there are many people who would love to come to this country and you're going back to Jamaica today." She directed her comments at my wife who of course was moved to tears. As soon as she said this, I immediately started praying in my heart simultaneously, while I was speaking and being asked questions by the lawyer and judge on the stand. I knew that we were dealing with a spirit that was trying to abort our future, abort God's purpose for us, and destroy not only ours but our children's lives.

We had tremendous spiritual support at this hearing, whereas, our spiritual father, Bishop Earl Palmer, was there as well and I sensed that he, my wife, and myself all instantly went into prayer and intercession. The great thing is that we all knew what to do and we convened against the spirit of destruction at the same time. Lo and behold, after a brief break, we reconvened, and the first thing the judge said after she banged the gavel was, "Why are we here? Someone needs to tell me a good reason of why this woman needs to be separated from her children and her husband or this proceeding is going to be over!" Have you ever heard a shout in the spirit? Well that's what happened right in the courtroom. She proceeded to say after all the preliminaries were done that, "I'm only doing this on the account of your husband…." However, we all knew and know that she was doing it because of the work of the Holy Spirit:

Proverbs 21:1

The king's heart is in the hand of the LORD, as the rivers of water: he turneth it whithersoever he will.

It didn't matter how bad of a day that she was having or her bias towards people that have made honest mistakes, God had turned her heart toward His will and it was and is one of the greatest confirmations that He has given us regarding our union and our manifest destiny.

Heart praying is an essential skill to hone to go through the daily experiences that life will undoubtedly bring you. You can pray from your heart with your eyes wide open, even while someone else is speaking to you and God hears and Heaven is activated. While your boss is telling you that He is going to have to let you go, pray from your heart for direction. I commonly start praying when I realize that a total stranger or even a friend involves me in a conversation where they really need to hear a Word from the Lord right at that moment. When this happens, I will start praying from my inner man and ask God for wisdom. I'll pray, "God what would you have me to say to your child?" I'll pray this right while I'm looking at the person in the eyes.

Praying with awareness is an essential key to a deliverance minister or anyone that God is using in spiritual warfare. Praying with your eyes closed is good because it allows you to focus without distractions, but there are many times when you need to pray with your eyes wide open. Archbishop Desmond Tutu, a South African Anglican cleric who in 1984 received the Nobel Prize for Peace for his role in the opposition to apartheid in South Africa said this one time: "When the missionaries came to Africa they had the Bible and we had the land. They said, 'Let us pray.' We closed our eyes. When we opened them, we had the Bible and they had the land." Woah right? I can come from the many scriptures that tells us to watch as well as pray, but I think that Desmond Tutu has this point covered for us at the moment. It's okay to laugh beloved.

But when we learn to consistently pray heart prayers, guess what? We can pray all day. The Bible says pray without ceasing. That doesn't mean that you have to cut all of your hair off and go and join a monastery. It means that we have to know how to use our weaponry. There are many weapons of war in our arsenal. It's not by form or fashion that will make God incline His ear towards you. It's based off of an intentional relationship that we build with Him. He promised us that if we draw nigh to Him, that He would draw nigh to us (James 4:8).

I keep telling you to push. Let me give you the definition of push. Push: A **vigorous** (strong, healthy, forceful, full of energy) **effort to do or obtain something!** Your prayers are a force to be reckoned with and the more you pray the more power you're putting behind your request from the Lord. More prayer, more power. Less prayer, less power.

Supplication, again is a key part of most Heart Prayers. Most of the time when we get to the point of praying like Hannah prayed at the altar we are almost undoubtedly supplicating as well. Supplication is that act of earnestly begging someone for something with humility. It could be for yourself, it could of course be for someone else. But God instructed us to supplicate just like Hannah was doing, on her knees, at the altar, crying out to the Lord. He told us to supplicate in Paul's letter to the church in Philippi:

Philippians 4:6–7

6 Be careful for nothing; but in everything by prayer and supplication with thanksgiving let your requests be made known unto God. 7 And the peace of God, which passeth all understanding, shall keep your hearts and minds through Christ Jesus.

God totally expected us to come to Him before Him in supplication at certain points in our life. Of course, we don't have to beg, we can come before His throne of Grace boldly the Bible says. However, one must understand, that the spirit behind the word supplication means that you have to understand that there is no other place to go. If God don't do it for you, it won't get done. It's the feeling of Lord if there is anything that I can do to enlist your help in my cause, I'm here for it, and I'm willing to beg. That's why we all have so many instances in our life to bring us to this point because God desires it. Remember the scripture say *but in everything by prayer and supplication with thanksgiving.* God didn't say you might supplicate, He said you will. Pray and supplicate and don't forget to be thankful because God has been so good to you.

Purpose (definition): the reason for which something is done or created or for which something exists. Beloved, we must understand that we were created to worship God. We were created to Praise God. And we were created for relationship with God. The number one reason why most relationships fail after finances is communication. We must communicate with God in order to learn more about Him. We must communicate with God to grow stronger in Him. And we must communicate with God to learn His secrets. He who dwelleth in the secret place of the Most High, shall abide under His shadow. In order to live in this place of His presence it's going to require a push beloved. A push in the spirit realm. You're going to have push pass every gravitational pull against your destiny. In God there are no boundaries. In God Grace defeats law. And in God all things are possible. Your destiny is calling, when you pray, pray for His grace.

The Greek of the word gifts in the New Testament is charisma. Which can also be translated as grace. When God blesses us with a spiritual gift he has graced us with an ability. Every gift is in fact an individual grace, and we all have a measure of each one. Do you have the gift of healing? Well then God has given you the grace to heal in His name. Do you have the gift of prophecy? Well then God has given you the grace to prophesy in His name for His glory. And so on and so on. Somebody is saying, "I don't know what to pray for." Pray for more of His grace beloved. JEHOVAH, the name given in the Old Testament Scriptures to the Supreme Being, the great Creator of the universe, is described by the Apostle Peter as the "God of all grace." (I Pet. 5:10).

1 Peter 5:10-11

10But the God of all grace, who hath called us unto his eternal glory by Christ Jesus, after that ye have suffered a while, make you perfect, stablish, strengthen, settle you.
11To him be glory and dominion for ever and ever. Amen.

Pray to Him while He is near beloved. God bless.

Blessings and Curses

Ephesians 1 *(NKJV)*

1 Paul, an apostle of Jesus Christ by the will of God, To the saints
who are in Ephesus, and faithful in Christ Jesus:

2 Grace to you and peace from God our Father and the Lord Jesus
Christ.

3 Blessed be the God and Father of our Lord Jesus Christ, who has
blessed us with every spiritual blessing in the heavenly places in
Christ, 4 just as He chose us in Him before the foundation of the
world, that we should be holy and without blame before Him in
love, 5 having predestined us to adoption as sons by Jesus Christ to
Himself, according to the good pleasure of His will, 6 to the praise
of the glory of His grace, by which He made us accepted in the
Beloved.

7 In Him we have redemption through His blood, the forgiveness of
sins, according to the riches of His grace 8 which He made to
abound toward us in all wisdom and prudence, 9 having made
known to us the mystery of His will, according to His good
pleasure which He purposed in Himself, 10 that in the dispensation
of the fullness of the times He might gather together in one all
things in Christ, both which are in heaven and which are on
earth—in Him. 11 In Him also we have obtained an inheritance,
being predestined according to the purpose of Him who works all

things according to the counsel of His will, [12] *that we who first trusted in Christ should be to the praise of His glory.*

Beloved many churches and preachers tend to focus on getting a blessing. What they tell you is that if you pay one thousand dollars that God will bless you. Or what they will say is that if your works surpass some man drawn line, that it will move God to bless to you, right? Guess what? I want to let you in on something. According to Ephesians 1:3 and Ephesians 2:10, God has **already** blessed us. He's not getting ready to bless us. He's not manufacturing a blessing. He's not conjuring up a blessing. Our blessings are already determined. But we have an enemy and forces that keeps them away from us. Unfortunately, sometimes that enemy is **us**! As I routinely tell my congregation in Carlisle, PA regarding delays and denials concerning our blessings, "Sometimes the issue iss-ue!" Get it? I'm saying that sometimes the issue is you. I also like to say this regarding the enemy; "Sometimes the enemy is inna me!" I'm laughing right now and hopefully you are too but the point that I'm making is still valid and true.

Even though we are definitely in a spiritual battle and are daily fighting against unseen spiritual forces, many times we give the enemy too much credit, because we refuse to even admit that we're not where we need to be, for some of us. And for the rest of us, everybody else and their mother has a problem except for us. All of this is demonic but not always being driven one. How many of you know that a human can be enact far more wickedness on this earth than any fallen spirit ever could. As a matter of fact, these fallen spirits can't do anything without a willing vessel. They need you. They need us.

Let's get real for a minute. Is it a demon's fault that we don't have the discipline to get out and exercise so that our natural body will remain in good condition? How many demons have ever manifested and stuffed Ice Cream and Cheesecake and Soda down your throat? Can demons force us to think about things that God say we shouldn't? I didn't ask you how many suggestions that they've tried to lob into your hearing. I asked can they make you think on their evil suggestions? Of course, the answer to all of these questions is no, they can't make us do any of these things. How about our money though, can they affect that? Hold your answer to that one until after you finish this chapter.

What is a blessing? A blessing is a spiritual endowment that only God can give you. A blessing is also a gift that God has placed in you to do what you can't do on your own. It is the raw material that comprise the good things that God has planned for our lives. Such as a good marriage, a good job or career, and even healthy children. These are all blessings from God. These are things that God giveth and God taketh away.

Likewise, a curse is a spiritual endowment that comes upon you through **legal** means in the spirit realm to **stop** that already pre-ordained blessing. According to the Oxford Dictionary a curse is the following: a solemn utterance intended to invoke a supernatural power to inflict harm or punishment on someone or something. Which tells us what? Words can curse us! It doesn't matter who's mouth they come out of.

Proverbs 18:21 (KJV)

21 Death and life are in the power of the tongue: and they that love it shall eat the fruit thereof.

Message Bible: *21 Words kill, words give life; they're either poison or fruit—you choose.*

We have the ability to bless ourselves and agree with the blessings that God says are ours and we have the ability to abort those same blessings and hence, receive the curse. Just like we are what we eat in the natural, so it is in the spirit world and we have to learn to speak life over our lives so that we can live the purpose filled life that God created us for. How do we eat life? By digesting the Word of God in our hearts. We have to get the Word of God in us and not just by way of head information, like a seminarian, but in faith, because we are more spiritual than physical. This is a spiritual battle. And we have to actually believe and understand that the scriptures are the laws and principles of God that gives us the authority to wield spiritual power. I like the way that Solomon puts it in the Old Testament:

Proverbs 4:21-22 (KJV)

[21] Let them not depart from thine eyes; keep them in the midst of thine heart.

[22] For they are life unto those that find them, and health to all their flesh.

I also like how Paul put it in the New Testament:

Romans 10:17

[17] So then faith cometh by hearing, and hearing by the word of God.

The Bible is the key that God has given us to unlock spiritual things, especially blessings. God said to us in Jeremiah 29:11 that above all He wants to prosper us and keep us in good health. We just have to learn how to unlock the blessings that God has for us.

Get rid of the **God is getting ready to** doctrine and understand that **God has already done all things.** We don't serve a halfway God, we serve an **all**-powerful God and does **all** things well. When we read in the Bible that God rested on the seventh day, it meant that there was nothing else left for Him to do. He has already blessed in the Heavenly realms with every spiritual blessing that we'll ever need. I know this is the first time that some of you have ever heard this, but it's true. All of the blessings that you'll ever receive in this life has already been determined, planned, and scheduled according to the providence of God. The key is to come in agreement with what God has already established and ensure our receipt of these blessings on this side of life. That is what I'm going to teach you in this chapter.

What is it that you really need from the Lord? Do you need healing? Could you stand a little prosperity in your life? I'm not even going to ask you about money. But know this, **the truth is that you don't need the Lord to do anything for you.** He's already done His part. You've already got it, whatever "it" is.

You might be saying but the doctor's report is telling me one thing and my bank account is telling me another. I get it. But regardless of what the natural facts are, the truth is that God has already given you whatever you need. Paul is not the only person telling us this in the Word of God. Let's look at what Peter had to say:

2 Peter 1:3

According as His divine power hath given unto us ***all things*** *that pertain unto life and godliness, through the knowledge of him that hath called us to glory and virtue.*

Peter is saying that according to God's divine foresight and infinite power He has given us all things that pertain to this life to be Godly. This is a beautiful piece of knowledge. Because when you own this fact you start walking through this life looking for His provision and blessings.

I can't tell you how many times since I've learned this principle, that these scriptures have filled my heart with peace. There have been times when I didn't have enough money in my bank account to pay the mortgage and the mortgage was beyond due and God came through. One time I was two months behind in my mortgage, while at the same time Pastoring a church, and had just been released from my job. Unfortunately, the church I was pastoring wasn't financially stable enough to pay me a salary so all I had to lean on was this principle that according to God's divine power and foresight, He had already pre-positioned everything that I would ever need to make it through this tough season. All I had to do was look for it, trust God, and then do the hardest part, which was wait on God. Waiting on God is not easy, but it is something that we all will have to do at one point or another in our Christian walk. That's why my favorite scripture is in the book of Isaiah:

Isaiah 40:31

[31] But they that wait upon the Lord shall renew their strength; they shall mount up with wings as eagles; they shall run, and not be weary; and they shall walk, and not faint.

See, you don't know what it is like to wait on God until you don't have any recourse but to wait on Him. Some of us can go through these seasons privately and endure it personally. I had to wait on God and still encouraging people every day. I still had to preach that God will come through for you. I had to yell from the hilltops that our God will never leave us nor forsake us, at the same time, waiting for Him to show up in my own life. If you've ever been in one of these seasons, you need to say "Amen" beloved. If you're in this season right now read another scripture in Paul's letter to Ephesus:

Ephesians 2:10

[10] For we are his workmanship, created in Christ Jesus unto good works, which God hath before ordained that we should walk in them.

God will always come through for us when we apply His principles and laws. However, like the Prophet Hosea said we can't apply what we don't know:

Hosea 4:6

[6] My people are destroyed for lack of knowledge: because thou hast rejected knowledge, I will also reject thee, that thou shalt be no priest to me: seeing thou hast forgotten the law of thy God, I will also forget thy children.

The only thing that the most of us lacks is knowledge. But now that is not the case for you because God directed you to this material. Now you shouldn't be anxious about anything, but in prayer and supplication with thanksgiving you should just make your request to God and dwell in His peace that surpasses all understanding.

Most Christians believe that God can do anything, but if you were to ask them how much God has done for them already they would look at you with a blank stare. We need to remember that God has done a lot for us already and stop living in a constant state of trying to get God to perform. Stop praying to get got to move and start praying a different way. Start agreeing with His already established Word, which is His spiritual principles and laws.

Stop begging God to move through revival, healing, prosperity, social status, etc. Stop running from church to church. Stop running from meeting to meeting, trying to obtain something that is already yours.

God is immensely powerful and what you've just learned is not out of the realm of His powers. He has no beginning or ending, and time is not linear in God. Time is more like a bubble for God, if that makes sense. He can see through it. If you were able to blow a lot of bubbles and then look at them, that is a good representation of how God looks at the bubble or dimension of our time and age. The many bubbles undoubtedly would represent the many universes that God is constantly monitoring.

So, I will say only one more time in this chapter that our blessings are already determined for us **(Eph. 1:4, Eph. 2:10)**. We have to learn how to come in agreement with the blessings and then we can receive our portion.

. [10] *For we are His workmanship, created in Christ Jesus for good works, which God prepared beforehand that we should walk in them.*

Dreams

Earlier, I said that we have everything but we 're lacking knowledge of this fact, and if we do know this, then we are ignorant of the devil's devices to steal **(John 10:10)** from us. One of the methods that the thief uses to steal from us is our dreams. Did you know that the enemy makes covenants with us in our dreams? The enemy initiate curses on us in our dreams. And sometimes chief demons show up in our dreams to thwart our purpose and sabotage our promise in God. These demons could be Poverty, Cancer, Premature Death, Anger, Unforgiveness, Pride, Bitterness, etc. These demons, when we come in agreement with them cast spells and perform witchcraft on us in our sleep. See, God wants to bless us, but we don't realize that we're in a spiritual battle **(Eph.6:12)** and hence, the enemy does malicious things to us while our body is sleeping.

Matthew 13:25

25 But while men slept, his enemy came and sowed tares among the wheat, and went his way.

When our body sleeps, the spirit is still awake. Our spirit doesn't need sleep. And what the enemy tries to do with us is enact curses from prince ruling spirits as well as human agents, such as wizards, witches, sorcerers, wiccan, warlocks, root workers, voodoo practitioners, psychics, tarot card readers, false teachers/preachers/prophets, and the like to our spirit. Why? Because whatever happens in the spirit world has to manifest in the natural. Sometimes we're even being bombarded by spirits sent to us by people that have spoken angry and condemning words concerning us. Bottom line, everything is spiritual and never ever think that the random dream that you had the night before was just coincidental or nothing to even think about again, because it's not true.

I want to talk about one of the main spirits that the enemy uses to keep us subject; Poverty. Do you feel like just like when things start going well something always comes up to mess it up? You take 1 step forward and then take 2 steps back? You are next in line for the promotion at your job, but they say, "Oh we have to give it to this person because of direction from management, but don't worry you're next." **These types of things are symptoms of the spirit of poverty in your life!**

Before I go all of the way there, let me explain some things about your dreams.
Do you have dreams of roaches and mice? These kinds of dreams are revealing the spirit of Poverty in your life. If you don't have the ability to conduct spiritual warfare in the dream, you should immediately wake up, rebuke the dream, renounce covenants, break ties, and ultimately cast down this dream. The other thing that you should do is send back every curse or witchcraft to sender in Jesus name.

Do you have dreams of walking around in raggedy and tattered clothes? That's the spirit of poverty. How about dreams of you looking down and noticing that your shoes has holes in them? That's the Spirit of Poverty. Have you ever seen yourself begging in your dream? Again, it's a threat from the spirit of poverty. How about losing your wallet? Have you ever dreamed of losing your wallet? The spirit of poverty is forecasting that the attack that he is trying to get you to come in agreement with will cause you to **lose what god has already given you.** Remember John 10:10, understanding that the enemy comes to kill, steal, and destroy.

When you see these things, know that **A. It's the enemy. B. He needs your agreement**. A dream that you can't find your money is a classic one. Which is showing a robbing or thief demon that will try to operate in your life unless you renounce, rebuke, and cast down his dirty works. Also, a dream that you just made it to the ATM but you can't remember your Pin number is showing that an attack of delay by mental routes can be expected.

Expect a battle in your mind. For example, after this type of dream if you find that you are dealing with conditions such as Depression or Bi-Polarism get to warfaring in the spirit realm right away. If you noticeably start becoming cynical and even negative about things that you were supportive of before, you want to get warfaring in the spirit realm right away. God gave you a spirit of power, love, and a sound mind, not an unstable mind. Schizophrenia and even anger come to take your peace and you must rebuke, renounce, cast down satan's dirty works and then call on Jehovah Shalom, the God of all peace.

I've been throwing around this word renounce. Renounce means to formally declare one's abandonment to something. It means to take away your right to a claim or possession. One of the first things that you have to do when you are possibly making these spiritual covenants, whether in your dream life, daily confessions, or otherwise, is renounce those things. The best way to do this is to speak it out. After we accept Christ as our Savior the very next thing that any minister should teach the new convert is how to renounce everything that was evil in their lives prior to accepting Christ. This is a spiritual act that can only be done by you, not for you.

Your mother or father, as well intentioned as they may be, can't renounce the works of the occult and all of the rest of the evil covenants that you have made in your life, only you can do that. Your Pastor, your Prophet, your Apostle, your Bishop, can't do these things for you, only you can do this for yourself.

What we would want to do, is renounce our past involvement with any works of darkness. We can take it further even by renouncing works of darkness engaged in by our ancestors. Renunciation of our sins cleanses us from all unrighteousness, however, it is the renunciation of the sins of our ancestors that releases us from their sins. A sample way to pray to renounce everything that we might have engaged in or is currently being affected by is the following:

I forgive any person who has ever hurt me, disappointed me, abandoned me, mistreated me, or rejected me in the name of Jesus.

I renounce all hatred, anger, aggression, resentment, revenge, retaliation, unforgiveness and bitterness in the name of Jesus.

I renounce all pride, haughtiness, arrogance, vanity, ego, disobedience and rebellion in the name of Jesus.

I renounce all envy, jealousy, and covetousness in the name of Jesus.

I renounce all selfishness, self-will, self-pity, self-rejection, self-hatred and self-promotion in the name of Jesus.

I renounce all backsliding, ingratitude, unthankfulness, murmuring, complaining and falsely accusing.

I renounce all lust, perversion, immorality, uncleanness, impurity, and sexual sin in the name of Jesus.

I renounce all addiction to drugs, alcohol, or any legal or illegal substance that has bound me in the name of Jesus.

I renounce all witchcraft, sorcery, divination, and occult involvement in the name of Jesus.

I renounce all ungodly soul ties and immoral relationships in the name of Jesus.

I renounce all ungodly covenants, oaths and vows made by myself or my ancestors in the name of Jesus.

I renounce all ungodly thought patterns and belief systems in the name of Jesus.

Congratulations, you have formally declared your abandonment to all of the things that we've just prayed about prior. Feel free to make all the prayers that I'm given you in this book your own. I'm sure that as you are engaging in spiritual warfare as you read this book, the Holy Spirit within you is speaking to you and giving you, even more explicit instructions concerning you and your specific bloodline and purpose. We have renounced just now generally after the fact, so to speak. However, if you are engaging these kinds of spirits in your dream you should renounce and rebuke these things while you're in the dream. However, if you wake up and find out that one of these things happened and you didn't bind, rebuke, or renounce in the dream it's okay. Just do it in your earliest waking moments.

Binding, rebuking, and renouncing while you are actually in your dream takes skill and experience, because many of us have gone our whole lives thinking that our dreams were just random thoughts and mental word pictures that we didn't have any control over. So, what happens is that we have been falling asleep and allowing our dreams to take us wherever it wanted to our whole lives. I'm here to tell you that we actually can control our actions in our respective dreams and that we should. The real you is your spirit, not your physical body, so you are never more real than when you are dreaming. So, conducting spiritual warfare in your dream is the best course of action however, let me reiterate, if you don't do it in the dream, all you have to do is renounce these things and rebuke these things **as soon as you wake up.** Write them down. Remember them. Forgetting them is part of the enemies' strategy.

I suggest that you buy yourself a prayer journal to record every dream that you can remember. If you notice, you're only able to remember a dream for about the first five minutes after waking up. That's because it's the enemy's job to steal your dream from you as soon as you enter physical non-sleep consciousness, if he can. He does this because he knows the power of God's messages, warnings, blessings, and other things that can be transmitted in your dreams. The other part is that he doesn't want you to remember that you were just cursed and made covenant with him in your dream.

If you don't renounce or rebuke these spiritual assignments, then you have just come into agreement with the witchcraft that has just been performed on you. For example, some of you have made a covenant with the spirit of Poverty. If you are having a dream of sexual intercourse between yourself and someone else in your dream, I guarantee that a demon has just initiated and sealed a covenant with you in the spirit realm that you have to wake up and rebuke, renounce, and cast down immediately. When you come into agreement with a demon you create a covenant. A covenant is basically a contract. And just like the terms of a natural contract the terms in the spirit will go in line with whatever kind of spirit you encountered in your dream. So, if you had sex in your dream with a poverty spirit, for example, you can expect gradual streamlining of all of your resources. Cars will mysteriously break down. People will suddenly get fired. Doctor bills will accumulate out of nowhere.

Another one, is if you go to an ATM and as soon as you get there, the power shuts off! This is the spirit of financial delay. You better rebuke that thing off of your life or nothing will work for you.

How do you know you're dealing with a spirit and it's not just life? Number one, would be unexplained rejection. Everybody else is getting approved and your portfolio is better than theirs but yours is getting rejected.

Another thing is that sometimes infirmity is connected to the root spirit of poverty. You're stressing and making yourself sick because of lack. But the truth is that there is nothing wrong with you. It is the spirt of poverty kicking your butt. Stress can cause more infirmity than infirmity can. Remember that.

That headache that you're having is because you're worrying about how you're going to pay your mortgage or your rent bill, or your car payment. But the Word of God tells us in **Philippians 4**, *not to worry about anything but in everything, with prayer and* *supplication to make our requests known unto God and the peace of God that surpasses all understanding will guard our hearts and minds through Christ Jesus.* So, when we look at our issues from a Godly perspective we'll understanding that worry is not of God and is in fact, a sin. And the wages of sin are death. So, let's stop worrying and let's start receiving the awesome and priceless gift of God, which is eternal life.

> **Proverbs 10:15** ~ [15] *The rich man's wealth is his strong city: the destruction of the poor is their poverty.*
>
> *Message Bible* [15]*The wealth of the rich is their bastion; the poverty of the indigent is their ruin.*
>
> **Proverbs 14:20** ~ [20] *The poor is hated even of his own neighbour: but the rich hath many friends.* ***Message Bible*** [20]*An unlucky loser is shunned by all, but everyone loves a winner.*

You might have been that unlucky loser or better yet be that poor man or woman of Proverbs 14 but I'm here to tell you that you can break every covenant that you've made knowingly or unknowingly. You can break every curse that you've made knowingly or unknowingly. You can make null and void every known or unknown agreement. And you can retract every daily confession.

Proverbs 18:21

King James Version [21] *Death and life are in the power of the tongue: and they that love it shall eat the fruit thereof.*

Message Bible: [21] *Words kill, words give life; they're either poison or fruit—you choose.*

Prayer against the spirit of poverty:

Father, if anyone have projected the spirit of poverty against my life or if it has entered into my life through generational curses, or if there are certain things that I have been confessing, this day I break the covenants. This day, I break every affiliation with these spirits, and on this day, I declare and decree that they will no longer work along with my consent to bring my own demise. I burn every covenant with the Holy Ghost fire from Heaven that Elijah used against the false prophets. I apply the blood of Jesus between me and every curse. Every known and unknown agreement in the spiritual or natural is cut and burned by fire and by force in the name of Jesus. And I cast down every self-defeating daily confession right now with the blood of Jesus and the work of His cross and today their works are done in my life.

Somebody needs to rejoice. God says above all He wishes that we prosper and be in good health. God says that we are lenders and not borrowers. God says that we are the head and not the tail. We are above and not beneath. God says that no weapon that is formed against us shall prosper. Every tongue that rise against us we shall condemn.

Stop agreeing with the world and condemning the Saints and start condemning the enemy and agreeing with God's Word. Come into agreement with the Word of God and let it do what it do. I know that you've been down for a while, but we have to remember that a diamond is merely a lump of coal that did well under pressure.

Why did I use the illustration of a diamond working well under pressure? Because many of us have the potential to win and succeed in spite of the pressure that we're enduring however, we're not all the same. Meaning that we don't all have the same emotional intelligence. We don't all have the same emotional toughness, let alone spiritual.

Another illustration would be a boxing match. Some people can get hit by the same person and endure the hit and remain in the fight to the end, whereas, given the same conditions and boxer, there are some that can't take a hit. Mike Tyson, considered to be one of the hardest punchers of all times, fought many people. Many of them couldn't endure but a few rounds of his offensive onslaught, while there were many that could endure them all and give it back. Buster Douglass did get knocked down by Mike Tyson, but when he was on the floor, he thought to himself, "Is that all it is?". Meaning, like is that the punch, or the force that I've been dreading all of this time? And he got back up and proceeded to knock Mike Tyson out. Evander Holyfield took all of Mike Tyson punches and beat him twice. The last time he knocked Mike Tyson out as well. See, the difference between winners and losers is in the attitude and mindset that says, I am not going to be defeated no matter what I get hit with. Some people get knocked down and then get counted out. However, just because you get hit, doesn't mean you have to fall. And just because you fall doesn't mean that you have to stay down for the count. Get back up somebody.

It's not the getting knocked down that makes you lose. It's how long you stay down. You're in a spiritual warfare but **Ephesians 2:3** states:

[3] Blessed be the God and Father of our Lord Jesus Christ, who has blessed us with every spiritual blessing in the heavenly places in Christ,

Don't give up! Don't give in! Don't lose hope! Keep hope alive! And if you're tired of starting over then stop giving up!

Now, let me relate all of this back to prayer because this chapter is specifically talking about blessings and curses. We all want to be able to endure a hard thing when we have to go through, but the truth is the strength to endure, only comes from God. Some of you (us) have been praying to God and wonder why it seems like our prayers aren't being answered or that He's not hearing us. I want to ask you a question. The question would be, how is your attendance in church? Consider Proverbs 28:

Proverbs 28:9

[9] He that turneth away his ear from hearing the law, even his prayer shall be abomination.

Did you know that not being under the hearing of the word of God, causes a curse on your prayer life? You might as well stop praying because God doesn't want to hear them. He that turns his ear from hearing the law, meaning the Word of God, the Bible says that this person's prayer is an abomination. Find a church that you are compatible with. That preaches and teaches the unadulterated Word of God, that you have the ability to serve in, if possible, and then watch your prayer life go to the next level.

Ecclesiastes 8:4

[4] Where the word of a king is, there is power; And who may say to him, "What are you doing?"

When I was a commissioned officer I had the power to enlist Soldiers into the United States Army by having them recite an oath that I would lead them through. The power in my body, specifically, my mouth to say the words would mean nothing without the authority given to me through my commission, that is signed and sealed via the President of the United States. There is a difference between power and authority. Anyone can recite the same words that I did in front of new enlistees, however, unless they were commissioned with the authority that I was given by the US Army and the President of the United States their words would've simply been just that, words. Likewise, our prayers are taken as serious as our lifestyle and relationship with God shows. If you don't like God's house, God's people, and especially, God's word and the hearing of God's Word, then what authority do you really have when you try to use it?

The purpose of this book is to ensure that your prayer life is successful. Success will never lower its standards to accommodate you beloved. Instead it will be you that will have to raise your standards to achieve it. God provides to all birds but not in their nests. Sometimes effort is better than skill. So, get up arise and face the challenge. Dare what others fear. Get in the house of God. Get in the Word of God. Live it and love it and let God fill you with more of His power, wisdom, knowledge, and understanding. Destiny is calling.

Spiritual Warfare Prayer Manual

I rather teach one person how to pray than teach ten people how to preach.

Charles Spurgeon

The following Spiritual Warfare Prayers are sample prayers. They are not to be used as rituals or as incantations. They are simply a guide to go by. I don't believe in praying every day from a piece of paper, however, there are times in our lives when it is hard to pray. And there is nothing wrong with having something that is written down on paper to focus your thoughts and get back on track with your prayer life. This has happened to me many times and I praise God that I had my own personal prayer manual to center myself, so to speak, in prayer, beneath a Holy God. With that said, many on the other side (occultists) pray from books and manuals all of the time. So, don't feel weird because even before I started using prayer manuals or the writing of this book I would find the scriptures that I wanted to pray back to the Lord so that I could pray them word by word and in excellence. Some or all of these prayers should be prayed daily, and sometimes often during the day. This is a manual, so it is not indented just like my favorite prayer manual before I created my own, The Moody Prayer Manual. Just like the Moody Prayer Manual, I don't mind you sharing these prayers and redistributing them throughout the world. We need everyone in the world to pray these prayers.

Before we get to the prayers, let me lay this foundation. Jesus said to the Pharisees in the book of Luke:

Luke 13:32 (KJV)

[32]I drive out demons and perform healings today and tomorrow and the third day I shall be perfected.

When Jesus was sending out the 12 Apostles He said:

Matthew 10:5-8 (NKJV)

[5] These twelve Jesus sent out and commanded them, saying: "Do not go into the way of the Gentiles, and do not enter a city of the Samaritans. [6] But go rather to the lost sheep of the house of Israel.
[7] And as you go, preach, saying, 'The kingdom of heaven is at hand.' [8] Heal the sick, cleanse the lepers, raise the dead, cast out demons. Freely you have received, freely give.

In Mark 16:17 Jesus said this:

Mark 16:17 (NKJV)

[17] And these signs will follow those who believe: In My name they will cast out demons; they will speak with new tongues;

If you have been praying for the same old problem time and time again and nothing has happened, I would like to submit to you that maybe deliverance is really the issue. Have you gone to the altar at your church for prayer regarding addictions, fear, alcohol, depression, abuse, or more things, to no avail? If it hasn't worked, you need deliverance. More specifically you need to cast those demons out.

When Jesus operated in deliverance, He casted demons out, He didn't pray them out. If you are being oppressed or being held hostage by demonic forces you must be delivered. If you are being held captive you can be set free with deliverance. If God has gifted you with the ability to deliver others from these kinds of situations just know that the captives can only be set free with deliverance.

Deliverance can help any problem or habit. If you have a drug addiction you need to be delivered. If you have a sex addiction you need to be delivered from the lust demon that is holding you hostage. If you are a drug addict then you need to be delivered from the demon of idolatry, because when you are using you are worshipping particular demons. Pharmakeia is the Greek word used for spell making, magic, and sorcery in the New Testament. It is the root of the word that we use in our modern English language, called Pharmacy. For this reason, many sects of Christianity do not partake in modern medicine at all due to the inception of it. The early medicine men and medicine women were really sorcerers and sorceresses. Now some take it to the extreme such as the Jehovah Witness and the Amish or Mennonite, but please understand that there is some merit to the discussion. I'm not saying that all medicine is from the devil, because it is not, however, please take the knowledge that you have just learned and apply it to all of your future decisions. Back to deliverance.

I have good news for you. Demons come out in Jesus name and it's free. You don't have to pay anyone hundreds of dollars. You don't have to pay big money for a sanctified scarf or handkerchief that will not work anyway. All you have to do is kick them out in Jesus name. Let's get to the prayers, however, say this prayer before you start kicking out any demons.

BEFORE DELIVERANCE PRAYER

Father God, I come before you in Jesus' name, and I thank you for giving me all power and all authority over all demons. I cover myself in the blood of Jesus. I cover all my family members in the blood of Jesus. I thank you for your giant warring angels that are surrounding us, protecting us from all harm of the enemy. I take my authority and I attack from the third Heaven, and I bind the strongman over my mind, will, emotions, and over my home, in Jesus' name. I command you to leave this area now in Jesus' name. I bind up every demon that was sent to me, transferred to me, or followed me, and I command you to come out of my conscious, subconscious, unconscious mind, all parts of my body, will, emotions, and personality, in Jesus' name.

ANOTHER SAMPLE PRAYER BEFORE DELIVERANCE

Father God, in the name of Jesus:

According to Romans 10:9, I confess with my lips that JESUS is Lord, and in my heart I believe that You raised Him from the dead. According to Luke 13:3 I repent of my past sins and I admit and confess that I have sinned, and I believe that You are faithful and just to cleanse me from all unrighteousness. So, I call upon You, Lord Jesus to cleanse me from all sin and unrighteousness by Your Blood as you said you would in 1 John 1:7. And as Your word says in Romans 10:13 Everyone who calls upon the name of the Lord will be saved.

I confess and repent right now of occult practices such as (witchcraft, black magic, santeria, voodoo, juju, fortune telling, horoscopes, astrology, water witching, and anything else that you need to declare.)

I renounce all occult practices and satan and break all curses associated with those occult practices. According to Galatians 3:13 Christ purchased our freedom, redeeming us from the curse and doom of the Law along with its condemnation by Himself becoming a curse for us. For it is written in the Scriptures, *Cursed is everyone who hangs on a tree* (meaning crucified); Deut. 21:23.

I confess and repent of all sins listed in Deuteronomy 27 and 28 and break the curses associated with these sins.

I confess and repent of my iniquities and my father's iniquities according to Leviticus 26:40 and I break the curses associated with these iniquities.

I break and loose myself from all evil soul ties with my mother, father, brother, sisters, spouses, former spouses, former sex partners, pastors, churches, friends, etc.

Lord Jesus: I forgive my mother, father, brothers, sisters and anyone else who has ever hurt me, including all races, including whites, blacks, Spanish, Russian, German, Indians, Arabs, etc. Matthew 6:15, 18:21, 22, 35; Luke 11:4 [4]***And forgive us our sins; for we also forgive every one that is indebted to us. And lead us not into temptation; but deliver us from evil.***

I break and loose myself and my family from all curses that have been and are being placed upon me and my family, including any demons being sent to us: curses of witchcraft, psychic thoughts or prayers, ungodly intercessory prayers; all words spoken in anger, hurt, sorrow, or bitterness; all incense being burned for or against us, in Jesus' name. AMEN!

PRAYERS AGAINST EVIL ALTARS

Father God, there is none like you in all of the earth. You are God alone, seated on your throne and there is none like you. I confess that I am not perfect and in fact have sinned. Please forgive me for all of my sins. I repent of every evil work and of every evil way that I have ever sinned against thee, according to 1 John 1:9. I also release and ask that you release anyone of any consequence regarding their sin and transgression towards me. Because you said that you are just and able to forgive me for my sins, I take you at your Word and believe that I am forgiven. Lord God, according to Mark 16:17 I have the authority to cast out demons. Lord Jesus, I cover myself with the blood of Jesus. I cover my spouse and family with the blood of Jesus and I apply the blood of Jesus between me and any altar that has been erected against me. According to Ephesians 6:17, I have the authority to use the Sword of the Spirit. I take my authority and attack from the Third Heaven with the sword of the Spirit, my weapon of choice, and I strike and break the Altars of Balaam off of my life in Jesus name. I strike and break the Altars of Poverty off of my life in Jesus name. I strike and break the Altars of Infirmity off of my life in Jesus name. I renounce, rebuke, and rescind any covenant and/or

allegiance to any altar, especially the Altar of Balaam. Break Altar in the name of Jesus! Break Altar by the power of the blood of Jesus! Break Altar by the finish work of the Cross! I bind every witchcraft in every form that has been launched against me with the blood of Jesus. I apply the blood of Jesus between me and any anti-progress spirit in the name of Jesus. And I bind any kind of witchcraft that has been sent to me or my family, transferred to me and my family, or that has followed me and anyone in my family, in the name of Jesus. I rebuke every delay, I destroy every denial by the Holy Ghost fire that Elijah used against false prophets on Mt. Carmel. I return every spell, incantation, judgment, and/or witchcraft that has been sent to me or anyone in my family. I bind it to them by the blood of Jesus and decree and declare that their evil works shall not and cannot work! In Jesus name, I pray Amen.

When you are praying for God to break family curses you have to also go deeper and ask God to forgive the iniquity that is in your blood, or should I say, blood line. Iniquities are like the sins of the fathers.

INIQUITIES

Leviticus 26:40 (NKJV)

40 *'But if they confess their iniquity and the iniquity of their fathers, with their unfaithfulness in which they were unfaithful to Me, and that they also have walked contrary to Me,*
41 *and that I also have walked contrary to them and have brought them into the land of their enemies;*
if their uncircumcised hearts are humbled, and they accept their guilt—
42 *then I will remember My covenant with Jacob, and My covenant with Isaac and My covenant with Abraham I will remember;*
I will remember the land.

So, to break it down even further, you have to do three things when you are asking God to forgive iniquities:

A. Confess

B. Repent

C. Ask forgiveness of:

1. Own iniquities

2. Ancestors' iniquities going back 4 generations (or further as the Lord gives discernment)

3. Spouses, former sex partners, and their ancestors' iniquities going back 4 generations

PRAYER:

CONFESSION

Heavenly Father, I confess my iniquity of ___________________

I confess on behalf of my ancestors going back 4 generations their iniquity of ___ ______________________. I confess on behalf of my spouse and my previous spouses and former sex partners and their ancestors going back 4 generations, for their iniquity of ________ _________________________.

REPENTANCE

I repent of my iniquity of _________________. I repent on behalf of my ancestors, spouse, previous spouses and former sex partners and their ancestors going back 4 generations, for their iniquity of ________________ ________.

FORGIVENESS

Lord, I ask your forgiveness for my iniquity of ___________. I ask your forgiveness on behalf of my ancestors, spouse, former spouses and former sex partners and their ancestors going back 4 generations, for their iniquity of ___________.

SOUL TIES

I break all evil soul ties with these people in JESUS' name

CURSES

Before I give the verbiage for the prayer on this one let me just explain why we're breaking generational curses back to 4 generations.

Exodus 20:3-5 (NKJV)

3 *Thou shalt have no other gods before me.*
4 *Thou shalt not make unto thee any graven image, or any likeness of anything that is in heaven above, or that is in the earth beneath, or that is in the water under the earth.*
5 *Thou shalt not bow down thyself to them, nor serve them: for I the Lord thy God am a jealous God, visiting the iniquity of the fathers upon the children unto the third and fourth generation of them that hate me;*

Exodus 34:7 (NKJV)

7 *Keeping mercy for thousands, forgiving iniquity and transgression and sin, and that will by no means clear the guilty; visiting the iniquity of the fathers upon the children, and upon the children's children, unto the third and to the fourth generation.*

God was clearly given instructions to us not to worship any Principality, to include fallen angels or any other type of spiritual entity, anything in Hell, or anything in the Marine Kingdom.

Numbers 14:18 (NKJV)

18 'The Lord is longsuffering and abundant in mercy, forgiving
iniquity and transgression; but He by no means clears the
guilty, visiting the iniquity of the fathers on the children to the
third and fourth generation.'

Deuteronomy 5:9 (NKJV)

9 you shall not bow down to them nor serve them. For I,
the Lord your God, am a jealous God, visiting the iniquity of the
fathers upon the children to the third and fourth generations of
those who hate Me,

Other places where God delineates His parameters for curses and blessings are **Deuteronomy 11:26-28; 23; 27 and 28.**

The curse of Robbing God:
Malachi 3:8-11 (KJV)

8 Will a man rob God? Yet ye have robbed me. But ye say, Wherein
have we robbed thee? In tithes and offerings. 9 Ye are cursed with a
curse: for ye have robbed me, even this whole nation. 10 Bring ye
all the tithes into the storehouse, that there may be meat in mine
house, and prove me now herewith, saith the LORD of hosts, if I
will not open you the windows of heaven, and pour you out a
blessing, that there shall not be room enough to receive it. 11 And I
will rebuke the devourer for your sakes, and he shall not destroy
the fruits of your ground; neither shall your vine cast her fruit
before the time in the field, saith the LORD of hosts.

So after confessing, repenting and asking for forgiveness of sins and iniquities you can pray the following prayer:

Upon the authority of Jesus Christ, which I have as a Believer, and in the Name of Jesus and by the Power of His Blood I break the power of every curse due to sins and iniquities of:

drunkenness, adultery, godlessness, faithlessness, idolatry, etc.

committed by:

ME

My Mother and Father (Name each)

My Aunts and Uncles (Name each)

(and all spouses and former sex partners)

All ancestors going back through the generations to Adam AND Eve.

I break the power of each one of these curses due to:

sins of drunkenness, etc.

as they fall upon:

ME

My wife or husband (Name)

Our children (Name each)

as they fall upon:

Former sex partners and their spouses and children and ancestors

as they fall upon:

My mother and father (Name each)

My brothers, sisters (Name each)

My Aunts and Uncles (Name each)

My Cousins, their spouses and children (Name each)

By the power of the Blood of Jesus, I declare each of these curses due to sins of drunkenness to be broken and now powerless and of no effect, according to Galatians 3:13

I command all demons associated with these curses to come out in the Name of Jesus.

PRAYER THAT CANCELS WORD CURSES

To EVERY word curse blown in my direction, I stand proxy and declare, that the mouth of my enemy is short of breath!

Every word curse that is released from the mouth of my enemy, GRAVITY shall pull them down right now and they shall shatter upon hitting the ground!
Every spirit that travels thru water, I decree that the waters shall freeze, every spirit shall be trapped, and every block of ice shall be consumed by Holy Fire and die in, Jesus name!

Every strange spirit that's in my body, I command you to come out and burn by the fire of the Holy Spirit right now in the name of Jesus!

Every talisman or object that has become portals and/or gates, for demonic entry/possession, I break and close off, forbid and prevent your access, right now in Jesus name!

One of my prayers when I am in a serious encounter with a demonically possessed or oppressed person is this:

Father God, I now cover myself with the blood of Jesus Christ, and pray that the Holy Spirit would bring all of the work of the crucifixion, resurrection, and glorification over my life right now. I affirm that I have all the dunamis power that was received by men at Pentecost (Acts 1:8) and in the name of

Jesus, I command any ungodly spirit to leave this man or woman right now. I command you to a dry and desolate place. Go and never return, in the name of Jesus!

WEATHER DEMONS

It may be hard to believe, but foul weather can be caused by demons as well. Which means we have authority over them in that area too. We know that this is true because Jesus demonstrated it in Mark 4 and Matthew 8. We also saw Joshua tell the sun to stand still in Joshua 10 and Elijah had such a strong relationship with God that he declared that it wouldn't rain for 3 ½ years and it was so. So, if you truly believe that God has given you dominion over everything in this Earth we need to understand that this even includes the atmosphere of this Earth, which includes the second Heaven and the principalities, powers, and rulers that reside there. I have prayed against severe weather and have seen God either stop the storm or redirect it. However, please understand that sometimes God allows the storm for other reasons that we sometimes could never understand from a human perspective. So, don't just randomly challenge weather patterns unless the weather is about to impact a revival for instance. Or if there is a tornado or hurricane directly coming in your direction and there is no recourse.

Job 1:19 tells us of a great whirlwind from the desert that killed Job's children, showing us that even the winds are being directed by something outside of this earth realm. Because remember this didn't happen until after God and satan made their wager, so to speak. Of course, God controls everything and can affect the atmosphere including the winds, rain, and seas, in any way He wants too, just like He did for Moses at the Red Sea. However, in addition to that we have to remember that there are principalities and rulers of darkness in high places that can and do affect the winds, rain, and seas as well. **Acts 27:14** tells us of a typhoon type wind that came upon Paul at sea. This was a spiritually charged storm levied at Paul and he knew it. A sample prayer would be like the following:

In the Name of JESUS, I bind all demons that cause hail, excess heat and cold, lingering domes, fire, earthquakes, tornados, lightning, damaging winds, floods, hurricanes, bad weather of all kinds. I bind CHANGO, OXUN, EUROCLYDON, BAAL, SEIR, LEVIATHAN, HADADRIMMON, AMURR, BASILISK, and all others. Father, I ask you to send your warring angels (Matthew 26:53) into the heavenlies to do battle with these demons, to knock them off their thrones, take their crowns from their heads, and to write on their foreheads that they have been defeated by the Lord JESUS Christ. Father, I ask that you send the warring angels to block these demons from coming into our city, state, or county. I ask for warring angels to be placed around our property and home for protection from these demons. In JESUS Name, I cover my property, home, possessions and family in the Blood of JESUS. Amen.

SOME WEATHER DEMONS BY NAME

CHANGO - (prince) controls thunder, lightning, fire.

OXUN - god of thunder and lightning.

EUROCLYDON -east wind (Acts 27:14) Levant - a surge of the sea, raging, wave

BAAL - god of thunder

SEIR - prince

LEVIATHAN - Job 41:1; Psalm 74:14; Psalm 104:26; Isaiah 27:1

HADADRIMMON - west semitic storm-god, thunder

AMURR - amorite storm god

HURRICANE - means god of evil

TORNADO

HAIL

LIGHTNING

FLOODING

WIND

FIRE

EARTHQUAKE

BASILISK

SENDING THE JUDGMENT OF GOD

These Scriptures, Deuteronomy 30:7, Psalm 25, 109, 140, and Isaiah 54:17 are just five of many Scriptures that offer us some protection against people coming against us.

I personally know that there has been certain people who have come against me and have met with terrible judgment from the Lord. God has showed me people that were my mortal enemies in my dreams and turns out that they were scheming on me in real life. They went through many things such as being unexpectedly fired from their jobs, husbands and wives divorced them, and some of them were in major accidents. One person that really grieved me even died, not that I prayed for that. However, these prayers are to be prayed daily and I pray them daily because God instructs us to put on the whole armor of God in Galatians 6. But the truth of it is that sometimes when you are praying this way, God will show you someone close to you that is falling in the "enemy" category and you will have to pray for that person individually. One time, God showed me someone that was very close to me at one time. He showed me that the judgement for the way that they had and was dealing with me was Alzheimer's Disease. I woke up crying and started pleading with the Lord for that person. I promised God that I was okay with everything and had truly forgiven the person. He instructed me to Fast as well as Pray for the person and I have been assured that this cup will not be this person's portion. I had a former military boss that literally went for my career at one point in my life. This person lost their career in three years after their attempt on me.

These kinds of things happen to people all the time. Sometimes it happens really quickly, and then sometimes it takes days, weeks, months, or even years before the judgment of God falls on them. If you are under a lot of attack, you may want to specifically pray these scriptures against someone or even an organization. Before you say anything ignorant or stupid, let me tell you that this is biblical. Just read through the book of Psalms to see David praying against His enemies every other chapter. Also, you must remember that God took a second and third look at Sodom before He destroyed it because of the pleas of Abraham. Also, the judgement and fire of God relented due to Moses' prayers of mercy for the Hebrew people after they were delivered from Egypt. It is God's business when and how He deals with that person. If the person is innocent, nothing will happen to them. I make it a point to warn people, especially about **Psalm 109**, so they don't make fun or mock God's ministry or ministers, regardless of title.

This is not practicing witchcraft. We do not pray for bad things to happen to people. We rightfully pray to God to protect us and fight for us if necessary. Once we have done this, it is God's business how He handles it. Vengeance is mine saith the Lord. Prayer is just a vehicle and in fact a weapon. And anyone that plays with the Holy Spirit or even a Holy Spirit filled individual is playing with fire. Let me give you a little bit more Bible concerning this.

Psalms 79:12 (KJV)

And render unto our neighbors SEVENFOLD into their bosom their reproach, wherewith they have reproached thee, O Lord.

Genesis 4:15 (KJV)

And the LORD said unto him, Therefore whosoever slayeth Cain, vengeance shall be taken on him SEVENFOLD.

Genesis 4:24 (KJV)

If Cain shall be avenged sevenfold, truly Lamech SEVENTY and SEVENFOLD.

I believe a person can avoid the judgment of God in these matters by repenting. However, the scriptures say, *My people are destroyed for lack of knowledge.* One note to remember though. A person's ignorance regarding these things will not stop God for rendering vengeance and ultimately judgement on those who continue to live in sin.

Pray this way:

Father God, in the name of JESUS I send the judgment of God to (name names). I pray Deuteronomy 30:7, Psalms 25, 109 and 140, Isaiah 54:17, and any like Scriptures on them, and anyone else coming against us, in the name of JESUS.

When I know that I am going into hostile territory, physically and spiritually, and I want to be armored up, I pray this way:

Father God, in the name of Jesus, I bind Isaiah 54:17 to my spirit and decree and declare that no weapon formed against me shall prosper, every tongue that rise against me in judgment is condemned right now in the name of Jesus. Also, God I bind Romans 8:28 to my spirit and I decree and declare that ALL things shall work together for my good because I love you and am called according to your great purpose.

I pray this prayer or a variant of it every morning after praising God with my lips and giving Him thanks for a new day of life. I also ask God to forgive me for any sin that I've might've committed in the spirit (dream) world as well.

SENDING FALLEN TORMENTING ANGELS TO EARLY TORMENT

We can pray for tormenting angels to be sent for early torment according to Matthew 8:29. It would go something like this,

Father God, according to the principle that I understand according to Matthew 8:29, I send every tormenting demon that is oppressing me right now for early torment in Jesus name. I apply that scripture and I pray that each and every one of them be rounded up by mighty warring angels, chained, and taken to place scheduled for their torment right now. God, you said that greater works shall we do than even our Lord and Savior Jesus Christ and by His very blood we consume every work of the enemy and burn every chain by fire and break its grip by force.

PRAYERS AGAINST THE SLEEP PARALYSIS DEMON (Being choked in your sleep,etc.)

Father God, as I lay me down to sleep cover me deep in the Blood of Jesus. Blood of Jesus fight for my physical body, spirit, and soul, right now in the name of Jesus. To any and EVERY dark power pressing me down in my dreams, I command that you die by the power in the blood of Jesus.

Father God, I put on your armor that you said is mine in Ephesians 6 and I ask you to fight for me.

I lay a fire to EVERY agenda of the enemy for my life through EVERY satanic oppression. To EVERY satanic power, your time is up, the blood of Jesus is against you, and by the authority of the name of Jesus I command that you die by fire, in the name of Jesus. By the power of the blood of Jesus and the authority of His name, I declare that EVERY power that is sitting on my peace, good, and expected end, be unseated by fire, in Jesus name.

ANOTHER ANTI-WITCHCRAFT PRAYER

Father, In JESUS Name, I break and loose myself from all witchcraft curses and evil and demons being sent to me and my family. As your war club (Jeremiah 51:20-23) and weapons of war, I break in pieces the walls of protection that the satanists and witches have put up and I return the evil and demons back to them. Exodus 22:18 I send the judgment of God to the satanists and witches sending anything our way, in JESUS Name. I heap coals from the altar of God upon their foreheads in JESUS Name. I cover me and my family with the Blood of JESUS and ask for warring angels to be placed around us for protection. I break and loose us from psychic power, thoughts and prayers. I break and loose us from words spoken in hurt, anger, sorrow or bitterness. I break and loose us from the power of incense and candles being burned on our behalf. I break and loose us from ungodly intercessory prayers in JESUS Name. Amen.

FINANCES

Father, In JESUS Name, I bind all demons that would cause me to have job failure or money failure. I bind all demons that would keep me from receiving all money, possessions, inheritance, jobs, promotions, bonuses or raises that are rightfully mine. In JESUS Name, I command the demons to return these to me sevenfold. Father, I ask that you send your angels out to gather these and bring them to me in JESUS Name. I loose the blessings of Deuteronomy 28 upon me in JESUS Name. Amen. (Note: having unicorns in your home or an Italian Horn can cause finance problems. This can be statues or anything else.)

HEALTH

Father, In JESUS Name, I bind all demons of infirmity, sickness, disease, illnesses of all kinds. I loose myself from

these demons and I loose the healing virtue of JESUS Christ into my body. (Be sure and cast out all of these demons).

SLEEP

Father, In JESUS Name, I bind all demons of the night, nightmares, bad dreams, torment, sleeplessness, torture. I command these demons to loose me and come out of me, and I ask that you protect my mind while I sleep, in JESUS Name.

SPIRITUAL WALK WITH THE LORD AND ANOINTING

Father, In JESUS Name, I ask for wisdom, knowledge, and understanding of Your Word. I loose the sevenfold Spirits of God in me in JESUS Name.

Be sure to anoint your home. Include all doors and windows and bind the demons and command them to leave. You can do this in your office also.

CONSECRATION PRAYER

Father God, forgive us for failure to align ourselves perfectly with God's will, known sin and rebellion, emotional stress and trauma, submissions to an ungodly cover, inherited curses, worldly art and music, ownership of unclean objects, failure to cleanse property and places; unforgiveness, idolatry or a lack of separation from the things of the world. We ask for forgiveness, confess contact with the occult, close doors to Satan, break curses, renounce psychic bondage, cut evil soul ties, loose the mind, restore the fragmented soul, confess sins of the fathers, surrender to Jesus, and renounce all evil.

ANY UNGODLY THOUGHTS, OR THOUGHTS YOU DON'T WANT, PRAY THIS IMMEDIATELY:

Father God, In Jesus name, I circumcise these thoughts.

You may have to pray this several times before the bad thoughts leave. This really works too!

WHEN ENTERING YOUR OFFICE, GROCERY STORE, ANYONE ELSE'S HOME, ETC., PRAY THIS BEFORE ENTERING:

In Jesus name, I cover myself and this place with the blood of Jesus. I bind up every demon in here, and I ask for giant warrior angels to protect me.

AFTER HANGING UP THE PHONE, LEAVING WORK, GROCERY STORE, NEIGHBORS, OR VISITORS LEAVE YOUR HOME, ETC., PRAY THIS IMMEDIATELY:

In Jesus name, I command every demon that has followed me, was sent to me, or transferred to me, to leave me now.

BEFORE DOWNLOADING EMAIL OR OPENING WEB PAGES ON THE COMPUTER, PRAY THIS:

In Jesus name, I bind up every demon coming across the computer lines, and I return them and any curses.

BEFORE OR AFTER GETTING INTO ANY VEHICLE, PRAY THIS:

In Jesus name, I cover myself in the blood of Jesus. I cover this vehicle and the road I travel in the blood of Jesus. I take authority and dominion over all animals and demons of the road, so they do not cross my path. I dispatch angels ahead of me to protect me.

BEFORE GOING TO SLEEP, PRAY THIS:

In Jesus name, I cover myself and all my property with the blood of Jesus. I take authority over all demons of the night, bad dreams, nightmares, and sex dreams, and anyone or

anything trying to get into my dreams, and I command them to stay away. I ask for giant warrior angels to protect me and my property as I sleep, through the night and the day. I ask for a fiery wall of protection around me.

ANY SHARP PAIN THAT COMES ON YOU SUDDENLY IS ALMOST ALWAYS WITCHCRAFT. WHEN THIS HAPPENS, PRAY THIS IMMEDIATELY AS YOU USE YOUR INDEX FINGER AND THUMB ON THE SPOT OF THE PAIN, LIKE YOU WERE PULLING OUT A VOODOO PIN:

In Jesus name, I pull out all fiery darts, pins, needles, spears, voodoo, all witchcraft and curses and anything else, and I return it to the sender, one hundredfold. (Then motion with your hand towards a window or door like you were throwing it out.) If it is witchcraft, the pain will go immediately. This is a highly effective Spiritual Weapon.

TO RETURN ALL EVIL BEING SENT, PRAY THIS SEVERAL TIMES DURING THE DAY, AND ANY TIME THE HOLY SPIRIT PROMPTS YOU: (A silver cord is a spiritual cord that keeps your body and spirit connected. Those who practice voodoo and/or many other types of black magics attach false silver cords with you in the spirit realm, while you are sleeping to cast spells on you in your dreams, while you're sleeping.)

Father God, in Jesus name, I cut and burn all ungodly silver cords and lay lines.

As your war club and weapons of war, I break down, undam, and blow up all walls of protection around all witches, warlocks, wizards, satanists, sorcerers, and the like, and I break the power of all curses, hexes, vexes, spells, charms, fetishes, psychic prayers, psychic thoughts, all witchcraft, sorcery, magic, voodoo, santeria, all mind control, jinxes, potions, bewitchments, death, destruction, sickness, pain, torment, psychic power, psychic warfare, prayer chains, incense and candle burning, incantations, chanting, ungodly blessings, hoodoo, crystals, rootworks,

and everything else being sent my way, or my family member's way, or any ministries way, and I return it, and the demons to the sender, one hundredfold, and I bind it to them by the blood of Jesus.

SPIRITUAL WARFARE PRAYER AGAINST WITCHCRAFT
(Pray this daily as well)

Father God, in the name of Jesus Christ of Nazareth, I come against the prince-ruling spirit and all spirit guides. I come through the blood of the Lord Jesus Christ, in the name of Jesus. I paralyze you and silence you, forbidding you from influencing or strengthening them (the witch or witches) in the name of Jesus, right now!

We are destroying your very works: the spirits of hate, bitterness and murder, spirits of envy and jealousy, spirits of wizardry, sorcery and all your co-spirits, your works, your powers, your influences are destroyed in the name of Jesus!

I paralyze you, all, right now. You will not be able to use these souls any longer against the church (or, a particular person or Christian organization), in the name of Jesus.

I come against the spirit of blindness, binding the spirits of bondage and heaviness, fear and hate.

I pray, Lord, that you will open their eyes, so they can see the glory of Jesus. Open their hearts so that they can hear your voice. Break the yokes in their lives and give them liberty in their souls, that they may be free to repent. Show them every evil work and every evil deed they're guilty of, and Lord Jesus, convict their hearts unto repentance. Bring these souls out of darkness; save these souls so that you may have the glory.

Satan, I silence you in the name of Jesus, binding all your interference. You will not interfere with these souls and they

will have their own free will choice to make up their own minds if they want to repent. They will do it without your interference. Also, Lord Jesus, I pray that you will release warring angels to wage war against these demonic activities and will send ministering spirits to minister to their souls.

JEZEBEL

Jezebel is a ruling spirit that tries to overthrow prophets and prophetic people. The spirit of Jezebel can be detected by seasoned men and women of God because it is also a spirit of "false" prophecy. Normally, this spirit will operate within a person that will prophecy some half-truths and a whole lot of error, normally based off of emotions and personal opinion. This spirit attacks churches, families, and individuals. She is a ruling and controlling spirit that is prevalent in many men-demeaning groups, such as pro-women groups. Not saying that all of the pro-women groups are bad or being led by this spirit because there are many women only or for women groups that are extremely Godly and on point. But nevertheless, this spirit shows up in the highest levels of many spiritual organizations. Such as the "First Lady" of a local church. The First Lady is one of the main reasons that many "called" men of God gives up on the ministry and sometimes get distracted and discouraged. It's a "I'm going to let you have the title of the Senior Pastor as long as you know that I'm in charge." Spirit. If you are a female and just got mad you might be affected by this spirit, get over yourself. However, I should say that this spirit can be found in men as well, especially in this day and time.

When you are under attack from a Jezebel spirit everything can seem overwhelming and even hazy. The Jezebel of the Bible was literally possessed by one or all the demonic deities, Anat, Hathor, Asherah, Baal, and Astarte, that were worshipped before her and by her in her life. However, the Lord Jesus has given us the power to defeat the attacks of Jezebel.

God is well able to defeat every demonic force and He does it by prayer. There is no force of darkness strong enough to withstand the power of sustained intercession. God hears and answers your prayers, especially if you are praying in accordance to His will. He will muzzle that thing and cast it out.

When you want to pray against a spirit or demonic force you must pray "against" it. By against it I mean to pray "opposite" of the spirit that you're dealing with. So, whereas, Jezebel is a false spirit of prophecy, we would come against this spirit by praying for the true spirit of prophecy.

What is the true spirit of prophecy? Good question. The answer is that the testimony of Jesus is the true spirit of prophecy.

Revelations 19:10

And I fell at his feet to worship him. But he said to me, "See that you do not do that! I am your fellow servant, and of your brethren who have the testimony of Jesus. Worship God! ***For the testimony of Jesus is the spirit of prophecy."***

So, all we have to do is release the testimony of Jesus into the situation and He will shut down and muzzle every voice of Jezebel in your life. How do you do that? By applying the blood of Jesus over your family, your home, your church, and your business. You do it by worshipping specifically using the name of Jesus. Sing songs about Jesus stating that He's a Waymaker, Miracle Worker, Promise Keeper, Light in the Darkness. Let the devil know that Jesus is Lord and He is the Lord of your life. Do this especially in the areas that have been affected by the venom of this spirit and watch the atmosphere change. No matter what it looks like, keep on worshipping our Lord Jesus, in spite of what it looks like, because Jezebel is an intimidator, but is not in any way stronger than our God. Just like the real human Jezebel was thrown out of the window by her own eunuchs, tramples on by Jehu's horses and then eaten by his dogs (**2 Kings 9:30-37**), God will do the same to any jezebellic spirit that has chosen to come against you. Stand firm, keep on praying and interceding, and watch God kill that spirit and feed it to the dogs.

Pray this way:

Father God, I come against the spirit of Jezebel right now in the name of Jesus. I apply the blood of Jesus over every false and subversive spirit that would and has come against me and the body of Christ. God search my heart, close any open doors that I may have opened to the enemy, and remove any influence that the Jezebel spirit may have over me. I command everything in me, in this place (insert your church name if necessary) and/or situation to line itself up with the Word (John 1:1) who is Jesus and furthermore, I command that everything in this situation to change its appearance and look like Jesus, sound like Jesus, speak like Jesus, act like Jesus, and smell like Jesus. I remind every Jezebel spirit and demonic spirit at the sound of my voice right now of Philippians 2:9-11, in that God the Father has given, God the Son, Jesus, a name that is higher than every name. And at His name every knee that is in Heaven, on the Earth, and under the Earth, shall bow and confess that He is Lord. And right now, in the name of Jesus, I invoke the authority and power of the name of Jesus and command every Jezebel spirit, every Ahab spirit, and every other demonic and ungodly spirit to bow at the name of Jesus and confess that He is Lord. Leave this place now and never return. I command you to lose your hold of every person that you are and have inhabited and go to the abyss right now in the name of Jesus. The blood of Jesus is against you. The name of Jesus is against you. And you must obey. Everything that I have just prayed has been recorded as a witness against you and since I'm praying in the name of Jesus, it is so and so it is. Amen.

Now, one last thing before we get off of Jezebel. If you really want her out of your life you have to get rid of and ban everything Jezebel in your life. This includes even the foods that you eat, the beverages that you consume, and the businesses that you support. For example, Starbucks. Do you know that Jezebel has been and is being served to the world every day in every cup of coffee and/or tea that they sell?

The Starbuck Siren is representation of the most powerful siren in the world. When Starbucks was first formed the logo of their company was a siren, complete with breasts, nipples and all; holding her twin tails apart in a sexual manner. Since then, they have tried to slowly desexualize the image. And now, because of the reemerging of ancient knowledge that has been lost over the millennia's, it is a close up of the siren with long flowing hair.

According to The Woman's Dictionary of Symbols and Sacred Objects the siren had a connection to the ancient symbol of the Sheila-Na-Gig, a pagan goddess, who posed with her legs spread, showing off her "vesica piscis", her vaginal area, which, in Latin, means "vessel of the fish." That shape, representing the yoni or vulva, is ubiquitous in goddess-worshipping cultures, and it's not a coincidence that a vulva shape appears to surround the Jezebel figure or Our Lady of Guadalupe figure that is on the logo. I almost inserted a picture of what this deity looks like but there are architectural grotesques found all over Europe on churches, castles, and other buildings, and I'll let you do the research for yourself. So, leave Starbucks alone, because its inception and worldwide popularity has been due to the pledge to this demonic deity from the beginning and it will only get stronger and stronger. Every time you're sipping you need to understand that you are sipping and eating food that offered unto idols.

COMMANDS

Mark 11:23 (NASB95)

[2]"Truly I say to you, whoever says to this mountain, 'Be taken up and cast into the sea,' and does not doubt in his heart, but believes that what he says is going to happen, it will be granted him.

Father God, I return all curses and demons back to the senders right now in Jesus name. I use our weapons of warfare according to Ephesians 6 against the kingdom of darkness. satan I am closing every door that you may have

opened in me from any evil contact or association. Jesus Christ became a curse on the cross for me and blotted out the handwriting of ordinances against me. I break the curses going all of the way back to Adam and Eve and destroy every legal hold and grounds that the demons have to work in my life.

We bind the spirits power and loose ourselves from their holds. We break demonic soul ties. We ask for the necessary spiritual gifts and especially the gift of discernment to minister to the people. We ask for the anointing of the Holy spirit and the authority of Jesus Christ. We have been given power and authority over Satan and his army.

We send angels with boxes to separately seal each demon in, chain and gag the demons, read scripture to the demons day and night, and fill the boxes with the Glory of God. We loose the angels to spin the demons minds round and round, to chase and harass, to bruise, crush and flatten the heads of the serpentine spirits, and to snip off the tails of the scorpion spirits.

We order the princes and rulers to be bound with chains and thrown down before the other spirits, and their foreheads to be written in red letters that Jesus Christ is my Lord. We command the lesser spirits to attack the traitors in the camp and throw them out. We release the spirit which attacked the Midianites in Gideon's day.

We command the demon's answers to stand up in the Judgment We send the warrior angels with swords to chain the rulers and throw the fire of God on them. We ask that the demons be cut into pieces and scattered over the dry places.

You are defeated by Jesus and must obey His commands. We adopt each other as spiritual sons and daughters and cover them with the Compassion and Love of God. We use love as a weapon. We command the demons to manifest only as

God permits. We use tongues of men and angels to expel demons.

We bind powers over our area, break assignments from powers in the heavenlies to demons in the people and ask for legions of covering angels for protection. We bind the strong man and his spirits in everyone.

The Lord Jesus rebuke you. We command that you confess that Jesus Christ is your Lord. We ask for the leadership of the Holy Spirit. We anoint with oil symbolic of the Holy Spirit. We intercede for our loved ones.

We command the ruling spirits to cast out their underlings. We command the angels to assist in the work of deliverance as directed by God.

We break evil curses, vexes, hexes, jinxes, psychic powers, bewitchments, potions, charms, incantations, spells, witchcraft and sorcery. We break all cords, snares, controls and bondages. We ask that the Power of God be manifested. We command the demons to go to Tartarus, or wherever Jesus sends them.

Warnings

Real truth is never afraid of questions.

Apostle Dr. Larry Birchett, Jr.

Ephesians 3:10 (KJV)

To the intent that now unto the principalities and powers in heavenly places might be known by the church the manifold wisdom of God

I want to give you some additional information beloved on various subjects because prayer sometimes is hindered by the things that we're engaged in that we simply don't know is sin or witchcraft or otherwise.

At one point in my life I had a question in my heart regarding gambling and God revealed some things to me besides the obvious.

CARDS

Satan is a master at camouflaging witchcraft into all aspects of humanity's culture. A prime example is the deck of playing cards, something that can be found in every household Christian and Non-Christian. The deck of cards was known by the Puritans, our early Christian forefathers, as the "Devil's picture book." Did you know that the first deck of playing cards was created by sorcerers in 1392 for King Charles of France, who they say was insane? Of course, we know that he wasn't insane he was demonically touched. They were and are also utilized by witches, psychics, and satan worshipers for divinations to cast spells and curses. They were and are also used as a form of silent communication. King Charles of France believed in the magical power of playing cards. And even now if you encounter a person that always has one particular card on them, for instance, a Jack of Spades or Joker in their wallet or pocket, get away from them. Never give them anything of your personal items, watch your words around them, never invite them to your house, and cover yourself with the blood of Jesus if you have to be in their presence; they are in the occult.

CERN

The European Organization for Nuclear Research, known as CERN, is a European research organization that operates the largest particle physics laboratory in the world. It is located in Geneve, Switzerland.

They use the world's largest and most complex scientific instruments to study the basic constituents of matter – the fundamental particles.

They are asking questions such as “What is the universe made of?” “How did it start?” And Physicists at CERN are seeking answers, using some of the world's most powerful particle accelerators.

Everything that you’ve read so far about CERN is almost word for word quotable from their websites and credible sources. But one thing that you won’t find is that they’re dabbling into the spirit realm and even the occult. Their whole intent is to tear the fabric of our dimension so that whatever is on the other side can come through. The particles are made to collide with each other at the speed of light ripping the visible dimension. They’re using particle accelerators and decelerators as well as this thing called the Large Hydron Collider.

The Large Hydron Collider might be the very thing that opens up the portals of Hell on Earth. In Matthew chapter 24, Jesus said that as it was in the days of Noah, so shall it be at the time of His return. As already taught in this book, during Noah’s time there were giants, demons, monsters, and a whole lot of supernatural things going on before the flood killed all or most of these things and the portal was closed to most of the demons and things that were not supposed to run around in the human part of our Earthly existence.

Revelations 9:3-11 (KJV)

3 And there came out of the smoke locusts upon the earth: and unto them was given power, as the scorpions of the earth have power.
4 And it was commanded them that they should not hurt the grass of the earth, neither any green thing, neither any tree; but only those men which have not the seal of God in their foreheads.
5 And to them it was given that they should not kill them, but that they should be tormented five months: and their torment was as the torment of a scorpion, when he striketh a man.
6 And in those days shall men seek death, and shall not find it; and shall desire to die, and death shall flee from them.
7 And the shapes of the locusts were like unto horses prepared unto battle; and on their heads were as it were crowns like gold, and their faces were as the faces of men.
8 And they had hair as the hair of women, and their teeth were as the teeth of lions.
9 And they had breastplates, as it were breastplates of iron; and the sound of their wings was as the sound of chariots of many horses running to battle.
10 And they had tails like unto scorpions, and there were stings in their tails: and their power was to hurt men five months.
11 And they had a king over them, which is the angel of the bottomless pit, whose name in the Hebrew tongue is Abaddon, but in the Greek tongue hath his name Apollyon.

The last time that humans tried to do this God destroyed our works. This happened at the Tower of Babel beloved, under the leadership of Nimrod. The Tower of Babel was being erected as a Monolith to some of the deities that we've been discussing in this book and satan himself. It was one big ritual that Nimrod, the Giant Hunter and Slayer, had knowledge of from ancient demons.

Wouldn't it be ashamed if we (humans) are the ones who reopens that portal to all of those demons to physically crossover, once again? Oh, and by the way for you gullible Christians, these scriptures are not allegorical or meant to mean something spiritual. The fact that John, the Revelator, wrote that the scorpions couldn't eat the grass of the Earth in Revelations 9:4, let us know that this is the case. Throw that Hermeneutic book away beloved and go back and read the Bible all over again after reading the entirety of this book.

A few more things about CERN. They are openly mocking God. One of their experiments is said to yield evidence that the universe is left handed. This is openly mocking God in scripture:

Isaiah 48:13 (KJV)

Mine hand also hath laid the foundation of the earth, and my right hand hath spanned the heavens: when I call unto them, they stand up together.

Also, on the outside of their facilities CERN has a huge statue (idol) of Shiva. Who is Shiva? Shiva is a Hindu FALSE god. He is regarded as "the Destroyer" or "the Transformer" and is regarded as limitless, transcendent, unchanging and formless. This god fits perfectly with the "destroyer" of Revelations 9 doesn't it?

Beloved, they are on record as looking for the God particle. This "particle" could possibly rip a hole and create a Black Hole that will change the fabric of this world forever and allow for everything on the other side to cross over.

The other thing that they're trying to do is create time travel. Enough said.

Pray against these things men and women of God.

CATHOLIC CHURCH

Besides the fact that the Catholic Church is deep into idolatry and the tradition of men and fallen angels, we have a bigger problem with them that I need to warn you about because many will hear,

"Depart from me I never knew you." Due to affiliations such as secret societies and even so-called entities of Christianity.

The smaller things to discuss is that the Catholic church openly teaches and supports praying to angels, of which we should never do. We should only pray to the creator not His creation.

The Catholic Church also prays to dead human beings. They have a practice of turning people into so called "Saints" after death based on good deeds while living. Then they place value on a certain area that they were "righteous" at while living and ascribe prayers to these individuals. That's why you see people praying to St. Thomas when they lose something and another saint when they want healing and so on and so on. Wouldn't it make sense to pray to God, the Creator, instead of the creation? Not to mention that we know that this is big time error and very blasphemous. Many will go to Hell for these practices(blasphemy).

Stop your "hail Mary" because Mary can't hear you. The dead can't communicate with the living. She's in Heaven. Stop praying to her idols in these catholic churches, this is idol worship, plain and simple. And there are demons attached to every statue erected in these churches. When you're bowing in front of them you are standing in front of a demon. Yes, even the huge crucifixes. When you're bowing in front of these images, you are bowing in front of satan, because guess what? Jesus is no longer on the cross. Also, the Bible tells us to not make any image of anything in the Heavens, Sea, or under the Earth. Repent of these things, reverse the curse.

But the biggest thing to know in regard to this book about prayer is that the Vatican has a space program. Their space program is so advanced that it has a telescope called the Lucifer Telescope. They say that they are monitoring an interstellar planet or "star" that is getting closer and closer to the Earth. Of course, they are referring to "Wormwood" of Revelations 12. They're setting the stage for satan to make his entrance into this Earth. The Catholic Church is going to give him validation because unfortunately, many of the priests in this church are practicing the occult. That's why there is so much sin and corruption in their priesthood. They smoke, cuss, and drink with the best of them.

The Vatican, as corrupt as it is, holds many truths about planet Earth and our history as it pertains to biblical things. They have many bones of Nephilim, they have art work, they have ancient scrolls, they have extraterrestrial remains, they have everything and know the truth at the highest levels. Which is why the Pope is one of the most revered men on Earth, whether you like him or not. Many believe that the Ant-Christ will come through the Pope himself and that the Catholic Church will provide the spiritual leader of the anti-Christ movement in the last days, a platform. In fact, the last Pope will be the False Prophet talked about in the book of Revelations.

FATIGUE

Watch out for FATIGUE. It can cause you to lose focus and ultimately loose fellowship. NEVER make a decision when you are fatigued. Consider Elijah. The demon of suicide took over and some people say, entered into, Elijah because he was fatigued. If it could happen to Elijah, it could happen to anyone. Take care of yourself beloved, get your rest.

PRAYERS TO NEVER PRAY

This book is about prayers that literally make it into the heavenly halls of God but let me take a quick second to speak about prayers that you shouldn't pray. One of these unadvisable prayers is called a Pharisetical Prayer. Let's look at Luke chapter 18:

Luke 18: 9-14

9 To some who were confident of their own righteousness and looked down on everyone else, Jesus told this parable: 10 "Two men went up to the temple to pray, one a Pharisee and the other a tax collector. 11 The Pharisee stood by himself and prayed: 'God, I thank you that I am not like other people—robbers, evildoers, adulterers—or even like this tax collector. 12 I fast twice a week and give a tenth of all I get.'

13 "But the tax collector stood at a distance. He would not even look up to heaven, but beat his breasts and said, 'God, have mercy on me, a sinner.'
14 "I tell you that this man, rather than the other, went home justified before God. For all those who exalt themselves will be humbled, and those who humble themselves will be exalted."

Another trend that is going on in our generation is so called "Commanding" God to do one thing or another. I'm here to tell you that you should never attempt to pray this way because we have never and will never, ever, command God to do one single, solitary thing. As a matter of fact, it is only He that does the commanding.

Prayer is an act of faith. We pray and in faith believe that God will answer our prayer. Prayer is an expression of your trust in God's perfect will in any circumstance. Your prayer life is so vital to how you engage with Him that the enemy works to make sure you don't discover its power. I pray that this book has helped you to tap into the power that is contained in prayer. All that we are and everything that we do is tied to the way that we pray and how much we pray. Without God we can accomplish nothing of eternal value. His Word guides us in how to pray and teaches us that the earnest prayers of those who are righteous produce beautiful results. If you want to experience change, respond to God in prayer and watch Him transform your life. God bless.

PORTALS

The picture on the front of this book is called a Vortex Portal. Watch your environment and the places that you willingly enter beloved. Some Vaping shops are literally portals into other demonic dimensions. If you are high enough on a certain substance you can walk into these places and literally be somewhere else. Some Cigar shops are in the same category. Smoke is a conduit that helps humans to reach other dimensions. Every Native American tribe and ancient culture knows this and their "holy men and women" still use these practices. Marijuana is a gateway drug or substance that many use to start embarking into these dimensions. It gives you access to certain demonic forces and information and these stores and places of business are not into the business that you think they are. As a matter of fact, Evangelist Ramirez, a world known ex-satanist, testifys that there is a certain store in New York on 42nd street that he used to buy his occultic paraphernalia from. He explains that in the back of the store, seances, witchcraft, and high level sorcery was being performed all the time and only he and other high level occultist knew this.

Another portal business is Tattoo Parlors. If you are even a baby Christian, the Holy Spirit in you should be screaming at you before you even walk into one of these establishments. These places are extensions of Hell on Earth. You're literally walking in a gate of Hell when you walk into these places and allow witches and warlocks to mark your flesh and shed your blood. Many ex-tattoo technicians admit that they were in one of the disciplines of the occult when they were doing these activities. You have been warned.

THE MARK OF THE BEAST

Revelation 16:2 and 19:20 cite the "mark of the beast" as a sign that identifies those who worship the beast out of the sea and the other beast that came out of the Earth.

Revelations 13:1 (NIV) The Beast out of the Sea

[1] The dragon stood on the shore of the sea. And I saw a beast coming out of the sea. It had ten horns and seven heads, with ten crowns on its horns, and on each head a blasphemous name.

Revelations 13:11 (NIV) The Beast out of the Earth

[11] Then I saw a second beast, coming out of the earth. It had two horns like a lamb, but it spoke like a dragon.

I'm going to end this book on this subject, because hopefully after going through everything that I threw at you in this body of work, you have come to realize that there is so much that we should be praying for and even more that we should be praying against.

God showed me a vision of a coming destruction of the whole world. I was climbing up a very steep mountain. Ahead and above me was my Bishop, below me was a very good friend and minister colleague of mines. As I realized I was on the side of the mountain, I turned around to see the whole world fragmented and torn apart as if the largest earth quake imaginable had shaken the whole world. I got scared, or at least that's the best word I can use to describe my nauseous feeling by taking in the magnitude of what I was seeing. My friend below me then said, "Are you alright man of God?" This snapped me back into remembering who I was, and I shook myself and said, "Yeah, I'm alright." I started climbing again. My Bishop who was above me had just reached the cleft of the mountain and climbed up and was going into a cave that had an out of this world Amber looking light. I was right behind just about to reach the top to follow him and see where we were going. Right at that time, I woke up. I knew that we were going to a designated place that God had designed for us and other God-fearing individuals to go during this time. I don't know how I know this, but I know. It was the time of the end in the dream and no nation was spared.

What I want to tell you about the Mark of the Beast is that it relates to everything in this book. Remember two words, "Digital Biology". Even as I explained earlier in the book that the mark is already in the Earth in the technology of the cell phone, it gets deeper than that and now I'm going to be more specific. The cell phone that you carry in your pocket has more technology in it than the first spaceship that America sent to the moon. And it's all ran and powered by a chip that connects "radio" waves from another dimension to our earthly frequency to transcend space and time for communicative purposes. Think about that and let that sink in. The question is who gave us the technology?

This is digital technology. But what if I tell you that every app that is in your phone can be "in" you? All you have to do is think of a phone number and it'll appear in front of your eyes and dial by your voice command or thought. What if by a chip inserted "in" you, you could surf the net and pull up any information or video that you wanted? What if school for your children can be done right in your houses just by having them seated in their room and logging in telepathically or telenetically? Not to mention that when this technology takes over the world because of the coming crash of the economies, ALL monies will be digital, and you will not be able to buy or sell without this technology. But what they won't tell the masses is that this technology is demon powered and by putting it into your brain and nervous system, you have just literally become one with satan. It will take over your emotions, passions, and the like. Every time you have a child you the implant of this chip will be just as normal and mandatory as a circumcision is for a male child in America.

Let's go deeper. CERN is not only working on creating a portal to breach this dimension and let everything that is on the other side in. They are also working on genetically modifying human DNA and digital biology. To not make this a science paper, in short, all DNA can now be reduced to 1's and 0's. They have gotten so good and received so much help from the other side that even we, human beings, can be reduced to binary codes, which many physic expert and scientist say that we are anyway. We are all the sum of very complex and out of this world math equations. Did you know that? A movie should be coming to your mind right now. And that movie is the Matrix. Because that movie was demonically pushed, so that the devil could laugh at us because he is broadcasting what he's doing and doing it right in front of our faces. At the end of the movie the man was sitting there looking at every human being on his screens, and they were all just a bunch of codes. CERN has leaked this knowledge and information because it is powered by the occult, as we see this from the statue of Shiva, right on the outside of its premises and not to mention that their headquarters is built right over the ancient Temple of Apollos.

Right now, in many of our top Colleges and Universities, our young and gifted are literally "creating" organisms using digital biology. They are making living organisms because of this technology. Let that sink in. According to Anthony Patch, CERN has been and is doing the same thing, of course, on a much larger and malevolent scale.

Anthony Patch, since 1969 is a Christian Believer, and a published Author, Researcher and Speaker. He is best known for his extensive, leading-edge and revelatory research focused upon the experimentation underway in Geneva, Switzerland with the Large Hadron Collider, part of the CERN organization.

Let me make all of this make sense. He and others, has been uncovering and exposing CERN in an unprecedented way. Basically, CERN is not only trying to bring ancient demons directly into our dimension, they are trying to create them. CERN is being demonically led to find ways to alter the human body, to never get sick, to repair itself, to stay young, and be gods, so to speak, on Earth. The cult of CERN is basically trying to do what the serpent, satan, told Eve way back in the Garden of Eden. Eve got deceived because she thought that God was holding back, not realizing that she was already in the highest state that she could've ever been while on Earth. satan told Eve that if she did what he was proposing she would become as God. The ultimate Mark of the Beast will be a demonic chip that alters our DNA that will supposedly make us live forever and achieve the level of what Adam, supposedly was before the fall. MANY will take it because it means that they will no longer have Cancer, Alzheimer's, Diabetes, and on and on and on. This will be the Mark of the Beast beloved and the Catholic Church will be the first to endorse and push it. Again, the Pope will be the False Prophet.

Demons communicate to open vessels, that are not filled with the Holy Spirit, on this Earth that are seeking knowledge and fame. For example, I find it extremely ironic that Tesla Motors founder and CEO Elon Musk is escalating his warnings that our obsession with Artificial Intelligence technology (AI) is the biggest threat to our human existence. "With artificial intelligence, we are summoning the demon," Elon Musk is quoted as saying.

The truth is that the Founder of Tesla, Nikola Tesla, was constantly in contact with other world intelligence. He got deathly sick when he was a child and was revived by the demons of technology. Many believed that Nikola Tesla was a dangerous man; a man who believed that "black holes are the most powerful sources of energy and life." He was a man who conducted experiments, trying to discover "what to do in the Universe, so every being is born as Christ, Buddha or Zoroaster." Zoroastrianism is a pre-Islamic religion, revealed to man by a "god" named Ahura Mazda. It is my contention that this was a fallen angel entity. And yes beloved, that's why the Car line and technology of Mazda is so prevalent in the Earth. Are you waking up yet? The next paragraph is a quote from a published article from Salvation and Survival. The name of the particular article on December 4, 2014 was "Was Tesla The Conduit Between Fallen Angels & Our Technology?"

"In an 1899 interview, from his Colorado Springs laboratory, Tesla opened up about his "other-world views": that the Light of the Universe filled his six senses; about building a machine, that by vibration, provokes a feeling of bliss; that humans once had real and visible wings. He speaks of being aware, as a child, that there was an Energy in the Universe, and of trying to awake that energy, and figure out how it could influence people. He told his interviewer, "My eyesight and hearing are perfect and, I dare to say, stronger than other people. I hear the thunder from a hundred fifty miles away, and I see colors in the sky that others cannot see. This enlargement of vision and hearing, I had as a child. Later I consciously developed [it]."

In the end Nikola Tesla went mad. However, back to CERN. You should know that via technology, the demons that our computers have been able to pick up and decipher, is nothing but digital signals. CERN is converting these signals via help from the other side. They are in essence creating and constructing demon DNA. Do you think that cloning went away beloved? Get your head out of the dark and wake up. They are making animal hybrids, just like the Nephilim did when they were on the Earth physically during the days of Noah. They are using Eugenics and perfecting Cognitive AI

There was a series in 2016 called the Shadowhunters, that outright put this type of stuff into their plot. They have the Nephilim on the Earth as an agency and they have a sect of them that are turning "worthy" humans into other worldly beings with the blood of the Angel Raziel, a Watcher, that fell in the beginning. Watch the shows that are coming out beloved regarding all of this stuff. The Avengers, X-Men, Wolverine, and other Mutant shows are setting the stage for what's coming. Yes, I know this is some of our favorite movies, but don't be lulled to sleep.

They are speeding up our atmosphere using this collider and changing it. They are even using technology that is affecting what is going on, on Mars and Saturn. Do you know that many people worship the planet Saturn? That's for another book. But, in short, the occult prays for entities that are contained in Saturn to be released. They believe that this planet is full of the strongest of the fallen angels that were banished from Heaven. Because of all of the ancient evidence, that I won't get into right now, plus the NASA satellite images including video of the counter-clockwise spinning hexagram at its North Pole; so large you could fit four earths inside of it side by side. Also, the South Pole of Saturn has a gas hurricane which stays in the shape of an eye. Are you seeing the connections to our ancient symbols and Saturn? This gas eerily travels around this shape in the same way that the Muslim practice of walking counter-clockwise around the Kaaba in Mecca is performed.

Space magazine has reported that there is activity going on in Saturn because of the dark matter technology and energy that is being created by CERN. They literally are saying that the rings are starting to rotate as if Saturn is actually a planet that will be activated. The rings will start to wind up and either blow the planet up and unlocking the leadership of the nefilim, etc. or who knows. Again, this is just what the other side believes, but it's interesting. Yes beloved, that's why we have the Saturn Cars. That's why the symbol of Capital One is the rings of Saturn.

Toyota also uses it. The logo of Internet Explorer is using it and on and on and on. I'll leave this here, but lastly on Saturn, at one time Saturn was closer to the Earth than it is now as well as Mars. And that's why we have discovered that there is water on Mars and other stuff because spiritual entities were occupying this planet at one time.

Isaiah 13:5

5They come from a far country, from the end of heaven, even the LORD, and the weapons of his indignation, to destroy the whole land.

According to Isaiah 13:5, the Most High will be sending in an offensive attack descending from space. This is a powerful army and Satan knows he must match this power. Is the satanic army housed in Saturn? The plot of the movie Star Wars with the clones on a remote planet, is there something like that going on here?

CERN'S machine, the Large Hadron Collider is an incredible undertaking with a massive 27 kilometer radius. That is almost 17 miles in diameter. This is an extremely powerful machine. There is always a dual purpose for technology. One is for public consumption and the other is for a private agenda. This "agenda" is private for a reason.

ALIENS IN ANTARTICA

Watch the events that are happening and have been happening in Antartica. It is a pole of our Earth and many fallen angels reside and are trapped there. You can go as far back as World War II to find out credible stories from our own military personnel flying over Antartica and seeing things like Willy Mammoths and green plush land and beings. Mankind calls them aliens but they are demon Nephilim, probably some of the Fallen and the like. Many believe that whatever happened to reshape the topography of the planet Earth and whenever they were banished, that this was another one of the places that they are being trapped, until a certain time. ALL of the governments of the world know this and try hard to keep this knowledge under wraps. The snow that kept them trapped and kept humanity away is melting y'all. They have finally admitted that there is a big ginormous chasm that is located right under Antartica in the last few years.

Consider this as well, on the day that Hilary Clinton was apparently about to lose to Donald Trump, John Kerry, the then Secretary of State, took a weird trip to Antartica. Many believe that he went to appeal to the "aliens" which we know are demons, that are really running the world, to allow Hilary to win. As we all know, they denied his request. Senator Kerry came back very humble.

These types of things is the reason why I'm writing this kind of book, because it's one of he reasons why I was born, to be a shofar for the end of the age. Our government and every other top official, including the Vatican, knows all of this stuff and more.

Consider one more thing. In 2002, American troops was on ground in Kandahar, Afghanistan. As they turned the bin, one unit encountered a large being, they say about 15 to 18 feet tall in the mouth of a cave. He came out with impressive speed and speared one of their comrades, a Soldier named Dan. They immediately went into combat mode, and the one guy that came forth with the information say that something kicked in to tell them all to shoot for the face. They say that this giant had jet red hair that went down to his shoulders, a full red beard, 6 fingers on each hand, 6 toes on each foot, and two rows of teeth. He also said that his nails was thick like fungus nails, pointy, and gnarled. They managed to kill the giant. After they called it in, they were told to stay put two choppers was coming to transport the creature and them away to be debriefed. They were made to sign non-disclosure agreements binding them to silence. He broke the agreement because he realized that the Earth needs to know what is really going on. The race of the Giants, also known as the Nephilim, are still roaming the Earth, and the days of Noah are upon us.

My youngest son, Jayden, had a dream in September of 2018. His dream was that the rapture had happened. He was standing outside with one of his oldest sisters and niece. He said that me and his mother walked out of the house that we were living in 2018. He said it looked like us but it wasn't us because we had red eyes and he just knew. He's only 10 and he said we were clones. He said he asked sister about some of his other siblings and she told him that they were taken as well.

Let me conclude, the beast and the false prophet will trick the Earth into accepting this technology into our very beings. And the Earth will think that this is the greatest technological feat and will come together to fight against God if we could. This won't happen to me, but please understand how I am writing this. **The Mark of the Beast is the change of the DNA and this will be the last straw, the last Tower of Babel, the last offense that will culminate all things and allow for Jesus to come and smack everyone that will call themselves coming against Him down, once again.** Choose Jesus beloved, because it is only through Jesus Christ that we will have eternal life. It is only through Jesus that we will have eternal life. It is only through Jesus that we will have an uncorruptible body and live in peace. The light of Christ will shine brighter and brighter as the world gets darker and darker. Let your light so shine. I charge every reader of this book to disseminate ALL this information to the ends of the Earth. God bless.

Jesus answered: "Watch out that no one deceives you. For many will come in my name, claiming, 'I am the Christ,' and will deceive many. And many false prophets will appear and deceive many people. At that time if anyone says to you, 'Look, here is the Christ!' or, 'There he is!' do not believe it. For false Christs and false prophets will appear and perform great signs and miracles to deceive even the elect--if that were possible. See, I have told you ahead of time. "So if anyone tells you, 'There he is, out in the desert,' do not go out; or, 'Here he is, in the inner rooms,' do not believe it. For as lightning that comes from the east is visible even in the west, so will be the coming of the Son of Man. **(Matthew 24:4-5; 11; 23-27)**

"At that time the sign of the Son of Man will appear in the sky, and all the nations of the earth will mourn. They will see the Son of Man coming on the clouds of the sky, with power and great glory. And he will send his angels with a loud trumpet call, and they will gather his elect from the four winds, from one end of the heavens to the other. **(Matthew 24:30-31)**

For the Son of Man is going to come in his Father's glory with his angels, and then he will reward each person according to what he has done. **(Matthew 16:27)**

*As it was in the days of Noah, so it will be at the coming of the Son of Man. For in the days before the flood, people were eating and drinking, marrying and giving in marriage, up to the day Noah entered the ark; and they knew nothing about what would happen until the flood came and took them all away. That is how it will be at the coming of the Son of Man***. (Matthew 24:37-39)**

And the best one of all:
When the Son of Man comes in his glory, and all the angels with him, he will sit on his throne in heavenly glory. All the nations will be gathered before him, and he will separate the people one from another as a shepherd separates the sheep from the goats. He will put the sheep on his right and the goats on his left. "Then the King will say to those on his right, 'Come, you who are blessed by my Father; take your inheritance, the kingdom prepared for you since the creation of the world. For I was hungry and you gave me something to eat, I was thirsty and you gave me something to drink, I was a stranger and you invited me in, I needed clothes and you clothed me, I was sick and you looked after me, I was in prison and you came to visit me.' "Then the righteous will answer him, 'Lord, when did we see you hungry and feed you, or thirsty and give you something to drink? When did we see you a stranger and invite you in, or needing clothes and clothe you? When did we see you sick or in prison and go to visit you?' "The King will reply, 'I tell you the truth, whatever you did for one of the least of these brothers of mine, you did for me.' "Then he will say to those on his left, 'Depart from me, you who are cursed, into the eternal fire

prepared for the devil and his angels. For I was hungry and you gave me nothing to eat, I was thirsty and you gave me nothing to drink, I was a stranger and you did not invite me in, I needed clothes and you did not clothe me, I was sick and in prison and you did not look after me.' "They also will answer, 'Lord, when did we see you hungry or thirsty or a stranger or needing clothes or sick or in prison, and did not help you?' "He will reply, 'I tell you the truth, whatever you did not do for one of the least of these, you did not do for me.' "Then they will go away to eternal punishment, but the righteous to eternal life. **Matthew 25:31-46 (KJV)**

Are you going to be in the line of the sheep or goats? To assure that you will be counted as a sheep pray the most powerful prayer in the Bible which is the prayer of Peter. When he was sinking:

Matthew 14:28-30 (KJV)

28 And Peter answered him and said, Lord, if it be thou, bid me
come unto thee on the water.
29 And he said, Come. And when Peter was come down out of the
ship, he walked on the water, to go to Jesus.
30 But when he saw the wind boisterous, he was afraid; and
beginning to sink, he cried, saying, **Lord, save me.**

Pray the prayer of Peter beloved. **Call on Jesus** because He is near and is bidding you to come. *And everyone who* ***calls*** *on the name of the Lord shall be saved.* – **Acts 2:21 (KJV)**

God bless.

ABOUT THE AUTHOR

Apostle Dr. Larry Birchett, Jr., is the Founder and Senior Pastor of Harvest House Restoration Center, located in Carlisle, PA and the President of the Treasures of the Heart International Ministries that reaches across the globe. He is also the author of the acclaimed books *Reverence for the Storm* and *Processed for His Purpose-Purposed for His Promise.* He holds a PhD in Counseling and Communication from Calvary's Cross Institute; an Honorary Doctorate in Humanity from Glad Tidings Institute; on top of a Master of Science in Leadership and Business Ethics (MSLBE) from Duquesne University of the Holy Spirit. Him and his wife, Prophetess Dr. Joanna Birchett, Founder of Gospel 4 U TV and Magazine Ministries and author of the acclaimed book *Defeat was Never an Option*, are trailblazers for Jesus as they pastor together and travel the world together fulfilling the Great Commission of preaching, teaching, and baptizing every soul that is assigned to the work of their hands, into the Kingdom of God.

www.ingramcontent.com/pod-product-compliance
Lightning Source LLC
Chambersburg PA
CBHW051815090426
42736CB00011B/1484

9780989624978